RESISTANCE

RESISTANCE

THE WARSAW GHETTO UPRISING

Israel Gutman

Published in association with the
United States Holocaust Memorial Museum

A Marc Jaffe Book
HOUGHTON MIFFLIN COMPANY
BOSTON   NEW YORK   1994

For information about permission to reproduce selections
from this book, write to Permissions, Houghton Mifflin Company,
215 Park Avenue South, New York, New York 10003.

Library of Congress Cataloging-in-Publication Data
Gutman, Israel.
  Resistance : the Warsaw Ghetto uprising / Israel Gutman.
    p.   cm.
  "A Marc Jaffe book."
  "A publication of the United States Holocaust Memorial Museum."
  Includes bibliographical references and index.
  ISBN 0-395-60199-1
  1. Jews — Poland — Warsaw — Persecutions. 2. Holocaust, Jewish
(1939–1945) — Poland — Warsaw. 3. Warsaw (Poland) — History — Uprising
of 1943. 4. Warsaw (Poland) — Ethnic relations.   I. Title.
DS135.P62W2728 1994
943.8'4 — dc20 93-46767
                CIP

Printed in the United States of America

AGM 10 9 8 7 6 5 4 3 2 1

Maps copyright © 1993 United States Holocaust Memorial Council

In memory of Irit

CONTENTS

ACKNOWLEDGMENTS

I wish to acknowledge my gratitude to colleagues and friends who encouraged me along the way as this work was carried out.

I wish to thank my friend Mr. Jeshajahu Weinberg, the Director of the Holocaust Museum in Washington, who initiated the project of writing this book, and Professor Michael Berenbaum, Director of the United States Holocaust Research Institute, who contributed many constructive suggestions as well as his editorial skills.

Mr. Marc Jaffe, the editor of this work for Houghton Mifflin, has demonstrated friendship and patience. His experience and advice were of substantial importance in the process of shaping the structure of the book.

My thanks to Mrs. Ethel Broido, who translated the manuscript with dedication and skill from Hebrew to English.

This book is one of the initial publications of the United States Holocaust Research Institute. (Founded in December 1993, the Institute is the scholarly division of the Holocaust Memorial Museum. Its mission is to serve as an international resource for the development of research on the Holocaust and related issues, including those of contemporary significance.) Several of its staff members contributed to the publication of this book.

Betsy Chock graciously and selflessly assisted with the typing of the manuscript. Linda Harris and Bryan Lazar scanned chapters into the computer. Scott Miller assisted with some translation and fact checking. Genya Markon and Teresa Amiel of the museum's photo archives helped select the photographs and write the captions. Dewey Hicks and William Meinecke prepared the maps. Dr. David Luebke, former Director of Publications at the museum, assisted in preparing this work for publication. So too did Aleisa Fishman, who proofread the manuscript and handled other chores in preparation for publication. Janice Cook and Jeffrey Burridge helped in the editing of this work.

Lydia Perry and Deirdre McCarthy, who served as assistants to Professor Berenbaum, were gracious and able. Their assistance was invaluable. Ms. Perry typed sections of this manuscript and saw to it that other sections were ready for editing. Ms. McCarthy saw to it that the work was ready for publication.

I am pleased that telling the story of resistance in the Warsaw ghetto was so central a concern to this institution.

ISRAEL GUTMAN
Jerusalem
December 1993

INTRODUCTION

No ACT OF Jewish resistance during the Holocaust fired the imagination quite as much as the Warsaw Ghetto Uprising of April 1943. It was an event of epic proportions, pitting a few poorly armed, starving Jews against the might of Nazi power. The ghetto Uprising was the first urban rebellion of consequence in any of the Nazi-occupied countries and was a significant point in Jewish history. The Uprising represents defiance and great sacrifice in a world characterized by destruction and death.

The Polish writer Kazimierz Bradys called Warsaw "the invincible city." "Warsaw," he wrote, "was the capital of World War II," for the city symbolized all that was both sublime and tragic during the war — and the ghetto was the heart of the Warsaw tragedy. The Warsaw Ghetto Uprising is a historical event, but it also has become a symbol of Jewish resistance and determination, a moment in history that has transformed the self-perception of the Jewish people from passivity to active armed struggle. The Uprising has shaped Israel's national self-understanding. It is viewed as the first Jewish rebellion since the heroic days of the

Bar Kochba revolt in 135 C.E. The Uprising has become a universal symbol of resistance and courage.

The commanders of the Uprising were young men in their twenties, Zionists, Communists, socialists — idealists with no battle experience, no military training. With but a few weapons and limited ammunition, they knew that they had no chance to succeed. Their choice was ultimate: not whether to live or to die, but what choice to make as to their death.

We begin this work at the end: the ghetto, which only two years earlier had become the home of 400,000 Jews, is empty. Bereft of its population, the ghetto is reduced to rubble. Buried beneath its streets are the material remains of Jewish culture and civilization. Some sixty miles away in the skies around Treblinka are the ashes of the Jews of Warsaw who were brought in the summer of 1942 by train to its gas chambers. Within hours of their arrival, their material possessions confiscated, their hair shaved, they were gassed and their bodies cremated, sent up in smoke.

To understand the full meaning of the Warsaw Ghetto Uprising, we must sojourn among the Jews of Warsaw on the eve of World War II. Warsaw was a metropolis, the capital of the Polish Republic, and the largest center of Jewish life in Eastern Europe. It was also the heart of Eastern European Jewish culture during a time of transition and intense creativity. Political movements were centered in Warsaw; Zionists and Bundists, Communists and socialists competed for the allegiance of the young. Jewish theater and film thrived in Warsaw, Jewish newspapers proliferated. Jewish-Polish relations were changing as Jews entered the mainstream of Polish society. Jewish religious life was intense and devout. The religious community was piously observant, the secularists ardently secular. The religious community was deeply divided among the Hasidim and their opponents (*mitnagdim*), Mizrachi (Zionist Orthodox Jews), and the fiercely anti-Zionist Agudath Israel. The tensions and diversity within pre-war Warsaw's Jewish community continued in the ghetto and shaped ghetto life.

Just before World War II, Warsaw's Jewish population was 375,000, almost 30 percent of the city's total. One could not think of Warsaw without considering its Jews, who were to be found in every part of the city, though it was its northern part that contained the traditional Jewish neighborhoods. Jewish Warsaw was a city of contrasts. Offices of Jewish political parties and of many welfare, educational, and religious institutions were headquartered in Warsaw. Most of the Jewish periodicals, published in a variety of languages, were located in Warsaw. There were Jewish publishing houses, theater groups, and sports clubs. Warsaw was the home of writers and poets, including S. Anski (author of *The Dybbuk*), Y. L. Peretz, and the Singers — Isaac Bashevis and Israel Joshua. The Warsaw that was flourishing with Jewish culture stood in stark contrast to the depressed status and abject poverty of the Jewish masses who constituted so visible a part of the city.

The Nazi invasion of Poland on September 1, 1939, transformed and divided the city. By September 8 the Nazis stood at the gates of Warsaw. The Poles decided to resist as long as possible, thus the city was bombarded from the air; twenty days later it fell. More than one quarter of its buildings were destroyed or damaged. Casualties were high: fifty thousand dead or wounded. The German entry into Warsaw ended an era; the diversity, intensity, and distinctness of the pre-war city were gone. Three and a half years later, Jewish Warsaw stood in ruins, its ghetto reduced to rubble.

After occupation, the Nazis followed a familiar pattern established in Germany: Jews were first identified, and by December they were required to wear the Jewish star. Jewish property was confiscated and the remaining Jewish shops were marked. From local shops to art collections, from factories to private libraries, the Nazis followed a disciplined procedure of confiscation. All radios were taken. Collective responsibility and punishment were imposed: the deed of one endangered all. Jews were isolated from their former neighbors and concentrated into restricted living quarters. Forced labor was required, and the Jewish Council members were charged with the task of gathering the needed workers. The poor substituted for more affluent conscripts in response to ever increasing German demands. Class divisions deepened. They were soon to narrow: both the rich and the poor grew increasingly poorer. By the summer of 1940, more than

100,000 workers, more than 25 percent of the Jewish population, were conscripted by the Nazis. They faced long hours, no pay, and sadistic masters.

The Jewish Council was formed with the remnants of previous leadership. Adam Czerniakow, an engineer who had previously served on the Jewish Community Council, was appointed its head. The behavior of the Judenrat in Warsaw during the Holocaust has always been a matter of considerable controversy. The debate intensified with the charges made by Hannah Arendt in *Eichmann in Jerusalem* that had the Jews been leaderless and without formal institutions, the task of killing them would have been considerably more difficult. Arendt charged that Jewish leaders, wittingly or unwittingly, became tools of the Nazis. In the past three decades the ardor of this debate has not diminished. Czerniakow struggled to serve two masters — the Nazis, who viewed the Judenrat as an indispensable instrument of their policies, and the Jews, whose ever growing needs he desperately tried to meet.

On November 16, 1940, the ghetto was sealed. Over the next years, the population of the Warsaw ghetto would vary from 380,000 to 440,000 Jews. Death was pervasive throughout the ghetto. In 1941, 43,000 inhabitants died inside the ghetto, more than one in ten of its residents. Every day, ghetto residents struggled for survival. Jewish Self-Help manned the soup kitchens and provided fuel and coal, meager resources in the struggle for survival in the cold Polish winter. The formal structure of the ghetto as prescribed by the Germans and the Judenrat coexisted alongside the informal structure of the ghetto as it emerged in real life. The Judenrat developed into a multilayered government with a series of departments, which often functioned as fiefdoms for their directors. Those who worked for the Judenrat were seemingly protected. Tensions developed between those with "protection and connections," and those without. Religious tensions were rampant between the devout and the secular, and between Jews and Catholics of Jewish origin who were defined as Jews by the Nuremberg race laws. (Daily services were held for "converted Jews" at the ghetto's Roman Catholic Church, which in the end was the only building left standing in the ghetto.) The informal structure was more creative, but no less developed.

A political underground published a vital clandestine press; youth movements and cultural life continued; political movements pushed their partisan agendas; education, religion, and culture endured in this hostile environment. Often ghetto institutions had a double life, one legal and open, the other clandestine and secret. Youth movements and urban training communes were camouflaged as soup kitchens. Cells of the Jewish underground were disguised as agricultural workers' groups.

There were basic tensions between the formal structure of the ghetto and informal structures that filled the vacuum of leadership and alleviated, at least in some small way, the harsh conditions of ghetto life. Children were indispensable to smuggling food, and family life was preserved despite the strains.

By mid-July 1942 the ghetto was in a panic. Rumors of deportation were rife. Czerniakow heard these rumors, and sought reassurance for his people. The leader of the Judenrat sought exemptions for children and for orphans. In the end, the order for deportation appeared, without Czerniakow's signature. The wife of the Judenrat chairman was held hostage to ensure his compliance with the Nazi master. On the evening of July 23, the ninth day of Av — the day of mourning commemorating the destruction of the Holy Temple in Jerusalem and the exile of the Jewish people — Czerniakow completed the ninth book of his diary. To continue writing, he would have had to open a new book. Instead, that very same day he swallowed cyanide. There were no words of warning, only a final tragic confession of failure: "The SS wants me to kill children with my own hands." He could not participate.

Even in death Czerniakow remained controversial. Those close to him felt that his suicide was testimony to his personal courage, to his sense of public responsibility, an act of ultimate integrity. Underground circles were less charitable. They saw his death as an act of weakness. He had not even summoned the courage to warn the ghetto and to call for resistance.

During the days that followed, hundreds of thousands of Jews were dragged to the *Umschlagplatz* (assembly and deportation point) and transported in cattle cars to Treblinka. Initially, the task of rounding up the Jews for deportation fell to some extent to the Jewish police, but within a week the SS, aided by Ukrainian, Latvian, and Lithuanian soliders, as well as by the German gendarmerie — some two hundred men in all — took the lead and systematically laid siege to blocks, buildings, and streets. Those awaiting deportation were anxious; families struggled to stay together while some sought to escape the ghetto, to find a place to hide on the "other side of the wall." Others, such as Janusz Korczak and his orphans, went together — children and educators. Emanuel Ringelblum described the scene: "Korczak set the tone: everybody was to go to the *Umschlagplatz* together. Some of the boarding school principals knew what was in store for them there, but they felt they could not abandon the children in this dark hour and had to accompany them to their death." Korczak had firmly resisted all personal offers of safety.

The first to be taken were the weakest. Then came those who lacked papers and permanent jobs. They, in turn, were followed by relatives of those who had exemption papers, and finally even workers with proper papers were taken. Everyone was a potential victim. Families had to decide whether to stay together. Should mothers go with their children? What of the fathers?

Among the young and the resistance, demoralization set in after the deportations. Demoralization and recriminations were especially prominent, since in the early days of the July deportation a decision had been made that the time was not yet ripe for resistance. The survivors were frustrated and enraged that they had not fought the Germans or even struck out against the Jewish police. Remorse was deep. As Yitzhak Zuckerman reported on a conversation:

> Jewish resistance will never come into being after us. The nation is lost. If we couldn't organize Jewish force while there were still hundreds of thousands in Warsaw, how can we do so when only a few thousand are left? The masses did not place their trust in

us. We do not have — and probably never will have — weapons. We don't have the strength to start all over again. The nation has been destroyed; our honor trampled upon.

Because there was no choice, despair soon gave way to a firm determination to resist. Yet first, deep political divisions had to be overcome and alliances had to be forged among Jewish fighting factions torn by deep ideological rifts. Zionists of the right and the left, religious non-Zionists, socialists, Bundists, and Communists were at odds with each other, divided over what tactics and strategies to employ, when to strike, whom to trust, what contacts to make. Divisions were so deep that the Revisionist Zionists established their own fighting unit, with only marginal contacts with the major resistance organization. Even the Nazi threat of total destruction could not unify the Jews, but the unification that was finally achieved represented almost all major political and social streams in Jewish life.

The Germans were hesitant to destroy the entire ghetto population. They did not want to lose the assets of the ghetto, including enterprises they wanted to transfer intact. Furthermore, they required Jewish labor to gather, store, and guard existing property. The deportation of July–September 1942 reduced the ghetto population from 400,000 to between 50,000 and 60,000 people. After the summer deportations the ghetto was left a mere remnant consisting mostly of men, whose chances for survival were enhanced by their usefulness for heavy labor. Almost all were between the ages of fifteen and fifty.

Belated efforts were made to forge a fighting organization. Political solidarity was required as was a unity of purpose and program. These were not easily achieved amidst the tensions and anguish of the post-deportation ghetto. The Jewish Fighting Organization, the ZOB, its leadership and fighters, emerged from the shadows of the first deportation. The ZOB members saw themselves as rejecting a Jewish tradition of passivity and compliance and returning to the heroic days of Jewish fighters of biblical times. And they conceived of themselves as an expression of Jewish national redemption.

Mordecai Anielewicz, who was to emerge as the undisputed leader of the Uprising, returned to Warsaw after the deportations from eastern Silesia, where he was engaged in underground work. Because he had been outside the ghetto during the decisive days of July–September, he was also free of the hesitation and powerlessness that had eroded the spirit of some of the ZOB members when they recognized the full consequences of their failure. He was soon to become a hero because of his extraordinary accomplishments during the few months of dynamic preparations and at the height of the battle.

The first act of resistance was an assassination attempt against the chief of the Jewish police, Jozef Szerynski, who, in the words of one diarist, "aided in the execution of 200,000 Jews." Soon Jacob Lejkin, another prominent policeman, was assassinated. Within a month, the first Judenrat official, Yisrael First, was killed. The ZOB were convinced that the ghetto could not be transformed into a fighting force unless the fifth column elements were eliminated. They also understood that the Nazis would not intervene in internal Jewish vendettas.

The ZOB insisted that there could be no next time, no further deportations, at least not without a fight. They proclaimed, in a public manifesto:

> Jewish masses, the hour is drawing near. You must be prepared to resist. Not a single Jew should go to the railroad cars. Those who are unable to put up active resistance should resist passively, should go into hiding . . . Our slogan must be: *All are ready to die as human beings.*

On January 9, 1943, Heinrich Himmler paid a visit to the ghetto. Two days later he ordered the deportation of eight thousand remaining Jews, who constituted the "illegal element." This time, the Jewish reaction was different. Ghetto streets were deserted, many went into hiding. A group of fighters under the command of Anielewicz attacked the Germans, and the first street battle occurred in the ghetto. By the third day of the *Aktion* the Germans were reduced to shooting wildly — and for the first time Jews had shot German soldiers. Armed resistance had begun. The

Germans were suddenly hesitant and cautious. They did not go down to cellars, and each Jew they captured was searched. Streets became the scene of battle.

The *Aktion* ended within a matter of days. The remaining Jews were electrified. They falsely assumed that Jewish resistance, not Jewish compliance, had brought the deportations to a halt. Again they reproved themselves for their inaction during the fateful deportations. Hideouts were fortified, resistance units were strengthened. "The January revolt made the April revolt possible!" said one of the major leaders of the Uprising.

No doubt remained regarding the fate of the ghetto, and the only decision to be made was the response of those who remained. The ghetto had to be purged of dangerous collaborators. Money was desperately needed to purchase arms, cultivate contacts on the Aryan side, and acquire modest but substantial aid from the Polish underground. Planning for battle began in earnest. The leadership rejected a plan to transport some Jews to partisan areas clandestinely, and thus rescue at least a remnant. The reasoning was simple, Yitzhak Zuckerman said:

> We saw ourselves as a Jewish underground whose fate was a tragic one . . . a pioneer force not only from a Jewish standpoint but also from the standpoint of the entire embattled world — the first to fight. For *our hour had come without any sign of hope or rescue.*

The attitude within the ghetto had changed completely. When the Germans approached the leader of the Warsaw Judenrat, Marc Lichtenbaum, to speak to Jewish workers, his response was, "I am not the authority in the ghetto. There is another authority — the Jewish Fighting Organization." From January onward, Jewish forces stood on high alert, ready for action if the need arose. The high alert lasted eighty-seven days.

The Uprising itself, which began on April 19, 1943, the first night of Passover, continued until the final liquidation of the ghetto. Three days were allocated for liquidating the Warsaw ghetto. The battle of the bunkers continued for more than a month.

As the ghetto was set aflame, some Jews escaped through the sewers. One survivor reports:

> On May 10, 1943, at 9 o'clock in the morning the lid of the sewer over our head literally opened and a flood of sunlight streamed in. At the opening of the sewer Krzaczek [a member of the Polish resistance] was standing and calling us to come out. We started to climb out one after another and at once got on a truck. It was a beautiful spring day and the sun warmed us. Our eyes were blinded by the bright light, as we had not seen daylight for many weeks and had spent the time in complete darkness. The streets were crowded with people, and everybody stood still and watched, while strange beings, hardly recognizable as humans, crawled out of the sewers.

The Uprising was literally a revolution in Jewish history. Its importance was understood all too well by those who fought. On April 23 Mordecai Anielewicz wrote to his comrade in arms Yitzhak Zuckerman:

> What we have experienced cannot be described in words. We are aware of one thing only: what has happened has exceeded our dreams. The Germans ran twice from the ghetto . . . I have the feeling that great things are happening, that we have dared is of great importance. . . .
>
> Keep well, my dear. Perhaps we shall meet again. But what really matters is that the dream of my life has become true. Jewish self defense in the Warsaw ghetto has become a fact. Jewish armed resistance and the retaliation have become a reality. I have been witness to the magnificent heroic struggle of the Jewish fighters.

RESISTANCE

I

THE FIRST WEEKS
OF WAR

B Y MID-MAY 1943, the rebellion of the Warsaw ghetto had
come to an end. The last groups of Jews had been murdered
or sent to death camps. Perhaps a few thousand were hiding underground. The people were gone; so too their homes,
apartments, workshops, factories, public and welfare institutions, synagogues, makeshift houses of prayer, hospitals, and old-
age homes — all had been systematically erased from the face of
the earth, vanished forever.

On the fifteenth of May 1943, SS General Jürgen Stroop,
whose forces had destroyed the Warsaw ghetto, triumphantly
reported that the guards on duty the night before had encountered only six or seven Jews in the ghetto area. Only a handful of
Jews remained within the ruins of the ghetto. Stroop also noted
that he had blown up the great synagogue of Warsaw, located
outside the ghetto area. This imposing structure, the work of the
architect Leandro Marconi in 1878, was the pride of many Jews.
To the Nazis, its destruction symbolized the final victory of German power and spirit. The Jews of Warsaw had been destroyed.
The material remains of Jewish life would also be eradicated.

General Stroop began his report of May 15 with an enthusiastic description of the victorious military campaign. Heavy artillery had been employed; thousands of casualties had been inflicted on the enemy. In the words of his summary: "The Jewish quarter in Warsaw is no longer."

Indeed, Jewish life in Warsaw had ended. For nearly four years, Jews had fought for their lives, their children, and their homes. The non-Jewish world ignored their struggle or simply became resigned to the situation. Only a few, a very precious few, risked their lives by coming to aid the Jews.

The final chapter of the Jewish community in Warsaw had begun only four years earlier, on September 1, 1939.

In the summer of 1939, Germany presented Poland with an ultimatum demanding changes in the boundaries between the two countries; German inducements were tangible, its threats veiled. Poland stood firm. Along with the rest of the world, Polish leaders had followed the Reich's trail of broken agreements, dictates, and territorial expansion. Poland knew from the sad experience of Czechoslovakia and Austria that initially restrained German demands soon would be followed by ever-growing claims and threats to destroy the enemy and all European democracies. The Polish affair would end with the German occupation of its enfeebled neighbor. An attack could be expected; the only question was when.

Warsaw took some modest steps to prepare for war. Volunteers dug trenches around the approaches to the capital. Members of the Polish intelligentsia, who had never held a shovel, stood shoulder to shoulder with caftan-clad Jews, and they worked feverishly to protect the capital city. On August 29, 1939, Warsaw mayor Stefan Starzynski told residents, "Yesterday, more than 20,000 men dug trenches. Therefore, there are now a dozen kilometers of trenches already in a proper condition."

The Polish political crisis occurred just as Europe was abandoning its policy of appeasement, which was particularly strong in Great Britain. Public opinion was shifting against the Nazis. The abrogation of the Munich Agreement shortly after it was signed in March 1939 and the subjugation of Czechoslovakia, perhaps the most stable and successful democracy created by the

Versailles treaty, convinced many that Hitler would not be satisfied by redressing the inequities resulting from World War I or gathering all Germans into one state. The German leader was intent on conquests and war.

The British policy of appeasement and the country's desperate attempts at negotiation had convinced Hitler that Great Britain and France would be reluctant to defend Poland despite their treaty obligations. Unwilling to display any weakness, Hitler resolved to attack Poland, correctly assuming that Poland would remain isolated during a short campaign. The last step that isolated Poland and ensured Hitler's fast victory was the Nazi-Soviet pact signed on August 23. Hitler and Stalin, who were until then outspoken ideological and political rivals, united in the plot to give the Nazis a free hand in their invasion and to divide conquered Poland between themselves.

The first of September was a sunny summer Friday. Polish children were about to begin their new school year, but instead they were awakened by the sound of bombing. Zila Rosenberg, a Jewish girl who later became a member of the resistance in Vilna, remembered her terror: "I am lying in an open field, trying to shrink, to turn into a tiny invisible dot. Low-flying heavy German bombers are passing overhead. My heart is beating like a thousand hammers: oh, God, don't let them harm me."

No official declaration of war by the Nazis preceded the attack. Rather, German prison inmates were dressed in Polish military uniforms and armed with rifles, and they initiated what the Nazis claimed was a Polish attack on a radio station in the small German border town of Gliwice. The ruse was successful, and the bombing of Warsaw took its inhabitants by surprise. At about 7:00 A.M., hours after the bombing began, Polish radio broadcast the first warnings:

At 4:45 A.M., the German army, without declaring war, crossed the Polish borders from the north and the west . . . the first air-attack on Warsaw this morning caused damage in the airport area Okiecie and in residential quarters . . . the newspapers printed during the night do not give any news as yet of the beginning of these acts of war.

On September 3, Britain and France declared war against Germany. Euphoria swept through Warsaw. The national anthems of Great Britain and France were broadcast endlessly. No one asked how the Allies would reach the Polish battlefields or where and when the western front would be set up. Excited crowds streamed toward the British embassy, then continued toward the presidential palace. A young Jew grasped a microphone:

> Brothers, Poles, Jews. The enemy is beating and murdering us, burning and destroying our houses, our property, the effort of generations. I am a simple tinsmith, I don't understand politics. But it is clear to me that when we are attacked, we must defend ourselves. All of us — the rich and the poor, and even if we think there has been some injustice in the past, this must be set aside for the time being. Now we have to think of but one thing: if we all concentrate on a single purpose, we will be united — and we will win. But if we are not united, it will be bad. Long live our homeland and its allies and down with fascist Germany!

Still, despite the demonstrations and the war, the theaters and cinemas stayed open and were well attended.

On September 4, a newspaper reported, "The first transport of wounded reached Warsaw. Discouraging news is streaming in about the situation at the front, particularly about the advance of the German army in the southwestern sector. Escaping civilians turn up from Western Poland."

The Polish authorities ordered a partial evacuation of the capital. On September 5, President Ignacy Moscicki left town. On the same day, a railway station where refugees were concentrated was attacked from the air, resulting in many casualties. On the sixth, the prime minister, General Slawoj-Skladkowski, announced that "due to the danger facing the capital, the government was obliged to leave the city in the determined hope of returning after we have achieved victory." The chief commander of the armed forces, Marshal Rydz-Smigly, also fled. The situation deteriorated rapidly as the front was breached at critical points.

The commander of the Polish forces abandoned the defense of the western districts.

With the attack against Poland, the Germans launched their "blitzkrieg" for the first time, which shocked Poland and surprised the world. The speed of the attack was unanticipated by Poland's high command. It wreaked havoc before the defense forces of the country were even activated. One commentator noted,

> The pace of the Germans' advance during the first week of the war astonished us . . . the chaos, the unbalanced and faulty organization . . . From the very outset, there was a complete devitalization of the railways . . . and in the confusion surrounding the movement of the railways, one could explain the phenomena which made me realize that we were entering an entirely new phase in life: that of leaving Warsaw.

Warsaw was threatened from the air and on the ground by the German tank corps, artillery, and infantry. The colonel responsible for the information services of the Polish general command broadcast a call for all young men of recruiting age to depart for the eastern regions, where the new front would be established. His ominous words yielded unanticipated results, for masses of inhabitants started on their exodus from the city. Adam Czerniakow, who later headed the Judenrat, the Jewish Council, in Warsaw, noted in his war diary on the seventh of September, "With knapsacks on their backs, they set out for the unknown."

Government authority had completely broken down. The administration, the political party structure, and various public functions were on the brink of collapse. Individuals took their fate into their own hands, crowding onto the bridges over the Vistula River. The roads leading eastward were thronged with an endless procession of people, who made an easy target for low-flying German aircraft, which machine-gunned the exposed migrants.

Many Jews took to the roads along with their Polish neighbors. Among the first to leave were political activists and prominent public and cultural figures in the Jewish sector. Jewish leaders felt uneasy, however, about leaving the city. Some claimed that they were likely to be on a German "wanted" list because they had published anti-Nazi articles or had taken part in activities against the Third Reich, such as advocating an economic boycott. Among those heading east were the heads of the Zionist movement, such as Moshe Kleinbaum (Sneh), who was later to play a decisive role in the organization of Jewish defense forces in Palestine; Menachem Begin, the central figure of the Zionist Betar movement, who headed the right-wing Irgun underground in Palestine and later became prime minister of Israel; and Zerah Wahrhaftig of the religious Zionist Mizrachi party. They were not alone. Long-standing leaders of the leftist non-Zionist Bund, Henrik Ehrlich and Victor Alter, Communist leaders, leaders of the Left Po'alei Zion, and the head of the Warsaw Jewish community, Maurycy Meisel, also fled.

The top echelon of Jewish leadership in political life, in both municipal and civil affairs, escaped the city together with the wave of refugees. Some of those who did not flee during the first days of September took advantage of other opportunities to slip out of Poland before the summer of 1940, including Apolinary Hartglas and Moshe Kerner of the General Zionists, Abraham Weiss of Mizrachi, Shmuel Zygelbojm of the Bund, and Yitzhak-Meir Levin and the Rabbi of Ger and his retinue from the heads of the ultra-Orthodox Agudath Israel. As a result, when Warsaw Jewry faced its greatest crisis, its most experienced leaders — political and religious — were elsewhere.

The leaders and many members of the Zionist youth movements declared that the movement's activities had ceased temporarily, and they too moved eastward. In all, it is estimated that some 300,000 Jews were in the wave of migrants streaming eastward from western and central Poland prior to January–February 1940. While no figures are known, it is likely that nearly 20 percent of all those who left were Jews from Warsaw, although some returned or eventually lost their lives at the hands of the Germans. Many who departed were young men who had left their wives and children behind. Thus, from the beginning of the ghetto, the Jewish community was disproportionately composed of women, children, and the aged.

The flight of émigrés weakened the Jews remaining in Warsaw. Only a few top-level functionaries and public figures remained behind, generally for personal or family reasons. But there were also those who deliberately stayed behind because they would not abandon their people in distress. This spirit induced the historian and public figure Emanuel Ringelblum to stay in Warsaw during the time of the ghetto. In his diary he noted, "The nights of the 6–7th September. Thousands and thousands of young people — more than a hundred? — phone me: 'Are you leaving?'" As the hour of their greatest crisis approached, Warsaw Jews would be led by second-tier leaders. Ringelblum would not leave.

Unlike the Jews of Germany and the annexed countries, Polish Jews had no time to consider how to avoid the German snare closing around them. Jews of an older generation remembered the German troops who occupied Warsaw and parts of Poland during World War I — those soldiers had been polite and civil to the local population. Surely, they thought, the Germans could not undergo such an extreme and drastic change despite their professed ideology and territorial aggressiveness. Many Jews were convinced that the intended "solution of the Jewish problem" was the expulsion of Jews from Germany.

As the enemy approached the gates of Warsaw, two men who stood their ground earned the respect of the Warsawites, Mayor Stefan Starzynski and General Walerian Czuma, the man in charge of defending the capital. Their courage posed a stark contrast to a pathetically vague and fragmented government and the boastful arrogance of the establishment. Starzynski's voice and appeals had a calming effect and carried conviction.

The army decided to turn the city into a fighting fortress, surrounded as it was by retreating combat units lacking effective air defenses. Some thought that the city and its inhabitants could block the enemy's advance, demonstrating to the world the city's unwillingness to surrender and Poland's courageous spirit.

As the 16th Division of the German armored corps arrived at the gates of Warsaw on September 8, the 4th Armored Division attacked with air support. General Czuma announced that Warsaw was to be defended, and he called on its inhabitants "to go about their business as usual." According to Polish sources, the mission assigned to General Czuma was well beyond the power and means at his disposal. His forces consisted of several units in the city and what few troops could be realigned during their retreat.

The civilian population was asked to dig trenches and erect ramparts and barricades. Despite their enthusiasm and strong will, the many volunteers could not overcome the powerful arms and methods of the enemy. Defenses were improvised. The Poles were overwhelmed, yet still they refused to yield.

On the 12th of September at 10:00 A.M., Stefan Starzynski announced on the radio that General Czuma had been allowed to recruit an armed battalion of defenders of Warsaw made up of 600 men and expressed the hope that this unit would be raised within half an hour. Volunteers were asked to report at 11:00 A.M. before the Mostowski palace: "I need 600 dedicated, healthy, strong young men, who want to fight for Warsaw. The first unit must be ready at once. I call on 600 youths to come forward immediately; men who are determined and ready to die for their homeland and for Warsaw..." In a dozen minutes, there were some thousand at the gathering point — from young boys still in their teens to old men.

This hastily thrown together defensive body succeeded in arresting the advance of the invading Germans and even inflicted damage in direct combat. But the true obstacle to German domination was the city itself; its houses and citizens became the front, and they paid a heavy price for it. German forces surrounded Warsaw on all sides and continued to advance, subjecting the city to murderous air attacks and artillery bombardments.

The mayor and army commander appealed to the inhabitants to withstand the assault and prevent the city's occupation. It is unclear whether this stubborn defense of the city was part of a larger plan to provide a breathing spell for the Polish army which might change in the course of the war. For the first three weeks, the inhabitants of Warsaw displayed unbelievable endurance, discipline, and spirit of sacrifice, despite the intensifying attacks, wanton destruction, disturbing shortages, and the absence of any encouraging change. One commentator wrote:

> In such conditions, with no information about the real course of events, the eternally deluded Warsaw lives the life of a besieged city. The extended trenches and barricades prepared for street fighting were an aspect that the enemy had not considered at all, for there was no need or desire to sacrifice thousands of victims when such battles were absolutely unnecessary from the German point of view. They had two effective means of achieving the desired results: bombing from the air and attacking positions with heavy artillery, and in addition, there was always the possibility of letting the city starve.

During the first two weeks of the siege, the bombardment did not deter Warsaw's inhabitants, but then the Germans supported their air attacks with unceasing bombardment from their artillery. Fires spread throughout the city. In many instances, there was no attempt to save victims trapped under collapsed buildings. There were only a few reinforced shelters. The cellars in which people gathered for shelter proved helpful against the noise and quaking incurred by the bombing. In the event of a direct hit from the air, however, they were fatal traps.

Hospitals were destroyed, and in one, most of the seven hundred patients could not be saved. The water supply gave out. Hunger spread through the city, causing severe suffering among the thousands of refugees who had found shelter in public buildings. During the night, when the air attacks stopped, long queues of people formed outside the bakeries to await the distribution of bread before dawn. The supply was generally insufficient.

Even graver was the water shortage. The first signs of sickness began to appear, threatening the population with serious epidemics. The morale of the inhabitants, which had been high at first as people helped their neighbors, turned into nervousness, intolerance, and grumbling. The atmosphere was rife with rumors about battles that were supposed to have broken out on the western front on the border between France and Germany, or about Soviet penetration into the eastern part of Poland.

The desperation of Warsaw's inhabitants is detailed in one account of September 17:

> The third Sunday of the war was one of the most difficult days experienced by besieged Warsaw. From dawn onward, heavy artillery was shelling the city and in the course of a dozen hours, some 500 shells had fallen. Added to this, both during the morning and the afternoon, planes were bombing the town and dropping incendiary bombs. People fell in great numbers in the streets. Tens of houses were burning, collapsing or turning into rubble. Thousands were caught under the debris of bombed churches during Sunday services.

On September 21, Colonel Waclaw Lipinski, head of the information sector of the high command, announced on the radio:

> We are fighting. We are fighting in special circumstances but we have the will to fight and we shall continue despite the fact that the German general command claims that the war in Poland is at an end, although we are making a stand against the tremendous advantage enjoyed by the enemy in the air and in its armored division . . . We must remember the words engraved on the hearts and spirits of every Pole: to be defeated in battle but not to surrender, is victory.

But after broadcasting these statements, the radio went off the air. The water supply, the electricity, gas, and telephone systems were out of commission.

The heavy bombing on Yom Kippur, September 23, 1939, was deeply etched on the minds of the Jews of the city. On Friday, Yom Kippur eve, Adam Czerniakow wrote, "Today is Yom Kippur — the Day of Judgment. Throughout the night the sound of cannon-fire." The teacher Chaim Aaron Kaplan, who kept a detailed diary, described that Day of Atonement:

The forces of the enemy increased on Yom Kippur. We did not have a single hour of peace. The heavy artillery is showering fire and iron on our heads . . . the enemy is offering us two "treats": during the day — shells flying over our heads and houses, which, even if these are six stories high, become heaps of ruins together with its inhabitants . . . while at night, in the terrible darkness, the enemy drops his bombs.

Mary Berg, a young Jewish girl, not quite fifteen, told her diary:

On the 20th of September, the radios went silent and the water-pipes were destroyed. It seemed to me that here we were living on an island abandoned and cut off from the whole world. I shall never forget the 23rd of September, Yom Kippur of 1939, which the Germans intentionally set out to make a day of aggressive bombing of the Jewish quarter.

A Jewish youth of sixteen recalled:

Yesterday was Yom Kippur. At Kol Nidre in the evening, all the people assembled in the shelter were in tears. Until today, I haven't seen adults gathered together and crying from the depths of their hearts. Every year, with the advent of Yom Kippur, the Jewish women would usually be shedding tears, whether or not this was brought on by genuine emotions or merely out of habit. This time they were the tears of those who were struck by catastrophe. People's voices were choked and they held their heads in their hands. They did not take into consideration the fact that children were present, or perhaps the sight of the children was an even greater reason for their emotional reactions and tears. On the very day of Yom Kippur there was continuous bombing from morning to night and most of the bombs fell on the Jewish quarter. Perhaps this was a special token prepared by the Nazis for the Jews on this day.

Two days later, while Hitler was staying in the area at an advanced post of the Eighth Army command, Warsaw was subjected to a seemingly endless German attack, intended to break down the resistance and the spirit of the population. Unbeknownst to the citizens of besieged Warsaw, the entire Polish campaign had been resolved some two weeks earlier, and Warsaw's stand had only symbolic significance aimed at showing the world how Poland had fought for its freedom long after any chance of victory was gone. Although not the victors on the battlefield, the inhabitants of Warsaw had proved their courage and had been ready to sacrifice for their capital, their home.

However, when the city entered the first stages of total destruction, there were signs of hesitation, dissatisfaction, and disappointment. Planes appeared like vultures, bearing destruction and death. Whenever the whistling sound piercing the air was heard, and then the rumble of houses being destroyed, the response was trembling in the hearts and minds of thousands of people. With every whistling boom, one's mind measured the distance and one's heart skipped a beat. The sound of a hit, the impact of catastrophe, also brought with it a sense of reassurance to those who had not been the target. But this reassurance lasted only a fleeting moment, for it was soon followed by another whistle, signifying yet another bomb on its way to the earth.

On the twenty-seventh, the skies were no longer blackened by planes. The shelling had stopped. With fear and uncertainty, the inhabitants of the city crept out of the cellars and ditches to confront the sight of heaps of destroyed buildings blocking the streets, carcasses of horses, and the debris of war. Above all, there was a sort of cloud of down feathers hovering strangely about the city.

On the twenty-eighth, the people of Warsaw were informed that the city had surrendered. General Julius Rommel, commander of the German armed forces, announced on the twenty-ninth to "the citizens of the capital" that, as a result of the letter of surrender, enemy forces would enter the city on the following day at noon. The announcement ended with these words: "The fate of the war is changing. I rely on the population of Warsaw, which stood bravely in its defense and displayed its profound patriotism, to accept the entry of the German forces quietly, honorably, and calmly."

According to reliable estimates, some six thousand Polish soldiers died and sixteen thousand were wounded in the defense of Warsaw in September. Of the civilian population, there were ten thousand dead and fifty thousand wounded. An estimated 11–12 percent of the buildings of historic importance were destroyed, as well as all the hospitals and many houses.

A Jewish youth who strolled around the wounded streets of the city, with their mounds of ruins, was struck by the feeling that the days of his youth had come to an end and that the Warsaw he knew and loved was gone. The city, its people, and its life would never be the same again.

2

THE JEWS OF WARSAW
BETWEEN THE WARS

J EWISH LIFE and the place of Jews in Polish society was
rather different from what it was in Western Europe. From
the French Revolution onward, Jews throughout Western Europe pressed for equal rights as individuals and confined expressions of their Jewishness to the religious sphere. In contrast, most
Jews in independent Poland between the wars insisted on their
recognition as a people, with the rights of a national minority.
The Jews wanted to be recognized as a community — part of and
apart from other elements in Polish society.

In the Western European countries, Jews were a small percentage of the overall population, but one in ten persons in Poland
was Jewish, and in many cities, towns, and hamlets, Jews constituted a large percentage of the total population. In some cities,
Jews constituted a majority of the population. Unlike other minority nationalities within Poland, Jews were dispersed throughout the various parts of the Polish state. Thus, they were not in
the same position as the Ukrainian minority, which was concentrated in a specific territory and could demand a form of
territorial autonomy, such as governmental recognition of their

language as the official language of a region, or independent judicial and educational systems.

Polish nationalism was intensely Roman Catholic and far more immune to the pressures of secularization than the more Western countries. As a result, the gap between state and society was deep, and Jews were far more inner-directed than their Western European counterparts. Though the sojourn of Jews in Poland was lengthy — the presence of Jews can be traced to the year 963 — it was almost always uneasy. Jews had arrived in Poland at the invitation of Polish princes to perform economically complementary functions that could not be undertaken by the majority population. The economic utility of the Jews led the ruling class to be more inclined toward tolerance and pluralism; thus, Poland attracted Jews suffering from discrimination in Germany in the thirteenth and fourteenth centuries. Among the general population in the economically backward Polish society, the masses did not experience prosperity, or even economic security. Their resentment against the Jews was intense. The Roman Catholic Church, itself a late arrival to Poland, often pursued a policy of discrimination and hate toward the Jews. It perpetuated negative Jewish images present in Christianity; of Jews as outsiders, betrayers, and perpetrators of deicide.

After World War I, Poland attained independence after 136 years of partition and occupation. The restoration of the Polish state, which had been the objective of a prolonged and obstinate struggle by the Polish people for the right to national self-determination, was a direct result of the disarray (be it due to military defeat or revolutionary turmoil) among Poland's enemies and occupiers: Austria-Hungary, Germany, and Russia. This led to the political-territorial decisions made at the Versailles peace conference.

The political and territorial order resulting from World War I seemed to play into the hands of those seeking national minority status. Under the minority treaties that were authorized and imposed on Romania and a string of new or renewed states — including Poland — the new states were obliged to give minorities rights protected by law and supervised by the League of Nations. The decision to undertake these treaties and define their contents was largely due to the insistence of American representatives at

Versailles (including the American Jewish groups) and other European countries. Actually, the minority treaties granted rights to the Jews solely as a religious group, but many Jews mistakenly interpreted these treaties as offering them the rights of a national minority.

In Poland, the "minorities treaty" seemed to guarantee constitutionally the rights of Jews as one of Poland's minority groups. On paper, the treaty assured equal rights for religious and national minorities as a fundamental provision of the new constitution. Jews and other minorities were given political and civil rights. As a matter of right, they were entitled to equal justice under law. Even their linguistic and cultural heritages were preserved, including Jewish school systems. Discrimination in hiring and professional employment was outlawed.

When the Polish government, which was made up of right-wing and centrist parties, tried to adopt an electoral system that would affect the proportional representation of the minority in Parliament, the Jews responded by setting up a united front to contest the elections — a "minorities bloc." In the end, the bloc's list gained a substantial victory, winning 22 percent of all the votes to the first Polish Sejm in 1922. The Jewish faction alone had elected 35 representatives out of 444 members of the Sejm, some 8 percent. In the Sejm, warring political factions of the right, the center, and the left neutralized each other's power. None had the power to put together a government on its own or to tip the scales in its favor on decisive questions. Consequently, the influence of the minorities bloc was enhanced. However briefly, it enjoyed disproportionate influence.

Members of the Jewish faction in the Polish parliament differed in their assessment of the politics of the minorities bloc. Some believed that the bloc was a permanent parliamentary body that should be active in the general Polish political scene while serving to protect essential minority matters. Other representatives, particularly those from eastern Galicia, believed that the bloc was a marriage of convenience, speculative and tactical at best. One could not presume that disproportionate Jewish representation would continue. They were dubious of the long-term prospects for cooperation with the Ukrainians, who were noted for their deep-rooted animosity toward the Jews. Thus, they urged that Jews become less involved in the internal power struggle over the various political trends in Poland.

Over time, it became clear that the solidarity of the minorities was questionable. After Hitler's rise to power, it seems that the German minorities in various countries were not inclined to oppose anti-Jewish legislation in Nazi Germany. So, the Jews were constrained to leave the organization of European minorities when they were abandoned by other minority groups and by the general public.

During 1924 and 1925, prominent members of the government put out feelers that resulted in practical discussions with Jewish representatives to the Sejm. They sought an accommodation along the lines of traditional Jewish politics. Jewish representatives would be obliged to adopt the government's line on basic matters and support the power interests of Poland, a concept that could be interpreted as supporting the regime's conduct toward the Slav minority on Poland's eastern border. In exchange, the government promised concessions and relief in a variety of essentially Jewish areas, such as economics, employment, civilian rights, education, and religion. This political agreement, known as UGODA, was instigated by one of the heads of the nationalist movement Endecja and the brother of then prime minister Stanislav Grabski and was supported by the majority of the Jewish representatives in the Polish parliament.

Extreme nationalist Jews, Zionists, and Bundists alike, intent on preserving Jewish national rights, viewed the UGODA as a near-betrayal of the national Jewish principle and appealed to the wider Jewish public for support in the controversy. But the public was indifferent and disappointed in the results of its political and parliamentary efforts.

In the early days of the revived Polish state, the Jews had great hopes. But these hopes faded away. Fiery speeches in the Sejm had no power to sway the authorities or to alter patterns of economic discrimination. UGODA was also little help and was not even implemented.

In the first years after independence, the minorities bloc, to which the Jews belonged, temporarily held the balance of power between right and left. After impressive initial successes in 1922, the minorities bloc lost strength in the subsequent elections. There was also a marked fall in the standing and popularity of the main Zionist faction led by Itzhak Gruenbaum. The Jewish population learned that the parliamentary struggle had little tangible impact on their daily life and that the operative and decisive power in economic life was concentrated in the hands of the government and the ruling administration.

In May 1926, with the help of a group of officers and some loyal units of the army, Jozef Pilsudski organized a bloody coup d'état. A socialist in his youth, Pilsudski had founded the national armed forces in World War I and led the Polish army in the 1920 campaign that overthrew the Bolsheviks, who had penetrated deep into Poland and nearly reached the outskirts of Warsaw. The masses saw Pilsudski as a hero symbolizing the renaissance of Poland. He was greatly admired in leftist circles, but he chose to leave the political scene when he realized that he could not dominate it. The right, which had gained the majority's support in the elections, viewed him with suspicion. But Pilsudski's "retirement" was short-lived. He was merely biding his time in anticipation of the appropriate moment in which to take the helm and impose his authority.

Polish political thinking concerning the structure of an independent Polish state moved in two contrary directions. The rightist conception was that there should be a complete identification of the state with the Polish nation, while the left and the center were inclined toward a wider partnership in the state. Ethnic Poles were the first among equals, but Poland was to become the fatherland of many nationalities.

Endecja opted for a Polish Catholic state — a state that would be the domain solely of the ethnic Poles. They considered minorities as tolerated citizens or people who assimilated into the Polish state. Jews were seen as aliens who had no legitimate right to be in Poland — as unnecessary, even harmful. In contrast, Pilsudski and his supporters wanted to see Poland as a political power and the focus of a federated alliance of the smaller states in the region, rather than as a state exhibiting the expansionist tendency of Russia and Germany.

Rather obscure outlines of territorial autonomy for the minorities were drawn up, particularly in the eastern Slavic sector. What to do with Jews was a more complicated matter, for they were dispersed. Nothing definite was contemplated for them, but it was commonly believed that Pilsudski was interested in the integration of the Jews into Polish society.

With regard to the Jews, the attitude of Pilsudski's administration was positive and heartening, particularly at its outset. Marshal Pilsudski centered most of his attention on matters of defense and foreign affairs. He did not show any special interest in the Jewish question, nor did he display any anti-Jewish sentiments in either his public or his political statements, and he evidently curbed antisemitic leanings among his supporters. He was not prone to using the Jews as a scapegoat for his failures or his administration's errors, which was a common phenomenon not only in Poland but also in other European countries. Apolinary Hartglas, one of the Zionist leaders in Poland, wrote that the first year or so was a time of genuine change:

> That period was like a real "springtime among the nations." Antisemitic propaganda ceased . . . no one dared to publish blacklists of Poles who dared to buy in Jewish shops, no one assaulted or beat up the Jews. The governors of outlying regions forgot about the existence of restrictions that were valid in the Czarist times . . . Jewish secondary schools began to receive official recognition, committees were set up to assess matriculation results, and there were even some examiners who knew Hebrew. New Jewish lawyers were being registered while some Jews were even accepted into the ranks of the civil service. And the Jews stopped complaining about the heavy burden of taxes imposed on them.

The hope that Pilsudski would impose a multinational concept never materialized. The idea of a federation was not at all practicable because at the very outset of the new Poland's existence, there were tensions and claims regarding the regions in dispute, the dictated boundaries, and the areas taken over by force.

But even in the smaller area under Poland's authority, the assumption that, with Pilsudski at its head, Poland would experi-

ence greater liberality and democratic order was not realized. The
new leader believed that the source of Poland's weakness lay in its
excessive number of political parties and in its anarchic parliamentary structure, spreading corruption and generating a faulty
order of priorities. He therefore strove to undermine parliamen-
tarianism, to free the political establishment of its class interests
and corruption. He did not look to the left for support; on the
contrary, he turned toward the aristocracy organized in the conservative movement and to big business.

Pilsudski's authoritarian rule did not display the cast of a
fascist regime, although it took quite a few steps that were brutal
deviations from a democratic order. In its first years, the regime
enjoyed certain helpful economic proposals, but after the profound crisis that resulted from the 1929 crash the state was
subjected to a deep depression and mass unemployment. Planned
reforms were set aside in view of the need to cope with troubled
daily pressures.

No real analysis was made of the minority question, no plans
were made for improving their situation, and eventually there was
a regression in the attitude of the authorities and on occasion the
brutal use of force. In time, the Pilsudski camp changed from a
concept of statehood encompassing all the country's citizens to a
nationalist ideology.

The perceptible weakness of Parliament and the entire democratic structure did not lead to a revolt, nor did it work to the
advantage of the Jews. Discrimination against the Jews was hesitantly renewed, but until the marshal's death in 1935 a measure
of restraint was maintained. His passing undoubtedly marked a
turning point. The Jews were well aware of the fact that Pilsudski's strong personality, even during his illness, had restrained
sharp anti-Jewish outbursts, and they felt a sense of bereavement
and apprehension for the future. During the first year after his
death, an interim government ruled under the aegis of the president, Ignacy Moscicki. Because of its weakness or genuine intention, this government tried halfheartedly to guide the state along
democratic lines, but increasing economic difficulties and social
tensions overwhelmed it. In the government that was established
in 1936, power was divided between the president and Pilsudski's

heir to the high command of the army, Marshal Rydz-Smigly, who had not shown any marked ability in his country's military and defensive preparations. The results were miserable. The regime moved in a totalitarian-populistic direction and rejected out of hand any attempt to create a united front out of the various currents of opinion in view of the growing danger from Nazi Germany.

During the post-Pilsudski period, hatred of the Jews increased and an anti-Jewish policy was adopted by the administrative system as well as by the right-wing opposition. Pilsudski's death seemed to unleash all the forces he had restrained. From June 1935 onward, violent disturbances were carried out in a number of places on the initiative of extremists of the Endecja and radical right. At universities and schools, where anti-Jewish quotas were imposed, Jews were pushed increasingly onto separate "ghetto benches" despite objections voiced by Jewish students and the solidarity of their fellow Christian students and some members of the academic corps. This process of discrimination ended in most cases in the imposition of racial separation and the introduction of quotas. Proposals of an anti-Jewish and even racial nature were introduced in the Sejm, but these were never passed. Radical anti-Jewish proposals were soon overshadowed by the political crisis presaging the advent of the war.

Nevertheless, the anti-Jewish trend continued to spread among the ruling camp, and their leadership assumed a slightly different tone. In Pilsudski's day, the Jews were part of the large range of supporters within his camp. In the elections to Parliament, Jews, who were excluded as representatives of bodies supporting the Pilsudski faction, appeared on the lists of the broad nonpartisan body of government supporters and the nonpartisan bloc for collaboration with the government. Shortly after the death of Pilsudski, the "bloc" was dissolved and Walery Slawek, the man who stood at its head and had been close to Pilsudski, was ousted from the political scene.

At the beginning of 1937, a new body was formed that helped the ruling Diadochi (the successors) — the OZON, the "camp of consolidated nationalists." Within the OZON, emphasis was placed on totalitarian principles and Catholic ties. In its early stages, the new "party" tried to attach itself to the ranks of the antisemitic and profascist radicals who had left the Endecja because they found it insufficiently extremist. The leaders of OZON stated that they would not accept Jews because they considered the Jews a separate national entity, and that their organization was open only to Christians. In May 1938 the supreme council of this party was busy formulating its position on "the Jewish question" in Poland which would ban Jews from certain professions. The solution of the Jewish problem would be achieved by getting rid of a major part of the Jewish population. Antisemitic propaganda had reached its peak.

During the early years of the republic, antisemitism had been an accepted, albeit restrained, fact camouflaged by the formal pretense that everything was as it should be. By 1938 antisemitism united both the opposition and the government. The government refrained from using violence and physical terror — riots, assaults, and forced eviction — and insisted that the antisemitic policy must function through quasi-legal channels. The government was cautious — street violence directed by a totalitarian-inclined opposition could easily redirect the anger of the masses against it. The radical right spoke of the wholesale expulsion of the Jews and claimed that this could not be achieved without the use of pressure and violence. On the other hand, the spokesmen of the government feverishly sought out places that would accept Jews as immigrants. The emigration of Jews to Madagascar was even considered. Jews were described as a real handicap to Poland's progress. Many socialists on the left and the liberal circles opposed antisemitism and came to the defense of the Jews. There were also those who held liberal opinions, especially those who were sympathetic to Zionism, who spoke warmly of Jews' emigrating to Palestine, but they always made a point of stating that emigration or integration was a choice to be made by the Jews themselves and was not a matter to be dictated or forced from without. In the various polemics that occupied the press and public opinion in those days, there were active socialists who pressed for a large Jewish emigration for economic and social motives. Among the Jews themselves, some leaders called for a mass exodus of the Jews from Poland. Understandably, these outcries unwittingly added fuel to the antisemitic fires.

For example, in 1936 Zev Jabotinsky, the charismatic leader of the Zionist Revisionists, publicly broadcast his "evacuation" plan for Polish Jews. Government circles and the Enjecja were enthusiastic about the plan, but this proposal also encountered sharp criticism and anger from most Jewish journalists. The loudest protests came mainly from among the Bund and Agudath Israel, who, no matter how much they differed with one another, both sought to secure Jewish life in Poland. Yet even most of the pro-Zionist press considered Jabotinsky's views impractical, for they presumed the mass emigration of the Jews of Poland depended primarily on the Jews themselves.

The social tensions in Poland, the increasingly anti-Jewish mood, and the growing public demand to bring about the mass emigration of Jews undoubtedly spurred on the desire to emigrate. Prior to World War I, the Jews numbered 30 percent of the emigrants from Poland, Poles were 55 percent, and the Ukrainians 15 percent. This pattern changed during 1921–25. During the first years of Poland's independence, Jewish emigration was 69 percent of the total. In absolute numbers, some 270,000 Jews left Poland, of whom 190,000 went to the United States and 30,000 to Palestine, which was then at the very beginning of its development as the Jewish national homeland. After 1926, the percentage of Jews emigrating decreased somewhat (in 1926, some 40 percent of the total number of emigrants), but the absolute number of Jewish emigrants was still rising. The slowdown did not reflect an essential weakening of their desire to emigrate from Poland but could be ascribed to the increasingly difficult conditions devised by the countries that were their potential destinations. For the Jews to leave, they needed a place to go. In reality, the number of applicants eager to emigrate from Poland and other countries was in reverse proportion to the number of requirements and immigration laws imposed by the governments of their intended destinations. Foremost on the list of urgent international priorities at the time was the need to find a solution for the refugees fleeing from Nazi Germany. During these years the United States placed limitations on immigration by introducing a quota system that discriminated against applicants from Eastern Europe. Other spacious and underpopulated countries followed the American lead and refused to accept immigrants. The severity of the Great Depression and the pressure of unemployment brought with it the fear of low-priced immigrant labor. Those countries prepared to permit controlled immigration wanted farmers, and the Jews could not offer them much in the way of experienced farmhands. In the heated atmosphere of anti-Jewish incitement in the 1930s, many countries did not hesitate to declare their unwillingness to accept Jews.

IN THE PERIOD between the two world wars, Polish Jewry, and especially the Jews of Warsaw, played a central role in Jewish life throughout the world. Second only to New York in the size of its Jewish population, Warsaw contained a Jewish life that was both traditional and creative, religiously conservative and nationalist. Despite intense involvement in Polish culture, Jews in Poland saw themselves primarily as part of the Jewish people dispersed throughout the world and less as an integral part of Polish society.

From 1918 onward, Warsaw was the capital of an independent Poland, which comprised areas that for more than a century had been occupied by foreign powers intent on undermining Polish nationalism. Under Russian occupation Warsaw had been the major target of a policy designed to eradicate all evidence of Polish nationalism. Nevertheless, despite Russian efforts, the younger generation remained politically oriented and nationalistically inclined. Warsaw was also the scene of economic development and drive.

As in Western Europe, Jewish entrepreneurs played a trailblazing role in banking, railroads, international finance, and new industries. Jewish families figured largely in establishing a capitalist economy in Warsaw and in expanding it throughout Poland. Many of these economic pioneers were surrounded by aides and loyal agents, most of whom were Jews. Like the "uptown" Jews of New York City, some members of these leading families converted to Christianity when they were still young, while others of the second or third generation assimilated into the Polish aristocracy and bourgeoisie. Others remained within the Jewish community.

The impact made by these individuals and families was extended to the advancement of cultural and artistic institutions, journalism, and publishing. In philanthropy, Jews contributed extensively to education and to the founding of hospitals and public welfare institutions. Their charitable gifts also enabled like-minded Jews to advance in Polish society, yet their progress often attenuated their ties, loyalty, and utility to the Jewish community. Still, when these families were at their prime, their members gave generously to the public needs of both the Polish population and the Jews. Some of them — but by no means all — were also active in the affairs of the Jewish community.

The growth of Warsaw as an influential Jewish community was the result of Jewish migration over several generations. In 1781, when Poland was on the verge of losing its independence, there were 2,609 Jews in Warsaw. In Praga, a suburb of the city on the eastern banks of the Vistula River, the Jewish community numbered 244. On the threshold of the twentieth century, in 1897, the Jewish population of the city had reached 219,128. At the outbreak of World War I, the Jews of Warsaw made up 38 percent of the entire population of the city, a percentage that was to become even larger when refugees and displaced persons streamed into Warsaw during the war. In the independent Republic of Poland of the interwar years, the number of Jews living in Warsaw grew in absolute terms, but there was a comparative decline in the Jewish component of Warsaw's population. In 1921 the Jewish community comprised 310,300 people, or 33 percent of Warsaw's 936,700 inhabitants. In 1939, on the eve of World War II, there were some 375,000 Jews living in Warsaw, and they composed 29.1 percent of the city's 1,289,000 inhabitants.

Numbers alone do not reflect the importance of the Jewish community of Warsaw between the wars. Jewish Warsaw lacked the tradition and distinction that characterized other Jewish communities in Poland such as Cracow, Lublin, and Lwow, where Jews had lived for generations. Warsaw had neither ancient buildings nor the aura of glorious memories, the vestiges of an influential past. There were no ancient synagogues such as the one in Cracow; none that had been the home of world-renowned scholars. There was no tradition of greatness. In fact, the oldest tombstone in the Jewish cemetery in Warsaw was dated 1807. Nevertheless, there was ample opportunity for newcomers to make their impact, and the city had the feel of a community coming into its own. Warsaw's comparatively new facades and its fast-growing strength were a source of openness. New inhabitants and casual visitors could feel welcome. Social change was more prevalent than stability.

Partly owing to Polish society's rejection of these would-be assimilationists, ideas flowing from the East — regions of Russia and Lithuania, where Jewish nationalist culture had already taken on varied organizational forms and ideological maturity — gained increasing influence in Warsaw's Jewish community. Jewish life was characterized by a large number of political parties, overlapping institutions, violent public debates, and private quarrels.

Three far-sighted and politically realistic Jewish movements emerged on the eve of Poland's independence: Zionism, with its various orientations; the Bund and its organizations; and Agudath Israel, which united Orthodox, Hasidic, and *mitnaged* (Orthodox opponents of Hasidism) elements of Polish Jewry. All three movements viewed the Jews as a distinct nation separate from the Poles, though their differing definitions of what constitutes a distinct nation caused the three groups to be at times bitter rivals.

The Zionist movement in Poland adopted two fundamental principles: the resettlement of Jews in Palestine, and the national rights of Jews living in the Diaspora. The Zionists believed that a national renaissance in Palestine would also have to provide the Jews in the Diaspora, outside Palestine, with a sense of their national unity during their seemingly lengthy sojourn in Europe. In Poland, Zionism undertook intensive activity within Jewish society in the Diaspora as "work for the present," with settlement of Palestine as the future goal (though in the interwar period Hehalutz and other Zionist youth movements actively engaged in fostering immigration to Palestine as a "present-day activity"). Hebrew was revived as a spoken language, but Yiddish remained the movement's working language.

The Bund, the General Jewish Workers Union devoted to secular Jewish nationalism, used Yiddish both for organizing Jewish workers into a separate framework and for disseminating the idea of socialism among Yiddish-speakers. The Bund soon advocated national rights founded on national and cultural autonomy: the right of the individual or group of individuals to maintain a separate language, culture, and social life in a specifically socialist state.

The Bund worked on a national scale throughout Poland, and its primary connections were often class based. Thus, the Bund preferred to work with local non-Jewish socialist parties rather than with bourgeois Jewish organizations. At the same time, many Polish Jews converged in a separate socialist party, which rested on a national Jewish base rather than on international foundations. This phenomenon was unknown in Western Europe, yet it became a movement of considerable strength and impressive achievements in interwar Poland.

Agudath Israel — the Orthodox party that included large Hasidic groups — adopted certain aspects of modern political organization similar to those of other political parties despite its attachment to tradition and its meticulous observance of Jewish law. These aspects included representation in government institutions and limited reforms in the educational system. Agudath Israel had its own press, political leaders, and patronage system. For the most part, Orthodox Jewry rejected Zionism, for it sought the return of Jews to their land by human efforts rather than through divine fiat. Quietistic in its religious orientation, Agudath Israel believed in the return to Palestine and the renaissance of Jewish nationhood as a divine act.

Only a small but disproportionately influential group of religious Jews, organized in the Mizrachi movement, sided with the secularist Zionists. They opposed Agudath Israel by their advocacy of Zionism, and they opposed the secular Zionists with whom they worked closely and cooperatively by pressing for a religious and cultural character to the Zionist efforts.

The guiding principles of the political ideology adopted by the Polish Jews in the period between the wars was that Judaism was not only a religion defined by its rituals, beliefs, and practices, but that Jews constituted a national entity pursuing nationalist politics, education, and culture.

Warsaw was the seat of political party headquarters, representatives, and institutions of the state; the administrative center of welfare and self-help organizations; the hub of educational and cultural networks of varying kinds, writers' groups, and admirers of the Yiddish and Hebrew languages. Most of the newspapers and books were published in Warsaw, to be distributed throughout Poland and sent abroad.

The attraction of training for the free professions brought many Jewish students from Warsaw and other parts of the state to study at schools of higher learning. In some years, Jews composed a substantial percentage of the graduates of all high schools and universities, including many women. Jewish graduates applied to the universities to continue their studies in medicine, pharmacy, law, the humanities, chemistry, the Polish language and literature. The percentage of Jews in higher education began a steady decline in the period between the wars. In the years 1921–22, Jews composed 24.6 percent of all students; in 1925–26, 20.7 percent; in 1934–35, 14.9 percent; and in 1937–38, 9.9 percent.

During the last years of Polish independence prior to World War II, the number of Jewish students filled the limit laid down by quotas, a policy never formally authorized but carried out in practice. Bearing in mind that the percentage of students from the city areas was well above that of students from provincial districts, it appears that the number of Jewish students dropped in relation to the strata of the population to which they belonged.

Jewish students organized their own association, and founded the Academics' House, a boarding school for three hundred students and an assembly hall for many others. From 1928 until the outbreak of war, Jewish historian and Zionist leader Yitzhak Schiper was its last director. An umbrella organization of Jewish students and organizations, it was concerned not only with the defense of students who had come under attack from malevolent groups of Polish youths, but also with initiating cultural activities and sporting events.

At all levels, studies were conducted in the Polish language, even in the independent schools. Some mistakenly view this extensive use of Polish, especially as the everyday idiom of the young people, as indicative of spreading assimilation among the Jews in general and particularly among those in Warsaw. But the Jews were not drawn to assimilation. On the contrary, assimilation was on the decline in interwar Poland. Jews spoke Polish, and they were avid readers of Polish literature and Polish writers, who often portrayed Jews in a very positive light. Many Jews also supported the Polish struggle for independence. Yet, at the same time, they were conscious of their Jewishness, joined Jewish organizations, and thought in terms of the Jewish future. Unlike many German Jews, who thought of themselves as Germans, Polish Jews absorbed Polish culture but did not assimilate into it. For the most part, the assimilation of the Polish-speaking Jews was no more common than the assimilation of the English-speaking Hasidim of Brooklyn. Yet there were notable exceptions.

The contribution of Jews and those of Jewish origin to Polish literature, particularly to poetry in the period between the wars, was distinctive. Unlike American Jewish novelists in the post–World War II period, such as Saul Bellow, Philip Roth, and Bernard Malamud, few of the major writers of Jewish origin dealt with Jewish subjects and some even converted to Christianity. Even those who used Jewish themes portrayed Jews as figures outside their own spiritual world.

Despite political instability and economic weakness, Jewish culture in Warsaw had a unique vitality. Warsaw was the largest and most important center of creative and cultural activities in both Hebrew and Yiddish. Hebrew, the holy tongue, recalled the days when Jews were in their own land, a time of greatest creativity for the Jewish people. It was the language of the Book and of prayer — but Hebrew had become a dim memory in the minds and tongues of the Jews. The revival of Hebrew in the Diaspora in the nineteenth century was accompanied by attempts to renew the language in literature and periodicals. Popular in intellectual circles, it did not capture the masses and become the language of the people. Only when Hebrew was adopted by the Zionist movement and became an integral part of the national and social renaissance did it change from a symbol to a living language. The Zionists were the primary advocates of the Hebrew language. In contrast, the Bund opposed Hebrew, and certain elements of Agudath Israel were opposed to the secularization of the holy tongue.

In the Diaspora, especially in Poland, Yiddish remained the language of the people. Between the wars, the Jewish languages flourished in Poland, and in Warsaw in particular, even as they were being abandoned in the Soviet Union and the West. Outside immigrant circles in the United States, the use of the languages declined. In the last decade of the nineteenth century, Yiddish literature reached maturity, and in the twentieth century, literature, newspapers, and other publications developed culturally and commercially.

Most writers and poets, journalists and publishers in Warsaw were not natives but were drawn to the city from outlying eastern districts, from Lithuania, and from the provincial towns of Poland. The growth and consolidation of Warsaw as a cultural hub derived not only from its being the seat of the largest urban Jewish population in Europe, but also because of its stimulating social-nationalist tendencies and its shifting lifestyles.

In independent Poland there was an abundance of Jewish dailies and weeklies, most in Yiddish but some in Polish and Hebrew. In addition to the commercial press, daily party newspapers were also published. In the years shortly before World War II, according to YIVO, there were 230 newspapers in Yiddish, including 27 dailies, 100 weeklies, 24 biweeklies, and 58 monthlies throughout Poland. Evidently, these figures included short-lived publications as well as permanent institutions. Most of the larger papers appeared in Warsaw, where publishing houses also found markets for the original works of well-known Yiddish writers, as well as translations of fiction and nonfiction.

More than any other creative medium, the Jewish theater spoke to the masses, its productions arousing intense emotions among devoted theatergoers. Historians of the theater credit Abraham Goldfaden as the father of the Jewish theater with his establishment of a company in Iasi, Romania, in 1874. In 1885, when Warsaw was under the Russian sphere, Goldfaden brought his Jewish German theater to Warsaw and performed for two years (the company's production of *Shulamith* was greeted with much enthusiasm). The city was also host to occasional appearances by acting troupes who would perform in a German dialect similar to Yiddish, as plays in Yiddish were forbidden. Jewish theater had to cope not only with limitations imposed by the Russian authorities, but also with taboos from within the community regarding language, topics for theatrical performances, and modesty.

Jews inclined toward assimiliation considered Jewish theater a backward step that distanced the Jewish theatergoer from the Polish art theater. Indeed, historical sources note that the development of the Polish theater and music in Warsaw in the nineteenth century owed much to the patronage of wealthy Jews and Jewish audiences.

In 1905, establishment of the Literary Company brought permanent, officially sanctioned Yiddish theater to the Jews of Warsaw. The company relied primarily on the dramatic works of Jacob Gordin and performances by a number of outstanding actors and actresses, including the brilliant Esther Rachel Kaminska, who fascinated and delighted Jewish audiences in Poland, Russia, and the United States. According to connoisseurs of the theater, her forte was her ability to portray the personalities and lives of heroines in a manner that enchanted her audiences. The material was generally tear-jerking melodrama, burdened with moralistic instruction. It was a style that appealed to a public confident that their fate was largely within their own control.

Many writers, especially Y. L. Peretz, showed a marked interest in the development of the Yiddish theater. A society was formed to encourage the theater, and funds were raised to support theater on a high artistic level, with Peretz and Sholem Asch active in fund-raising. Though their efforts were not always successful, the theater maintained a reputation for quality through the performance of works by well-known writers.

Warsaw's Yiddish theater was noted for its enthusiastic audiences. Traveling companies and actors from the United States and other countries were frequent visitors. In 1917 the Vilna Troupe visited Warsaw, introducing a higher level of theatrical achievement with its modern treatment of Yiddish drama. The troupe met with great success in Warsaw, and some of its members remained in Warsaw to establish what became the city's foremost theater during the period between the wars.

THE INFLUENCE of Warsaw's Jews during the period between the wars also increased as a result of the disruption and decline in status experienced by the Jews under the Bolshevik regime in the U.S.S.R. and the horror that descended on the Jews of Germany with the rise of Nazism in 1933. In Europe, this period began with great hopes and expectations engendered by the legitimization of national self-determination and the recognition of the rights of national minorities promised by President Woodrow Wilson, and by the promise proclaimed in the Balfour Declaration of 1917, which stated: "His Majesty's government looks favorably upon the establishment of a Jewish homeland in Palestine."

However, the greater the hopes, the greater the disappointments. This era saw the escalation of aggressive nationalism, the growth of totalitarianism, and the predominance of an unrestrained antisemitic racism. In these two decades of naive expectations and short-lived hopes, Warsaw, with its variegated texture and contrasts, became the focus of unlimited and wide-ranging Jewish activity. In those days of confusion on the brink of the abyss, it was virtually the capital of the Jewish people, particularly because of the isolation and disconnection of the Soviet Jew.

Many — perhaps the majority — economists, political leaders, writers, artists, journalists, publishers, historians, leaders, rabbis, Talmudic scholars, and Hasidim who reached prominence in Warsaw between the wars were not natives of the city but arrived there in response to its magnetic attraction and promise, in much the same way that other Jews were drawn to Paris or New York. Many Jews came to Warsaw from the provinces and many others from the eastern border of Poland and parts of Russia and Lithuania. Jews arriving from the eastern towns encountered strong opposition on the part of Polish circles who viewed the arrival of the "Litvaks" (Lithuanian Jews) as an invasion of aliens who spread the use of the Russian language and culture and were responsible for the "Russification" of local Jewry, much as New York's Jews bemoaned the arrival of Yiddish-speaking Eastern European immigrants between 1881 and 1920. Considerable criticism of the "Litvaks" also came from more established members of the community who ridiculed the Yiddish dialect of the new arrivals. Yet Warsaw not only served as a refuge for outcasts, it also gave those who arrived at its gates the feeling of home and provided them with ample opportunity to participate in cultural and communal life. Common folk who wandered toward Warsaw or escaped to the city from afar quickly acclimated to the ways of the city and the local Jewish community, becoming true citizens of Warsaw in every respect.

In his saga *The Family Moskat*, Isaac Bashevis Singer revealed the thoughts of a rabbi from a small town who came to Warsaw:

> R. Dan Katznellenbogen now comprehended the full significance of the Talmudic phrase "In big cities life is difficult," yet Warsaw had other merits. Here he found books he could not find in his own townlet Binuv, or even in Lublin. The city was a place of study: wherever one went, there were synagogues, houses of learning, shtieblach, ritual baths. Collectors made the rounds and gathered the weekly tax for yeshivas. From the *heders* and the religious schools, one hears the voices of schoolchildren, by virtue of whose very breath the world exists. It is true that there are also many secular things here, modern things: clean-shaven men, women who retain their natural hair, students who study in the gymnasia, all sorts of Zionists, strikers, and just plain riffraff who have abandoned their Jewishness. But R. Dan did not take this into account. Gradually he became known to the scholars of Warsaw and they came to welcome him. In his own little townlet, R. Dan did not receive a tenth of the respect he received here in alien Warsaw: it happened just as it was written: "Get thee out of thy country . . . and I will . . . make thy name great."

The opportunity to enter Jewish life was not limited to religious Jews alone. A leading member of the socialist Bund, Bernard Goldstein, paints another sort of picture on returning to Warsaw from his travels in the east at the end of World War I:

> I was drawn to the wide public of the Bundists . . . and went to the "Club." . . . It was like a bee-hive. Already evening and the club was packed. They were all over the place, in every corner. There were meetings going on in all the rooms, the choir was rehearsing, the reading room was filled with people; one could hardly pass through the hallways. Different people confronted me. I recognize old friends from illegal work and new friends,

youngsters, unrecognizable faces . . . one of my first jobs was to help the strike of Jewish community employees and teachers at its schools. They already had a professional organization, but they were typical white-collar workers ("proletariat of the starched cuffs" as they were called) and completely helpless as to how to conduct a strike.

Entire streets and neighborhoods in the suburbs of Warsaw were inhabited mainly by Jews, with the greatest concentration inhabiting the northern sectors of the city. In certain streets, all the buildings were occupied by Jews, except for the janitor, who was not a Jew. Religious and secular Jews lived side by side as neighbors, often within the same family. In many families, the father would observe the religious precepts and conform to all the traditional rules in his dress. The mother would wear a wig and fastidiously see to the kashrut of her kitchen. Some adolescents followed in the footsteps of their parents, and others became Zionists, Socialists, and even Communists, who had "gone astray." Young people were avidly devouring fiction, theoretical books, forbidden newspapers, and periodicals, smoking on the Sabbath, and filling their homes with endless and noisy political arguments.

The religious life of Warsaw's Jews was expressed in the style of their home life, in the keeping of the commandments, in the many institutions and services, such as ritual baths, kashrut, the network of rabbis and *dayans* (judges), and the many houses of prayer. In the synagogues and the *shtiebels,* the religious and traditional Jews congregated for prayer on the holy days, the Sabbath, and weekdays, and for endless hours of study and discussion with friends. In the 1930s, there were three hundred such houses of prayer and almost everyone who came there had a permanent place. On the holidays, especially Rosh Hoshanah and Yom Kippur, the style of worship was considered important and cantors with sonorous voices were in great demand. The great synagogue on Tlomacka Street, which was actually evolving into one of the more enlightened places of worship, attracted worshipers inclined toward assimilation. They introduced certain reforms, such as holding sermons in Polish, when this was permitted by the government.

The educated classes and the assimilationists were convinced that if they were to have any influence they would have to introduce changes into the educational system, in dress and lifestyle, and to refrain at all costs from interfering with strict religious ritual. Thus, they were reluctant to establish Reform or Conservative Judaism, and religious life remained Orthodox. Organs were not introduced into the religious services of the more enlightened synagogues, as this was considered untraditional. On the other hand, services that included a male choir were considered entirely acceptable, and of course an important component of the service was the liturgical vocal music of the cantor. At the great synagogue such well-known cantors as Gershon Sirota, who died in the Warsaw ghetto, and Moshe Kossovicki often led the services.

The *shtiebels* of the Hasidim, in addition to being houses of prayer and study, were also used as quarters for the Hasidic rabbi's followers. Prayers in the *shtiebel* were highly emotional. This was the scene of deliberations over Hasidic literature, homilies given on such feast days as Pentecost (Shavuoth), and spontaneous dancing and singing. The most powerful group among the Hasidic sects in Warsaw was the Hasidim of Ger. The rabbinical seat was in the townlet of Ger, not far from Warsaw. The entire town lived under the patronage of the rabbi's court, and thousands of his followers streamed toward the place, particularly on holidays and feast days. The Admor of Ger, R. Abraham Mordecai Alter, maintained that in order to combat the secularization and erosion of the religious integrity of the Jews, it was necessary to move in new directions. The founding of Agudath Israel, and the leading role filled by the Admor and his followers, actually marked the adoption of hitherto unknown political methods by an Orthodox religious camp. Among the Hasidic rebbes who were seated in Warsaw was Klonimus-Kalmish Schapira of Piaseczno, who left a collection of his sermons from ghetto days which was eventually published as *Holy Fire*.

Members of the free professions and avowed assimilationists lived in streets and houses occupied by Poles or by a combination of Jews and Poles. It is difficult to estimate how numerous they were, but they could not have been more than 20–25 percent of the Jews living in Warsaw. The Jewish wholesale trade and its branches was concentrated on certain streets. Gesia Street was known as the source of textiles and related accessories; Franciszkanska Street was the place for leather stores and tanners; and Swietokszyska Street was devoted to publishing houses, shops for schoolbooks, and antiques dealers with second-hand and rare books. The Jewish quarter itself could be distinguished by its houses and the conditions of its streets.

The tenants' financial status and lifestyle to a large degree determined the appearance of the street: the sidewalks, the crowdedness and the noise, the cleanliness and the smells. Jewish alleys were congested and obviously neglected. Paul Tarpman described the pace of life in a typical alley of this kind:

> The street is buzzing with activity of a kind one finds only in the Jewish quarter, for it serves as the nerve-center of trade and work. The street was unfamiliar with sleep. Night-time had little meaning here. During the day the shops were filled with customers and porters, who carried sacks, boxes, rolls of fabric, entire households . . . on their sturdy shoulders. Sidewalks were crowded with people from daybreak onwards: vendors were selling rolls and soda-water, peddlers carried baskets full of peanuts, sunflower seeds, notebooks, and candles, loans and other bargains were being offered to any passerby in the most seductive tones, beggars in tatters and loafers praised their goods in the highest terms to all and sundry.
>
> Here a Jew from the provinces howled and bemoaned the fact that in a single second, his possessions had disappeared as if they had never existed. And there, a man who had come down in the world begged for a hand-out. Further on, a groom damned a friend with all the biblical curses and rebukes he could muster, and at the corner of the street, a Polish policeman was setting a trap (meta) for a Jewish peddler. Jews wearing the long, traditional black caftans (kapote), others wearing small, black caps with little visors and clean-shaven heads, elegantly dressed women or some in the simplest of garments. Filthy children and clean ones, some well-nourished and others thin as a rail — one could find everything here.

David Canaani, a native of Warsaw, described his street and the house he lived in as a youngster:

The street consisted mainly of residential houses. There were very few shops — merely enough to supply the simplest needs: groceries, shoemakers and tailors, a laundry, coal storage, a tiny stationery store for writing materials, where one could get anything from a shoelace to glue. Here you have the entire business of the street. Our street was partly street and partly lane. A street — for on either side there were blocks of houses of three, four, or even seven stories, and in each house there lived no less than forty to fifty families. A lane — for no tram passed through. It was lit by gaslight, not electricity. It was paved with cobblestones, and every passing wagon would make horrendous rumbling sounds and echoes that made one's heart stand still. It was a narrow street. A strip of grey sky would hang loosely overhead: sunlight barely managed to slip between the walls of the tall buildings. Only towards evening would the rays of the setting sun gild the slanting tin roofs and the flickering lights relieve the dark gloom.

In the winter, the street would get even narrower, owing to the piles of frozen, dirty snow heaped up along the sides of the road. But on a summer's morn, it would sometimes be scented from the produce on a villager's wagon, smelling of fruit and field-flowers.

Our street, the haunt of thousands of Jews, one of hundreds of the Jewish streets of Warsaw which would become heaps of bones and mounds of ruins. Our house on Nowolipki Street, No. 15, was one of the thousands of gray and anonymous Jewish houses in Warsaw. Its windows look out from distances of time and place. Nevertheless, there appears to be something singling it out, erasing its gray anonymity and dimness. There are undoubtedly many among Warsaw's inhabitants who remember this house because of the newspaper *Unser Express* (Our Express), which had its offices here for a short time.

For decades, many thousands streamed through the building on their way to the clinic of the welfare organization known as Achiezer (Brothers Aid). From this house, links were established

with the old settlers in Palestine: for some years it was the center
for Rabbi Meir Bal Haness' funds. Collectors for religious institutions, functionaries and just ordinary needy Jews could be seen
coming and going. Hundreds of pupils studied in Estherson,
the Litvak's Heder Metukan [at the Orthodox school, children
learned the Torah almost exclusively from a very tender age,
while at the Heder Metukan, a certain number of other subjects, such as arithmetic, the language of the country, and general knowledge, were taught], until he turned his school into a
hotel.

Hundreds, and perhaps thousands, of immigrants leaving for
Palestine and emigrants to America spent their last days and
nights in this "hotel."

But it was not the institutions which gave our courtyard its
character. Our house was essentially a residence for tens of Jewish families living there permanently. The house was old and had
been standing for some sixty or seventy years, with the typical
format of Warsaw houses and a courtyard closed in on all four
sides called "a box." There was a staircase at each corner, apart
from the wider and more elegant entrances to the street . . .
Almost all the apartments consisted of two rooms and a kitchen,
a small hallway in which the toilet was hidden behind a screen of
planks, and where a laundry basket and all sorts of junk could
be found as well. Apartments of this kind were considered re-
spectable and well arranged. At the heart of the Jewish quarter,
not only all the residents but all the institutions and all the
services were designed for the Jews and were essentially Jewish in
character. The Jews had the feeling of being at home among
themselves, in their own element. They were free to behave and
do as they pleased. The Yiddish language dominated the streets.
The motley crowd created a colorful and harmonious existence
within the teeming din and clamor. In the eyes of the Poles from
the more well-to-do and elegant streets but a few minutes away,
the Jewish quarter seemed a strange and alien world, while from
the point of view of many Jews, the specifically Polish streets
were an area of discomfort and at times the scene of attacks,
offensive name-calling on the part of hooligans, and even physical assault, particularly in the '30s.

The upheavals of World War I — military operations, mass movements of populations, and the change of rulers — paralyzed the economic life of Warsaw. The Poles displayed untiring and persistent enthusiasm in their struggle for restored political independence, but national freedom in itself did not solve the existential problems of a people. Poland between the wars suffered from the weakness of the Russian markets, which formerly constituted a consumer of Polish industrial production, and Poland was weakened by recessions and the great economic crisis of the interwar period.

IN INTERWAR POLAND, there was a marked tendency to oust Jews from positions of standing in the economy, most especially in Warsaw. It would be an overstatement to attribute to the Poles in general, and to all the nation's political bodies, the inclination to rid the economy of Jews and to view Poland's future through the prism of antisemitism, but anti-Jewish slogans were prevalent. There were many who saw in the elimination of the Jews from economic positions — and, from the late 1930s onward, the ousting of Jews altogether — the panacea for all of Poland's ills. This was the dominant opinion within the Endecja, with its large contingent of the bourgeoisie, the middle classes, and the intelligentsia. It was also the doctrine that permeated the ranks of many young students and political activists who, in the 1930s, abandoned the Endecja and founded a radical-nationalist branch, which, despite its self-avowed Catholic orientation, enthusiastically appropriated many elements of fascist ideology and adopted the anti-Jewish policies of the Nazis as its model.

The Jews were a distinctly urban element throughout Polish cities. Apart from a small minority of Germans, some of whom had obscured or rejected their former identity, the Jews were in many aspects the most distinct of Poland's minorities. A situation so rife with tensions and shortages naturally provided fertile ground for accusations against the Jews. The Jews, it was claimed, were responsible for the backwardness of the Polish cities, and Poland's poorly managed industry and commerce were a direct outcome of the excessive number of middlemen and their scramble for speculative profits.

Many Jews, or rather most Jews, were active in the world of commerce and trade and in certain skills and crafts that employed methods well behind those of the Western nations. However, instead of addressing the causes for the poor state of its cities and the backwardness of its commerce, and energetically introducing basic reforms and improvements in both the rural and urban sectors, Polish authorities frequently preferred to attribute the responsibility for this sorry state of affairs to the Jews, who were portrayed as the obstacle to eagerly awaited changes.

According to statistics, the Jews owned 73 percent of private businesses in Warsaw at the end of World War I, while in 1928 this percentage dropped to 54 percent, and it continued to decline until World War II. This regression is underlined even further on examining the categories of businesses in Jewish hands. It appears that the figure 39.5 percent, which represents the Jewish commerce in Warsaw in 1928, decreased to 23 percent in 1933. The fact that the Jews were mainly engaged in petty commerce and peddling did not lessen the antagonism. On the contrary, the small shopkeeper was seen by the consumer as an independent entrepreneur supplying all branches of production and responsible for the increasing gap between wages and prices, as well as for the problems of the unemployed who bought merchandise on credit and could not repay their debts in time.

The image of the rich Jew manipulating the strings of commerce was very common among lower-class Poles. In his book *The Republic of Many Nations,* a Polish scholar, Jerzy Tomaszewski, documented that apex of Poland's economy between the wars. There were ninety-two specific individuals in the ranks of the financial oligarchy who determined economic policy. Judging by the sound of their names and by other indications, at most fourteen of them were Jews — some had either assimilated or converted. As is traditional with antisemitic stereotyping, it is sufficient for only a small number of Jews or even one Jewish individual to be involved with an area of commerce in order to prove Jewish domination.

Jews were also the first to break down the barrier set up by the Union of Soviet Socialist Republics after the Revolution, and the Jewish Merchants Association organized a share-holding company whose expertise was in establishing commercial connections with the East. The nucleus of the Merchants Association, a powerful and prestigious body founded in 1906, was situated in Warsaw, and from there it spread to a network of branches throughout the country where it was organized according to specific trades. According to the Jewish historian Meir Balaban, this organization boasted some six thousand members in Warsaw in 1928. The association would arrange annual conventions, and, according to one of its members, these were "important events in the Jewish political calendar in Poland."

Businessmen from Warsaw were the dominant figures in the Merchants Association. By 1935 Abraham Gepner headed the organization. He was a man of enormous vitality, who had started life as a delivery boy in a commercial company and had reached a position of prominence in the metal trade as a merchant and manufacturer. In the 1930s, Gepner became known as a highly principled public figure and a philanthropist who was particularly sensitive to the fate of orphan children. During wartime and the ghetto, Gepner, then a man of almost seventy, was a member of the Judenrat and was responsible for supplies — that is, for the very sensitive and socially explosive area of distributing food to hungry people. In this unrewarding role, his good name was never questioned. In addition, he secretly supported the underground movement and the Jewish Fighting Organization. In his last days, Gepner wrote that he did not regret remaining in the ghetto with his brothers and sisters, and "if I could wipe away but one tear — I was well rewarded."

Within the ranks of the various types of manufacture, Jews excelled as developers, both within the framework of the Polish state and internationally. When the large companies left the arena of private enterprise and became share-holding companies, a number of Jews were appointed as their directors.

In general, the Jews preferred to work independently — that is, not to be wage earners but to maintain their own business or shop, no matter how small. Only under the heavy pressure of taxation, which affected the lower middle classes, and especially after the havoc inflicted by the severe depression, did the Jews who had been small businessmen experience the painful process of proletarianization. There were many artisans among the Jews of Poland, but the number of Jews working in agriculture in a country that was basically agrarian was markedly low. This reflected government restrictions against Jews' owning land, imposed time and again throughout Jewish history. In 1918 the Jews composed 37 percent of the artisans, and this percentage rose considerably during the years of Poland's independence. Jews were concentrated in certain branches of work, especially those demanding a degree of expertise, such as the manufacture of clothing, shoes, wood, hats, leather goods, haberdashery, and furs, among others.

In 1926 a government survey revealed that 55 percent of all workshop employees were Jews. In 1927 wide reforms were introduced with regard to workshop conditions and standards, and the workers were obliged to undergo an examination by the authorities which would entitle them to a license (patent), giving them the right to engage in their craft if they succeeded in passing. Many Jews failed, and quite a few complained that this was not due to faulty products but because the examinees were asked to prove their mastery of the Polish language. As a result, many Jewish workshops were forced to operate without an official license, and this had an effect on the prices they could demand. Work had to be done at the workers' homes. In the poorer Jewish sections, in Mila, Smocza, Krochmalna, and others, there were many tailors, shoemakers, dressmakers, and all sorts of temporary workers, who worked as independent artisans or undertook temporary job lots from contractors. Temporary artisans and workers, known as *chalupnicy,* lived in one small room and used the workshop for eating, sleeping, and daily family life. Children did their homework or played games in a tiny area of this one room, which was often gloomy.

In the course of time, these severe regulations were somewhat eased. The artisans were organized into a professional union called the Central Association of Jewish Artisans, and had some eight thousand members in Warsaw alone and more than five hundred branches throughout the country. The union attended to many aspects of the professional sector and protected the artisans' rights on the official and legal levels. The contradictory views that led to a split of this many-sided union were not only political, but were sometimes caused by a conflict of personalities and the ambition to dominate the union, according to Joseph Marcus, author of a book on the social and political history of Polish Jews between the wars. Until 1929, the union was headed by Adam Czerniakow, an engineer who was close to the assimilationists, but like other members with similar views, Czerniakow moved toward serving the Jews in other capacities and defended them against the discriminating policies of the authorities. Czerniakow was chairman of the Judenrat in the Warsaw ghetto from the beginning of the Nazi occupation, from October 1939 until he committed suicide at the start of the deportation of the Jews to Treblinka on July 22, 1942.

The larger Jewish unions also had a banking system and a welfare fund. The American Jewish Joint Distribution Committee (the Joint) had a large share in initiating and channeling funds into the maintenance of the financial and welfare network. According to Joseph Marcus, in the aftermath of the stock market crash, there was a decline in the Joint's involvement in and aid to these banking institutions. This only exacerbated the dire conditions of Polish Jews. Consequently, there was also a weakening of the effectiveness of the Jewish economic unions at the time when they were needed most. In response, independent mutual aid from local Jewish sources increased at this critical juncture.

In all, the decade of the 1930s was a period of dire poverty and widespread unemployment throughout Poland, but the greatest burden was placed on the Jews employed in the more vulnerable sectors of the economy who received less aid from the government, which proved incapable of dealing with the economic situation. From the middle of the 1930s, evidence of the increasing influence of the anti-Jewish course in the economy found its extreme and clear expression in the policies of the radical right opposition, which did not refrain from resorting to violent persecution and riots. At the same time, the ruling Pilsudski camp adopted anti-Jewish measures in the political and economic spheres by means of the "legitimization" process of an anti-Jewish boycott. When asked about his policy toward the Jews, the prime minister, General Felicjan Slawoj-Skladkowski, replied that he rejected violent means but that economic sanctions were mandatory. Economic sanctions directed against a sector of the population whose faith, language, and customs differed from those of the majority were deemed appropriate. About a quarter of all the Jewish inhabitants of the city were paupers in need of help, and some of them were on the verge of actual starvation.

The structure of Jewish society was that of a pyramid: at the top were a few of the wealthy. The middle layer consisted of most of the middle class, while the wide base contained the greatest number of people, those with low incomes or lacking steady incomes. In the course of time, these proportions changed, according to sociologist Jacob Lestchinsky. The top and middle layers of the pyramid thinned out, while the lowest layer of the pyramid swelled out of all proportion. During the entire interwar period, the Jews felt the need to reorient their professional lives and move from petty commerce and middleman positions to industry and established occupations. They sensed that a move in the economic status of the Jews would improve their image in the eyes of the gentiles. During the thirties, work in industry was regarded as a guarantee of stability and the promise of decent working conditions. There were innumerable petitions and attempts by Jewish public bodies to direct the many Jews without a livelihood to Jewish factory owners, but these had only limited results. Jewish factory owners were unwilling to employ Jews for several reasons. The enterprises owned by non-Jews employed only a few Jews as a rule, and hence the presence of a large number of Jews in a single factory was an unmistakable indication that the owner was a Jew — a matter the owner preferred to conceal. Second, most of the Jewish workers did not want to work on the Sabbath, which was then the Jewish family's accepted day of rest, even among the more secular circles. It was natural for an enterprise that employed large numbers of workers to keep Sunday as the compulsory day of rest, and exceptions to this rule caused discomfort and confusion in the production process. In certain industries, the non-Jewish workers themselves objected to the employment of Jews. At any rate, the acute distress as well as the antisemitic mood evidently moved some of the

Jewish industrialists to take on a number of Jewish workers despite the drawbacks involved.

The Polish government took an active role in directing the economy. Nearly a quarter of the capital, and ownership of some basic industries, was in government hands. The nationalization of entire branches of industry, such as salt, tobacco, alcohol, and lotteries, excluded Jews from areas in which they had formerly played a considerable role. Jews also claimed that credit policies discriminated against them. Jews were almost entirely barred from working in the national and municipal administrations. In his book *The History of the Jews in Warsaw,* Abraham Levinson indicated that

> in 1931, there were half-a-million administrative workers in the Polish government, with one percent of Jews among them — less than a tenth of the Jewish sector all together. In 1923, among the 3,177 clerks employed in national credit institutions — a sphere of the economy in which Jews were noted for their experience and native talent — there were 23 Jews or .66%. The Jews comprised 33% of Warsaw's population, yet among the 4,342 workers and officials in the municipal tramway services, two Jews, or .05%, were employed in 1928. Fifteen hundred additional workers and clerks were taken on in 1929, and after many efforts another . . . 4 Jews.

In an increasingly dire situation, the aid and advice given by the Jewish institutions concerned with mutual guarantees played a significant role. In addition to the professional unions organized according to their economic activities and employment, there were also funds for loans and urgent assistance within the Jewish communal framework. The Organization for Rehabilitation through Training (ORT) and the Society for the Promotion of Vocational and Agricultural Work among the Jews prepared Jewish youth for working as artisans and craftsmen and helped by providing the machinery and training for workshop personnel.

There were also attempts to direct young people toward agricultural training. The Hehalutz movement, made up of older

members of youth movements who were trained to join the kibbutz movement in Palestine, and other pioneers, who wished to
be part of a communal effort before emigrating, worked on agricultural farms and did other types of work in anticipation of their
future in Palestine. While some youth groups were no more than
reserves for a political party, such Zionist youth movements as
Hashomer Hatzair, the Young Zionist, or Akiva had defined ideologies but were not linked to a political party. Their members,
especially in the pioneering movements that prepared their members for life in Palestine, refrained from public and political activities in the Diaspora and focused on preparation for *aliyah,* the
ascent to the land.

The Jewish community of Warsaw maintained an educational
network that also stressed vocational training. The most efficient
and popular of the organizations was the group of companies
offering loans without interest to the needy — a form of assistance that combined the ancient tradition of mutual guarantees
with the Torah's dictum of not lending money on interest. The
Central Organization of Societies for the Support of Non-Interest
Credit and Promotion of Productive Work (CEKABE), which
became known for its organizational and practical achievements,
was set up with the financial assistance of the Joint in 1926.
Immediately after World War I, the Joint was drawn into helping
Jewish communities that had suffered from the havoc wrought by
war, and later on it returned in order to stand by the Jews of
Poland in their growing economic distress. The basic concept
guiding the Joint's assistance was one of constructive rehabilitation — that is, not philanthropic aid for daily needs, but money
that would enable the recipients to rebuild or strengthen their
source of livelihood or to undergo professional retraining. In the
circumstances prevailing at the time, this form of help was a protective measure for the Polish Jews. Those who received money
were obliged to return it in small specified amounts, while the
fund network was organized on the basis of membership and
membership fees. In the course of time, the Polish Jews' share in
the fund began to grow. Marcus writes that in 1937, CEKABE,
which gave loans without interest, numbered 825 local companies, with a dues-paying membership of 100,000.

The historian and chronicler of the Holocaust Emanuel Ringelblum, who was employed by the Joint in Poland, wrote a biographical study of Yitzhak Gitterman, one of the heads of the Joint in Poland and one of the driving forces behind the concept and organization of the fund network. (Gitterman was murdered by the Nazis in January 1943, more than a year before the murder of Ringelblum himself.) Gitterman maintained that there should be less charity but that the money at the disposal of the funds should serve as a stimulus to the economy. According to Ringelblum, the funds were a popular institution on the Jewish scene which had a role in every Jewish community and even in those towns where a community had barely established itself. The cooperative movement's activities among the Jews were also significant, in part because the movement abandoned the conservative inclinations ingrained in the Polish-Jewish mentality. It proved itself on many occasions by the effective means it adopted to counteract distress.

Among the different welfare institutions, such as old-age homes, hospitals, and so forth, the Association for the Care of Jewish Orphans (CENTOS) occupied the most respected position. It supported orphanages, among them the famous orphanage run by the pedagogue and writer Dr. Janusz Korczak and his assistant, Stefania Wilczynska, who not only created a model home for children but introduced original educational methods and self-instruction to both Jewish and Polish children which were studied by other educators. Korczak, Wilczynska, and the directors of other orphanages in Warsaw did not abandon their charges and in the days of the Holocaust Korczak's last journey, with two hunderd children on board the train to Treblinka in the summer of 1942, served as a beacon of dignity amid the appalling darkness of barbarity and slaughter.

The TOZ society was responsible for health and child care. The Central Agency for Aid to Jews in Warsaw saw to the most urgent needs of the poor and in 1936 gave assistance to some three thousand families. And perhaps the most original form of help came from a group of volunteers who made the rounds of the Jewish courtyards with large baskets in hand, asking for foodstuffs for the patients in hospitals. This group was called

"Good Sabbath, Little Jews" after the greeting with which they heralded their request for food for the sick. Children in these quarters excitedly awaited their arrival, carrying small packages containing food and sweets.

Youth movements played a primary role in the Jewish struggle and defensive action that was the last vivid manifestation of the Warsaw Jews' will to live. The youth movements, which treated adolescence and youth as an estimable period rather than simply as a transition to adulthood, originated in Germany at the onset of the twentieth century. According to Walter Laqueur's book on German youth movements, most members were middle-class young people who felt alienated and sought to change the social fabric. Within the intimate setting of the youth movements, they tried to improve the social climate.

While rudiments of the Jewish youth movements of Poland were evident prior to World War I, consolidation and maturity took place between the wars. The youth movements provided an ideology to those yearning for a purpose and for an intimate attachment to ease the dreariness of their lives. While it is not known how many belonged to the youth movements of Poland, sixty thousand is a reasonable estimate. During the occupation and the time of the ghetto, this reservoir of young people focused on local affairs and activities within the Jewish community.

Historians may ponder what might have been the fate of Polish Jewry had the Germans not invaded Poland in 1939 and not imposed the "final solution." What we can ascertain is that the two decades between the wars were a time not only of hardship and trial for the Jews, but also of achievements. And after all, the difficulties of relations with non-Jews were at least conflicts with a human dimension; the war and the Nazi occupation wrought a transition from an era of human troubles to one of inhumanity and destruction.

3

A NEW AND DIFFERENT
EXISTENCE

IN THE AFTERMATH of the German invasion in 1939, Poland
was divided into three areas. Western Poland was annexed by
Germany and incorporated into the Reich. Eastern Poland
was annexed by the Soviet Union as part of the Ribbentrop-
Molotov Pact between Germany and the Soviet Union established
just on the eve of the German invasion. Central Poland was
established as the General Government under German occupation, with Cracow as its capital. Still, Warsaw remained the center
of Polish and Jewish life.

Within the occupied area, Nazi rulers issued a seemingly endless series of decrees affecting both Jews and Poles. Incremental in
nature, these set the framework for ever-intensifying oppression.
The interval following each new decree allowed the captive population to adapt to deteriorating conditions. After each momen-
tous decree was issued, such as the confiscation of Jewish
property, imposed forced labor, or the transfer of Jews to work
camps, the Jews breathed a sigh of relief. The worst seemed to be
over and no greater trouble appeared likely. Few could envision
the future.

The mood of the Jewish community was somber. After the first few weeks of occupation, the Jews of Warsaw were fed up with the daily decrees and injunctions. Perhaps it would be easier, they said to one another, if Jews were told what was permitted and could then assume that everything else was forbidden.

At the outset of the occupation, the Nazis employed deceptive tactics. Military commanders of the Wehrmacht, which governed the city, mollified the community. Jews were told that "they need not be worried about their well-being." In October 1939 Hans Frank, a German attorney and top-ranking Nazi, was appointed governor-general of central Poland. He announced that "under a just government, everyone would earn his living by working. On the other hand, there is no room for political agitators, money-dealers and Jewish exploiters under German rule." Frank's remarks were ambiguous. No one was certain whether he would target only larcenous Jews or all.

On November 23, 1939, a Nazi decree was issued requiring that all Jews wear a white ribbon imprinted with a blue Star of David on the sleeve of their outer clothing. Jewish-owned shops also had to display Jewish identification. Three weeks later, on December 11, Jews were forbidden to change their places of residence within the area under the supervision of the governor-general. Within days, it was announced that Jews were obliged to register all their property and possessions, and on January 26, 1940, Jews were forbidden to use the railways without special permission.

The segregation and isolation of the Jews continued. Next, they were barred from various professions and excluded from entering restaurants, bars, and public parks. Jews were to use special carriages on public trams. A 7:00 P.M. curfew was imposed on the entire population in September 1940. For Jews, the curfew began an hour or two earlier.

Most of these restrictions were intended to humiliate, separate, and denigrate the Jews. Initially, they had a dramatic effect. A young man wrote of feeling that his arms were encompassed by a tight ring when he first had to wear the badge of disgrace, the Star of David. But in time, perhaps because they followed one

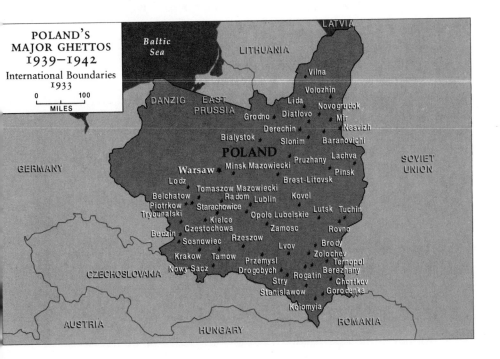

POLAND'S
MAJOR GHETTOS
1939-1942
International Boundaries
1933
0   100
MILES

Baltic Sea

LATVIA

LITHUANIA

DANZIG

EAST PRUSSIA

GERMANY

POLAND

SOVIET UNION

CZECHOSLOVAKIA

AUSTRIA

HUNGARY

ROMANIA

Vilna
Volozhin
Lida
Novogrudok
Grodno   Diatlovo   Mir
Derechin   Nesvizh
Bialystok   Slonim   Baranovichi
Warsaw   Minsk Mazowiecki   Pruzhany   Lachva
Lodz   Pinsk
        Tomaszow Mazowiecki   Brest-Litovsk
Belchatow   Radom   Lublin   Kovel
Piotrkow   Starachowice   Lutsk   Tuchin
Trybunalski   Opole Lubelskie
        Kielce
Bedzin   Czestochowa   Zamosc   Rovno
    Sosnowiec   Rzeszow
        Krakow   Tarnow   Przemysl   Lvov   Brody
Nowy Sacz   Drogobych   Zolochev
                Rogatin   Ternopol
                Stry   Berezhany
        Stanislawow   Chortkov
                Gorodenka
            Kolomyia

another so quickly, the restrictions and decrees were taken as a matter of course. The Jewish response was muted, resigned.

The public marking of Jews made life more difficult and prevented Jews from moving about freely outside the crowded Jewish quarter. Everywhere they went, they were identified and stigmatized as Jews. One man commented in his diary on the humiliation and the taunting of Jews, "Should one be offended? The oppressor is non-human after all!"

Some Nazi orders attacked the essence of the ability of Jews to survive. Jews were dismissed from jobs and offices without compensation. Others were deprived of their pensions and rights. Jews were excluded from the system of social welfare. Jews who had worked in industry, workshops, the free professions, teaching — that is, all who had received a monthly wage — were left without a livelihood, without any legal means of support. Refugees who were stuck in Warsaw or had been driven into Warsaw en masse at the beginning of 1940 found themselves in even more desperate circumstances. Unable to work, they could not return home.

Wealthy Jews, merchants, and factory owners were in a comparatively better position. They closed their businesses but moved the goods and materials in their warehouses to hidden places and cellars. Aided by Polish and Jewish informers, however, the Germans conducted searches and confiscated many of those goods. Germans appeared in uniform or in civilian clothes. Some carried papers that seemingly gave them the right to take what they found. Others bore no papers and were all the more dangerous and brutal. They confiscated furniture, pianos, medical books, clothing, and children's toys. Truck after truck loaded with goods taken from Jewish households could be seen leaving the Jewish quarter.

The attack on personal property was followed by the confiscation of savings and cash. Jews were forbidden to possess more money than was needed for daily expenses. If money was not handed over, Jews could no longer continue to operate their businesses. All money kept in bank accounts or owed to Jews by non-Jews was forfeited to the Nazis. The more affluent, some 5–10 percent of the Jews, could survive on their reserves or by disposing of their valuables. Temporary workers and the very poor were forced to live from day to day, selling whatever they had in exchange for basic necessities. Inadequate in the best of times, their resources soon were completely depleted.

Two general decrees issued during the first two months of the occupation shaped the entire course of the ghetto's existence: the appointment of a *Judenrat,* or Jewish council of elders, as a ruling body within the Jewish community, and the imposition of forced labor on the Jews.

On September 21, 1939, Reinhard Heydrich, head of the security police and second to Himmler in the SS hierarchy, ordered the establishment of a Judenrat, a body composed of "reasonable personalities and rabbis" from among local Jews. The Judenrat was to "bear the full responsibility for executing exactly and according to a time schedule, every order given at present or in the future." While appearing to be an institution of Jewish self-government concerned with protecting Jewish interests and looking after communal needs, in actuality the Judenrat was intended as an instrument of German control. Obedience and subservience were demanded; the duty of carrying out German orders was the main task.

The twenty-four leaders of the Warsaw Judenrat could not have been aware of what would be demanded of them. Jews who accepted these roles, or were forced to do so, could not fully understand the Nazi regime's intentions. They assumed that they would serve as representatives of the community under a hostile regime. It was not a pleasant task, but certainly a necessary one. Centuries of experience had taught them that even if the Jewish representatives could not influence hostile rulers, they nonetheless could intercede and request mercy in high places. They had learned that it was ultimately possible for Jewish representatives to alleviate the plight of Jews and offer solace if not protection in times of distress. And this was certainly not the first time in the history of Jews in the Diaspora when Jewish leaders would be forced to serve their community on behalf of a hated and oppressive ruler. One can assume that some Judenrat members undertook these positions reluctantly, while others were motivated by ambition.

Adam Czerniakow was the leader of the Judenrat in Warsaw from its founding until his suicide in July 1942. Throughout his tenure, he scrupulously maintained a diary, writing daily entries detailing his efforts and the conditions he faced. On October 4, 1939, he described his appointment as head of the Judenrat: "I was taken to Szuch Boulevard and there I was informed that I have to assemble 24 people to form a community council and act as their head." The offices of the German authorities in Warsaw were situated on Boulevard Szuch, considered by the people the Gestapo's fortress.

Czerniakow was born in 1880, the son of an assimilated Jewish family in Warsaw. After finishing his studies in chemistry at the Warsaw Polytechnic, he went on to study industrial engineering in Dresden, Germany. Returning to Warsaw, he married and started a family, but did not work at his profession. Instead, he became a teacher at the technical high school, headed the organization of Jewish artisans, and held a post in a public enterprise. He was also a member of the Warsaw municipal government, was active in Jewish associations, and was a candidate for the senate and a member of the board of directors of the Warsaw Jewish Community.

A Zionist leader described him as "a gifted man, lacking any political or public ideals, but a decent man." Czerniakow was ambitious, with talents that were not revealed until he saw the right moment to assume a leadership role. He was not a member of a Jewish party, nor did he identify with any of the dominant political or socioreligious movements, although at a certain stage he sided with the minority bloc and moved nearer the non-Zionists within the Jewish Agency.

Czerniakow was a staunch Polish patriot, completely at home in Polish and European culture. He was removed and almost alien to the life, culture, and history of the Jewish people. An assimilationist, he had been publicly active in the Jewish sector, yet he remained an outsider. According to one report, "until his appointment, no one had heard of him." Even his enemies claimed that he was a decent man with good intentions and high moral standards, perhaps too decent for a time that required much more than decency and morality to lead the Jewish people.

Czerniakow was a liberal in his views and inner world, sensitive to people and life, introverted and isolated, a book lover and a secret writer of poetry, and with little understanding of the masses. As head of the Judenrat, he may have longed for the Germans he had known in Dresden — straightforward and considerate people, with a sense of law and order, who could be depended on to keep their promises.

However, the police, the Gestapo, and the Nazi officials he came across as head of the Judenrat were an entirely different breed. When he occasionally encountered a humane response, he was momentarily relieved, but on the whole he was filled with bitterness and disappointment until his sad end. Bald and stout, Czerniakow was insulted and physically assaulted. Still he insisted on maintaining a civil manner. He would not submit or humiliate himself. Some two months before his tragic death, he wrote in his diary, "Have I the strength to maintain a decent level of behavior?" His concern to keep his self-respect in dealing with the Germans was foreign to most of the Jews around him but was characteristic of the man.

His state of mind is clearly and impressively reflected in the notation in his diary on January 26, 1940:

I was summoned to the police [Lieutenant Colonel Daume]. The community must pay 100,000 zlotys for having assaulted an ethnic German woman [*Volksdeutschin*] or else, 100 Jews will be shot. I appealed to the Gestapo to relieve us of this payment, and afterwards they agreed that I would not have to supply laborers for clearing the snow, so that we could save some money. Nothing came of it. We have to pay the money — tomorrow morning precisely. As this was the situation, I started to collect money from the community. Must borrow 100,000 and afterwards collect from those who owe taxes. At the same time, the police are demanding 6100 zloty for 61 Jews and Jewesses, who were caught without the Star of David band on their sleeves. In view of these experiences, I asked the SS to release me from my post as head [of the Judenrat], for in such abnormal conditions, I cannot lead the community. In reply, . . . they advised me not to resign.

Czerniakow made a great effort not to behave harshly toward the Jewish community or resort to coercive measures. In his diary, on May 17, 1941, he wrote about the visit of Mordecai Chaim Rumkowski, head of the Judenrat in Lodz. Rumkowski, who considered the Lodz ghetto a personal domain under his supervision and control, had gained a reputation for aggressiveness and despotic tendencies. According to Czerniakow,

Rumkowski reported on his activities in Lodz. The individual does not exist for him. He has special police authority in the ghetto [*Sonderkommando*] for confiscating and so he has confiscated diamonds and furs . . . this is an arrogant man, haughty and stupid. He is doing harm, because he tells the authorities that everything is in order in his sector.

Czerniakow's criticism and distaste are understandable. His methods were quite different from those of Rumkowski. Only under German pressure and threats would Czerniakow use coercion. But although his intentions were honorable, his methods did not suit the reality of the occupation of the ghetto and at times led to disappointing results. Czerniakow was reluctant to confiscate the property of the more affluent or to collect forcefully taxes from those who kept some of their possessions. He eventually had to impose a regressive tax on bread, which was officially distributed and rationed — throughout this period, the tax was paid equally by those who had no money at all and by those who had still enough edibles and hidden means. This type of procedure occurred with other decrees as well, indicative of a declining state of affairs in which people who were starving lived side by side with those who were overfed.

Czerniakow appealed to people's consciences, expecting them to behave with maturity and a sense of responsibility. He did not understand the difficulty of sustaining such values for desperate people involved in a struggle for existence and survival. His methods frequently harmed the weakest members of the community, as was evident when he was forced to fill a quota of Jews assigned to work camps. The well-heeled generally evaded being shipped to the camps through bribes or other forms of circumvention. So the hungry and weak were sent to the labor camps.

More accessible than the Germans, his presence more immediate, Czerniakow was a magnet for Jewish criticism. In diaries and memoirs of the Jews of Warsaw, Czerniakow was generally the object of bitter criticism. He was accused of preferring assimilationists or converts, of having an inclination for showy ceremonies and a limited understanding of the situation.

His diary included short entries noted every day in a series of small notebooks and written in a terse manner in Polish, with occasional ironic bursts of repressed anger. Following the celebration of his sixtieth birthday, he wrote, "Congratulations throughout the day. I wouldn't choose to be born again. It's too tiring." His pedantic attitude is confirmed, and he sometimes fumes against Jews in general. In 1940 he noted, "The color of the identity cards must evidently be changed every month. What would happen if these mobs were a state unto themselves." In July 1940 he wrote:

> I sit in a stuffy room resembling a jail. The Jews are constantly grumbling. They don't want to pay for the community, but demand intervention on private affairs or catastrophes. And if the intervention does not succeed or goes on too long, there is no end to their dissatisfaction, as if the matter depended on me. And frequently these are very loud complaints.

A year later, however, Czerniakow wrote, "The Jewish masses are quiet and balanced in the face of the intense suffering. In general, the Jews only shout when things are going well for them."

In some areas, Czerniakow's sensitivity was marked and constant. He lost all restraint when writing of human lives and the efforts to save them. Children, their well-being, their nourishment, and their education occupied him endlessly. Czerniakow's wife, Dr. Felicia Czerniakow, a teacher and faithful partner to her husband, sharing his heavy responsibilities, similarly showed a warm regard for children.

Czerniakow suffered personal as well as public tragedy. His only son, Jan Czerniakow, aged twenty-five, left with the stream of émigrés going eastward at the beginning of the war and had reached the heart of the Soviet Union, where he died in unknown circumstances at about the same time that his father committed suicide. In his diary, Czerniakow cried, "Where is my only son Jan?"

As head of the Judenrat, Czerniakow possessed considerable responsibility and power. Faced with a hopeless Sisyphean effort, Czerniakow reached a point of unending despair and helplessness, which led him to prefer death to participation in what he considered criminal acts.

By the time the ghetto was in full gear, the Judenrat was a caricature of the pre-war community. In the past, community activities centered on religious matters, including limited involvement in social aid and education. The Judenrat, however, had to deal with such matters as work, housing, food, justice, health, cleanliness, and public hygiene, and matters even more alien to the Jews in the Diaspora, such as the police and jails.

At the time of the ghetto, the Judenrat was also a caricature of an autonomous state cut off from the rest of the world (the Nazis sometimes cynically claimed that they had granted the Jews independence). The Jew as an individual or within an organization was not permitted to act or appeal to German authorities. Only the Judenrat, or, more correctly, the head of the Judenrat, could receive both the civilian orders of the German authorities and the complaints and fears of the Jewish public. And thus Czerniakow was caught between the hammer and the anvil.

The composition of the Judenrat in Warsaw was unusual. Some of its members served until the ghetto was destroyed, while others managed to escape, or they died, or were murdered. The first Judenrat consisted of well-known public figures, political activists, and leaders, including Professor Meir Balaban, Apolinary Hartglas, Moshe Kerner, Abraham Weiss, Shmuel Zygelbojm, and Yitzhak-Meir Levin, a historian and leader of a wide political spectrum. All left Poland with the last of the emigrants in 1940, except for the scholar Balaban, who died in the ghetto.

Czerniakow harshly described those functionaries who "escaped and escape," despite the claim by those who fled Poland that their pre-war anti-Nazi activities endangered their lives and that they could better assist Jews from outside the country. After some well-known political figures had left, few people of stature remained within the Judenrat.

Over time, the personnel and organization of the Judenrat increased. Before the war, the community employed some 530 individuals, while the Judenrat, together with all its departments, consisted of more than 2,000 employees, not including its various subsidiaries, which employed hundreds more. The police force, recruited with the establishment of the ghetto, numbered some 2,000 men at its most active stage.

The new employees were inexperienced in the areas they were responsible for, as very few Jews had worked in the administration of either the government or the municipality, and they understood very little of the activities of the Judenrat. In diaries and memoirs, a great many comments relate to the enfeebling corruption and bureaucracy within the Judenrat. The criticism drove the heads of the Judenrat to call for supervision by public committees. The committees, however, did not last long and changed very little. The corruption was the result of scarcity and the great gap between people's wages and their minimal daily expenses. The oppressors and their methods also contributed to the erosion of values and to the breakdown of accepted moral norms. Czerniakow was aware that he was surrounded by "malicious people," but accepted the necessity of functioning within the prevailing reality.

Throughout the occupation, Germans required virtual slave labor by Jews in the ghetto. Even before official decrees were issued, the German soldiers in trucks hunted down Jews on the street to work in barracks, load trucks, clear piles of debris, clean the streets, and so forth. They snatched people with no regard for age, sex, or physical condition. Men, who were the preferred objects of these snatchings, rarely left their homes. The appearance of a German soldier terrorized the ghetto. Men immediately fled from the streets.

Workers were given only the most primitive working tools. Instead of cleaning rags, they were forced to use their clothing. Even worse than the work was the brutality of young soldiers who had sadistic leanings or who were inflamed by anti-Jewish propaganda. To the accompaniment of raucous laughter, they cut off the long beards of the most Orthodox of Jews, or taunted workers with a barrage of continuous shouting and blows. At times, they confiscated the workers' identity cards in order to make them report again and again. A Bund activist in the Warsaw ghetto, Bernard Goldstein, described the hard labor imposed on the aged who lacked the strength to perform the work. He told of the killings that he witnessed.

He recalled a typical incident that he had observed. A group of men had to dig out metal bars from beneath the ruins of a ghetto building, load them on wagons, and then harness themselves to the wagons to drag them to an assembly point. An elderly German supervisor from Vienna showed some signs of sympathy, and even offered a piece of bread. But unexpectedly the German's manner changed completely:

> He suddenly started to shout wildly: Work! Work! and started to beat us with the butt of his rifle. This occurred when he spied an officer approaching us. "This is the way I have to behave," he explained to me afterwards when the officer had gone and thus excused his setting aside his Viennese passivity for Prussian brutality . . . Towards evening, after work, we were aligned in rows of 4–5, leading us away from the citadel [the military fortress in Warsaw which had once been a Russian jail]. While we dragged ourselves along the canal to the gate, the rows of German soliders standing on either side began to attack us with whips and sticks and rifles. We began to run and they ran after us, beating us mercilessly and shouting: "dirty Jews," "rotten Jews," and similar expressions. We were exhausted and covered with blood after a day's "work."

Nothing more vividly illustrates the impossible position of the Jewish Council than the solution it proposed to the kidnapping of Jewish laborers from the streets. After such snatching brought daily life and public activity to a virtual standstill, the Judenrat proposed a compromise. It would agree to supply a daily quota of workers on the condition that the roundups on the street cease. A more orderly process of forced labor, it believed, would better serve the ghetto. To fulfill its quota, the Judenrat established a work unit, complete with a group of organizers and supervisors which became the nucleus of the ghetto police. While the snatching did not cease, it was reduced. Systematic exploitation of Jewish labor in organized work details had replaced a chaotic and disruptive process. The Germans had their laborers whom the Judenrat would provide in an orderly process without requiring the expenditure of German personnel.

Every Jew had to have a work permit issued by the Judenrat which stated the days and hours the person had worked. The hours of mandatory work grew to eight days per month as the army, the railway services, and the municipal authorities increased their demand for labor. Jews who still had money could send surrogate workers, and, as Ringelblum says in his diary, the "profession of substitutes" was invented. For a day's labor, a substitute earned enough to buy a loaf of bread on the open market. Subsequently, the Judenrat organized a permanent work force of refugees and the poor to fulfill the communal obligation of supplying slave labor to the Germans. From that time onward, the community was concerned with raising sufficient money to pay the minimal wages of these workers. Its initial attempt to alleviate chaos on the streets soon propelled the Judenrat into the ongoing business of supplying the Nazis with forced labor.

In December 1939, Friedrich Wilhelm Krüger, who as supreme commander of the SS and the police was the officer responsible for security and Jewish labor within the General Government, issued orders regarding forced labor by the Jews. Krüger's order stated that "all the Jews of the General Government between the age of 14 and 60 are obliged to work . . . the duration of this obligation would be two years but this period will be extended if it was found that they have not achieved their intended educational goals."

In August 1940 the shipment of Jews to labor camps began. Among the first to go were those who had volunteered, hoping that conditions would be more endurable than in the ghetto. But these hopes were soon shattered. The recruits were sent to the Lublin area to drain swamps, pave roads, and build military fortifications. That year, an article appeared in an underground paper of the youth movement under the heading "The Work Camp," and it reported the following:

> I travel to the camp. Parted from my family and friends, and here I am at No. 10 Kawenczynska Street, the assembly point. I feel and heard there is no way back from here. No one will escape from this place. For the time being, the mood is good. As is the way with youth, they sing some songs, fool around, as if they were not being sent to a forced-labor camp. But the mood disappears the minute they begin to line us up and the SS personnel turn up . . .
>
> The camp in Lublin is situated right in the town itself, on a

former sports ground, on which some wooden huts have been constructed. We just arrived when some officers asked angrily: Who's sick? Suddenly there were tens of sick men. We looked on to see what was going to happen. They were lined up in a row, and the first in line was given a metal bar, which was attached to an electric wire. After a few moments, the man was writhing with pain. Then he began to shout that he was healthy. This was done to everyone who claimed to be sick. Afterwards we were taken to a hut where wooden bunks were arranged in tiers of three levels . . . and finally we arrived at Cieszanow, our camp. There I stayed for the rest of the time.

There are some thousands here in the camp; the work would not have been so hard if it were not for the daily appearance of the SS, the "blackberries" [black-uniformed units], the devils, as we were wont to call them. The most difficult part was on the way to work. One had to walk in a single line, without talking. Sometimes we would receive a blow from the butt of a rifle, even if we did not utter a sound. The terror and fear is dreadful. Even while we are working, we are likely to get beaten.

The work consisted of digging trenches and preparing the ramparts alongside them. For the slightest defect, one would be beaten. Someone who did not hold the shovel properly or someone who lifted his head while working, would get from 25 to 50 blows. The brutality is tremendous — to the point of getting shot to death. There were many such cases. On returning from work, it is the same as on the way to work. One is forced to sing, to run, to drop to the ground, and again clouts and blows. We worked not very far from the border and sometimes some youngsters would try to cross the borderline. Whoever managed to cross the border had little chance in any case, for the Soviet soldiers beyond the border returned him . . . Most of the time we had to sleep on the damp ground. Many took ill. There was insufficient food.

I spent two months in this atmosphere of terror, fear and torture. I returned a sick man, convinced that if I actually managed to return from the forced-labor camp, I would be able to withstand the hard times of Nazi subjection.

The Jews were not permitted to return to their former jobs, and all branches of the economy were barred to them. Small-scale artisans who had to provide their families with food and shelter showed an astonishing ability to adjust to the circumstances, as well as a surprising imagination. One account describes how this class of simple artisans secretly returned to skilled work:

> The production of wooden sandals was begun and workers in the wood-branch found work in this fashion. Cutters of old rubber would attach a layer to the soles and thus repaired shoes. Farmers smuggled leather into town for boots and the manufacture of shoes was in the hands of the Jews.
>
> Tailors turned clothes inside out and repaired old clothes, cleaning and adjusting used clothing for men and women. The "market" in the streets, courtyards, stairwells, and similar spots, was flooded with this kind of apparel. Gradually the hat-makers began working on hats — also a Jewish skill.

In the bakeries they were making bread from smuggled wheat, and in the underground mills, barley was ground by the most primitive methods. Swine hair was unobtainable, so they used fine wooden strands to create toothbrushes and clothes brushes. To replace electricity and gas, skilled artisans devised carbide lamps, which could only work for a few hours. Illegally, they started to manufacture soap and candles, which had been sorely lacking since the beginning of the occupation. Chemists contrived saccharine out of the remnants of vegetables. Syrups were used to make preserves and a honey substitute.

This inventiveness and use of substitute materials, however, could only supply work for a handful of artisans. The first winter of the war was very difficult due to the absence of food and the raw weather. At the beginning of the siege, welfare organizations renewed their activities. Ringelblum pointed out that the majority of social welfare workers stayed on the job.

At first, social welfare for the needy of Warsaw was carried out by an institution set up at the beginning of the war called the SKSS (*Stoleczny Komitet Samopomocy Spolecznej*), which administered the finances allocated by the Polish government for this purpose. The SKSS combined various public and philanthropic welfare institutions. The Jews also set up a coordinating committee for welfare, assisted by funding from SKSS. Help was given to those who had lost their property or whose houses had been burned down. Soup kitchens were established. The Germans were quick, however, to forbid any collaboration between the Poles and the Jews with regard to welfare.

In one way or another, the Jewish committee remained intact, encompassing such institutions as CENTOS, for children; TOZ, for medical care; and other welfare organizations that had been initiated and financed independently. Fortunately, as the Jewish welfare system faced overwhelming challenges, assistance came from the American Jewish Joint Distribution Committee, which was permitted to work in Poland until the United States entered the war in December 1941. Self-help quickly incorporated a wide network of public activities. Organizational names changed occasionally. The title given to the entire structure was ZSS — the Jewish Public Self-Help — which apparently did not please the Germans because of the inclusion of the letters *SS*. It was changed to JHK (Jüdischer Hilfskomitee), or the Jewish Committee for Help. In Warsaw, however, the terms *Joint* and *Self-Help* were used from force of habit.

Although the institution's offices moved from time to time, its most permanent location was in the building of Jewish Sciences. With its emphasis on self-help, the welfare network — unencumbered by the need to serve German masters — emerged as an alternative to the Judenrat. In some sense, this distinction was justified. The scope of the Joint's activities is detailed by a listing of its major departments: kitchens, food, housing, refugees, clothing, finances, health, social sectors, religion, youth, legal and statistical departments, and others. It employed hundreds of workers, including a core of people experienced in social work who enjoyed a certain autonomous status within this manifold organization. Unemployed artists, actors, writers, religious party activists, journalists, and the working intelligentsia, educated people with some experience in social work, were recruited into the ranks of the Self-Help personnel. In his diary, Chaim Kaplan frequently ridiculed the artists and writers and doubted their efficiency and inclination to help their own people, but he and others expressed great admiration for the initiative and devotion to the work of Self-Help. Unlike the Judenrat, which was performing an unfamiliar function under the watchful eyes of German rulers, Jewish Self-Help worked in continuity with traditional Jewish communal activities.

Emanuel Ringelblum, one of the organizers of this body and head of its social welfare department, explained the public significance of Self-Help:

> The war presented the public with very important questions. It was necessary to put an end to the relationships based on political differences which existed before the war. There had to be a united front from the left to the right. The Nazi war against the Jews had become a war of annihilation. It was being waged against every class and level of the entire Jewish population. As far as the Nazis were concerned, there was no difference between the Zionists and the Bundists, they were equally despised . . . the Jews were faced with the cardinal questions of life and death, and no factor could take upon itself the sole responsibility for such issues. Only by joining forces could we face such crucial and constant problems.

Through the efforts of Ringelblum and his friends, the Joint also had a covert identity as supporter of the civilian and political underground, and particularly of the pioneer youth movement, which later spearheaded armed resistance. Under the aegis of Self-Help, kitchens were set up, where the workers and most of their clientele were the starving and needy, as well as members of the youth movement or the political underground movement. Thus the kitchens, in addition to being places to eat, served as meeting places for an underground political body.

Ringelblum described a large assembly of the underground youth movement held in the building that housed the Self-Help offices. At the peak of the working day, ordinary social workers would be working side by side with those responsible for the underground archives set up by Ringelblum, who had taken on the obligation of gathering information and documenting Jewish life during the occupation.

In mid-1942, the Joint, operating without direct American support, lent financial aid to the Jewish Fighting Organization and its branches as it prepared for the uprising and rebellion. Ringelblum also had a hand in the establishment of a network of house committees, the first of which was created at the height of the September 1939 invasion. In every apartment house, a small group of individuals prepared for danger and emergencies, enemy attacks, and assisted refugees and tenants. Such committees operated in both Polish houses and Jewish houses, as well as in houses with mixed inhabitants. In most cases, these committees dispersed after the German occupation began.

Ringelblum conceived of the idea of turning the house committees into a locus of activity under the guidance of the Self-Help organization. The Self-Help organization divided the Warsaw ghetto into sectors, and committees were organized on both a sectoral and general scale. With the inhabitants forced by curfew to remain in their apartments during the long evenings, a vast opportunity developed for home activities. As a result, a local leadership emerged that was able to adjust quickly and resourcefully to changing conditions.

The backing and supervision of the Self-Help organization strengthened the house committees. Urgently improvised, the committees evolved into an institution that watched over the tenants of the houses and their situation, facilitated the relationship between families and tenants, and coped with such complex tasks as the organization of kindergartens, arrangement of cultural evenings and general meetings on the holidays.

Thanks to pressure imposed by the social department of Self-Help, those houses were in a better state and supported hostels and refuges, which were known as the refuge's "points." For a house with up to fifty inhabitants, the committee comprised five members; larger houses had seven. In April 1940 there were 778 house committees in Warsaw. Eventually, this number reached 1,518, covering more than 2,000 houses. They functioned for quite a long time, and their effect could be felt during the first and second years of the war. In the last year of the ghetto, conditions became more severe and reduced what help an individual could offer his neighbor. Frequent changes in the ghetto's borders and the expulsion of its inhabitants made the house committees unable to function.

Another organization guided by the social department of Self-Help was the *Landsmannschaft,* an association of refugees who had fled from the same cities and villages to Warsaw. Jews had been expelled from distant towns in western Poland in territories annexed by the Third Reich. Many affluent Jews arrived in Warsaw from towns such as Lodz with only hand luggage, in the hope that here they could manage better in the larger city. Other refugees had been expelled from towns and localities around the capital and forcibly evacuated to Warsaw.

In all, until the establishment of the ghetto, some ninety thousand refugees settled in Warsaw — more than one in five of the ghetto's population. The problem of their housing, food, work, and social services was the responsibility of the Judenrat and the Self-Help. In the memoirs of many refugees, one finds bitterness and many complaints about the indifference of the Warsaw Jews. In time of trouble, however, individuals tend to focus their compassion and sense of justice on their own families and fellow townsmen and less on the general population.

Refugees were housed in poor neglected cells where illness was rife. The Self-Help organized refugees into related groups, but only the more well-placed and aggressive found a niche in the Warsaw community. The majority of refugees were starving and reduced to a state of apathy and gradual acceptance of their fate.

A number of efficient and gifted personalities within the Self-Help organization confronted the problem of scarcity and suffering. During the war and the time of the ghetto, the directors saw themselves as the enlightened missionaries of salvation as long as they were dealing with local matters. Yitzhak Gitterman, the most outstanding and influential of these individuals, was a native of Ukraine, and during the war he moved to Vilna and tried to sail via the Baltic Sea to Sweden to seek help for his people. He was caught in mid-sea, placed in a prisoner camp in April 1940, and returned to Warsaw, where he became the Joint's head of personnel. He devoted himself to public service, with sympathy and loyalty to the underground and, later on, to the Jewish Fighting Organization.

The Joint enjoyed official American patronage and was permitted by the U.S. government to work in Germany and the occupied countries until the United States entered the war in December 1941. In that year, the worst experienced by the Warsaw ghetto, the Joint reduced its aid to the ghetto by 40 percent. Why this American-Jewish institution lessened its assistance to the Jews of Poland during the time of their greatest need is a question we cannot answer. But as a result of that withdrawal of support, the Judenrat was forced to increase its role in social welfare. Even while it attempted to assist the most needy, the Judenrat could hardly ignore orders by the German authorities to supplement the rations of their own employees at the expense of refugees, children, and the starving.

In February and March 1941 Dr. Fritz Arlt, who was responsible for the welfare of the population as head of *Bevölkerungswesen und Fürsorge*, put out the first feelers to the Judenrat and self-help organizations in the ghetto. From conversations with Dr. Arlt, it appears that German authorities were planning to introduce a welfare section to assist Ukrainians and Jews as well as Poles. This approach to Jews and self-help organizations (which lacked official recognition and thus operated in a gray area between legality and illegality) was surprising, since the Jews had not been entitled to pensions or welfare services.

Both Jews and non-Jews were inclined to interpret Dr. Arlt's approach as a humane gesture by someone sensitive to their terrible distress. His motives, however, seem far from benevolent. Arlt represented the same extreme racism as the rest of his party, and he took an active part in the expulsion of Jews from the small towns and villages in the Cracow district, viewing the wretched situation of the Jews in the ghetto as convincing evidence of their racial inferiority. In fact, the willingness of German authorities to implement a welfare program that included Jews stemmed from a demand by representatives of such international institutions as the Red Cross and the Commission for Polish Relief who visited occupied Poland in 1940. These organizations promised to assist with general relief only if it included the Jews, who would also have to be represented on the local bodies responsible for its distribution. In their desire to obtain needed aid, as well as foreign currency at a low legal rate of exchange, German authorities submitted to the international demands.

In 1940 the welfare program was officially authorized under an umbrella organization called the NRO (the General Council for Welfare), headquartered in Cracow. Dr. Michael Weichert, who represented the Jewish Self-Help organization, represented the Jews on the council, along with some members of the Warsaw and Cracow Judenrats. Heading the united framework and the Polish sector were Polish aristocrats such as Janusz Radziwil and the Baron Adam Ronikier, who had had contacts with German authorities during the German occupation in World War I.

The welfare program did alleviate dire conditions in the ghetto as the Poles who headed the NRO recognized the desperate situation of the Jews and granted them a considerably larger portion of relief funds than their numbers warranted. At the same time, the Joint and the Self-Help organization remained the primary source of relief amid ever increasing distress.

As conditions continued to deteriorate, the organizations faced an insoluble dilemma in determining to whom to give aid and how much. Should they give the same ineffective pittance to all, or give more generously to the few and ensure that they, at least, had enough to survive? Emanuel Ringelblum described these doubts in his diary in May 1942:

Social welfare is not solving the problem. It only draws out people's existence for a longer period. The people must die in any case. It merely prolongs the suffering but there is no way out. In order to arrive at genuine results, millions of zlotys are needed monthly and these are not available. The most striking fact is that the inmates of the refugee hostels are all dying, because their food consists only of soup with a crust of rationed bread. Which poses the question of whether it would not be more useful to give the money at our disposal to a selected group from among the public activists or the intellectual elite. But the real situation is such that, firstly, even the number of intended chosen consists of too large a group and is therefore not feasible, and secondly, there is no respite from the question of whether one may condemn the artisans, the workers and the ordinary masses, who were productive in their hometowns and villages and only in the ghetto as a result of the war, have been made into the dregs of humanity, ready for the grave. The tragic question still stands: what is to be done? To hand out tiny spoonfuls to everyone and then no one will survive, or to give handfuls [to the few] and then but a few will remain.

4

THE GHETTO IS SEALED

A T THE BEGINNING of the occupation, the Germans had no defined policy toward the Polish Jews. Heydrich's order of September 1939 regarding the establishment of the Judenrat did not establish a concrete plan toward the visible future, but it did articulate a two-stage policy. The first stage provided for a Jewish council (the Judenrat), the concentration of Jews from smaller localities in the major cities situated near railways, and the removal of Jews from certain branches of economic life *if* this did not have adverse effects on the wartime economy. The second stage, according to Heydrich, was a secret and final *plan (Endziel)*. Some historians have linked the term *Endziel* with the final aim of the *Endlösung,* the "final solution," the complete annihilation of the Jews. However, in September 1939 there was no such far-reaching decision to kill all the Jews, and it is doubtful whether Heydrich or Himmler had already conceived of such a plan at that time. Such a plan developed over time and was fully implemented from the second half of 1941. From January 1942 onward, the total annihilation of all Jews everywhere was the announced policy of the Reich.

Heydrich's instructions in September 1939 were intended for the *Einsatzgruppen,* the mobile killing units, subordinate to the police and the SS, who accompanied the Polish administration. Ever sensitive to his status, Hans Frank, the governor-general, preferred to ignore Heydrich's instructions. The transfer of the Jews to the General Government from the western parts of Poland which had been annexed by Germany was, after a certain stage, opposed by Frank, who put a stop to some of Himmler's plans in this area.

On the eve of the Polish invasion, the German high command received many orders directly from Hitler. According to a report of the meeting, Hitler said, "I have placed my deathhead formations in readiness — with orders to send to death mercilessly and without compassion, men, women, and children of Polish derivation and language." During the days preceding the invasion of Poland, Hitler was not especially concerned with the Jews. Frank's diary during the first months of his rule are full of anti-Polish declarations. On November 4, 1939, following consultations with Frank, Hitler confirmed his decision to destroy the royal palace in Warsaw and not to repair the damage in the city from the bombing of the first days of the war. On December 2, 1939, Frank declared that the major directive of the General Government was Hitler's desire "that this area should be the first colonial possession of the German nation." At a conference of government department heads on January 19, 1940, Frank held forth on the status of the General Government, its relationship to the Poles, and the fusion of the area into the ruling German structure, saying that "although the final destiny of the General Government was still in abeyance, one could be certain of one thing . . . no part of the area under German rule would be freed."

Frank later recounted that on September 15, 1939, he had received orders to take under his wing the civilian administration of the eastern occupied areas, and to exploit the areas without restraint, turning them into heaps of ruins (*Trümmerhaufen*) economically, culturally, socially, and politically. He boasted that after two months the General Government had become a worthy component of a unified German territory. Polish labor was exploited for the sake of the war effort. But if these changing tactics toward the Poles were not matched by the anticipated results in production, Frank said, "he would have no hesitation in using the most drastic means."

Nevertheless, the invasion of Poland brought 2 million Jews under German rule. It outdid in one month the efforts of six years within Germany (and eighteen months within annexed Austria and the Protectorate) to be rid of the Jews. There was no consistent policy toward the Jews during the initial months of the war. Some German officials wanted to remove the Jews; others felt that the continuing presence of Jews was essential to economic stability. A memorandum issued in November 1939 by the SS Department for Racial Matters recommended that antipathy between Poles and Jews be encouraged and exploited to German advantage. Frank was intensely involved with the issue of evacuation of the Jews from the western districts annexed by the Reich into the General Government. He complained of disturbances on the part of Jewish speculators as a threat to the stabilization of the Polish currency. However, Ludwig Fischer, governor of the Warsaw district (one of four districts of the General Government), pointed out that in certain commercial areas controlled by Jews, such as textiles, leather, and the slaughtering and provisioning of meat, no replacements were available and the Jews had to be returned to their occupations temporarily.

However, major decisions regarding the Jewish policy were not made locally but came directly from Berlin, apparently from Hitler. Whatever the Führer said was accepted as a directive and implemented. Still, it would be a mistake to view German policy as a seamless whole. Bureaucratic and personal rivalries continued among central factions of the party and the General Government administration over key positions and influence on many issues. Jews were just one of these issues. The principal competing factions in the General Government were the police and the SS, backed by Himmler, and Frank and his official machinery, supported by Göring. Each faction tried to anticipate the other in implementing Hitler's directives. In July 1940 Frank announced that Hitler "ordered that Jews should no longer be transferred to the General Government. Moreover, those Jews who were already in the General Government would be handled as a unit in the form of a separate, basic plan, so that in the foreseeable future the General Government would be free of Jews (*Judenfrei*). For some time a project of concentration of the Jews in a reservation was considered and experimented with. Later Frank claimed that when movement on the high seas would permit the shipment of Jews, "they will be transferred one by one, man after man, woman after woman, and maiden after maiden." Clearly, as late as July 1940, Frank viewed the solution to the Jewish problem in terms of their transfer to Madagascar. There were two ways to rid Poland of Jews: expulsion or annihiliation. Expulsion required a destination; annihilation required an infrastructure for killing. Until the "final solution" was set in place, officials assumed that the Jews would be evacuated. Madagascar, an island off the southeast coast of Africa, was the contemplated destination, since other countries were unwilling to accept Jews. Nine months later, in March 1941, Frank told a conference of government administrators, "Not long ago, General Göring said: 'It is more important to win this war than to pursue a racial policy.' We can now be happy with every Pole working in a workshop. If the Poles or the Jews do as we wish, it is not important now." In November 1941, five months after the mass murder of Jews had begun in the German-occupied territories of the Soviet Union, Frank told students at the University of Berlin:

> Not all these Jews are parasites from our point of view. Surprisingly there are Jews of a different category — I have seen this for myself. It is hard to believe but there are really Jews who work and are employed in factories as transport workers or building workers or skilled tailors, shoemakers and others. With the help of the Jewish artisans, Jewish workshops were set up in which, in exchange for food and other basic necessities, their production went far towards lightening the load of German industry.

The Jews were unaware of the political power struggle among the Germans. They did not know about the lack of clarity from above on matters of principle, and the diverse responsibilities and motivations of local officials. They viewed German authorities as unified and following one well-defined blueprint for Jewish policy and thus could not understand the conflicting signals they received. Through contact with local police and the SS on the one hand, and with Frank's administration on the other, the tension was dispelled and at times reversed, especially regarding the issue of Jewish work.

Daily life in the ghetto was filled with humiliations and dangers. Wehrmacht soldiers insulted, attacked, robbed, and injured the Jews. Jews had to doff their hats to a passing German in uniform. Many were beaten for failing to do so, while those who complied might be beaten because the German claimed that he did not know the passing Jew and had no reason to greet him. In diaries and memoirs, such acts were described as evidence of sadistic impulses by German soldiers. But it seems illogical to assume that sadism was common to an entire generation of Germans. Rather, racial and ideological brainwashing had succeeded in dehumanizing Jews to young Germans, as well as eroding humane inclinations. The story was told among the Jews of Warsaw that a Jewish girl had said that she would rather be a dog than a Jewess, for Germans loved dogs and would not kill them. Professor Ludwik Hirschfeld wrote in his biography:

> Every nation has its games. The English have football, the Spaniards have the bull-fight, and this generation of Germans are skilled antisemites, in order to get rid of the sense of pity and conscience and their corresponding human reactions before conquering the world. I assume this is the major source of German antisemitism — to learn to ridicule and hate. These teachings have gone down well.

While orders and directives generally came from Berlin, the ghettoization of the Jews emerged at the initiative of cities and local leaders. In a November 1939 discussion with Frank and administration heads in Cracow, Ludwig Fischer stated that in Warsaw "a separate ghetto must be set up for Jews, and his excellency, the Governor General endorses this step." Three days earlier, on November 3, Dr. Rudolf Batz, an officer of the SS and one of the local Gestapo personnel, appeared in the Judenrat offices and informed those present that according to the orders of

General Karl von Neumann–Neurode, military commander of the city, a ghetto had to be established in Warsaw within three days. A map of the intended ghetto was shown to the members of the Judenrat, and some of them were taken as hostages to ensure the execution of this order.

This news came as a bolt from the blue to the Judenrat, whose members were in a state of shock and despair. A population of some 150,000 was to move to the intended ghetto within three days — a decree more extreme than any previously imposed and an order that could not possibly be carried out in time. The Judenrat decided to take a risky step. Contrary to their common practice and perhaps even in contradiction to their own expectations, the members decided to play one authority against the other. Well aware that Batz was a Gestapo officer responsible for Jewish affairs, and that General von Neumann–Neurode commanded the Wehrmacht, the Jews dared to circumvent Batz by sending a delegation to the general to appeal the order. The delegation, which included Czerniakow, Hartglas, and Abraham Weiss, was received by von Neumann–Neurode, who had no knowledge of the order purportedly issued by him. During subsequent days of discussion between von Neumann–Neurode and the Gestapo, it was not clear whether the establishment of the ghetto would be postponed, its layout changed, or the decree annulled. On November 14, the Judenrat hostages were freed, and Czerniakow noted in his diary, "I was at the SS. The matter of the evacuation is not actual at the moment."

The threat of the ghetto, however, was merely delayed. Unbeknownst to the Jews, the plan for the ghetto was brought up by the central authority of the district and was endorsed by Frank himself. By March 1940, signposts were erected at the entrance of streets densely populated by Jews, bearing the message that anyone entering these streets was entering an "Infected Area." During the the same month, the Judenrat received a map of the "infected area" and was told to build a brick wall around it. The area consisted of some 4 percent of the city of Warsaw.

Czerniakow tried to convince the authorities to cancel this decree, but his efforts were in vain. In August 1940 the Germans officially announced that the city would be divided into three sectors: German, Polish, and Jewish. Jews were evacuated from houses in central streets in the Polish quarter; apartments and their contents were being requisitioned, a new euphemism for stealing. Jewish owners tried to save something of their property, but faced the cruelest challenge in seeking a place to live in the crowded Jewish quarter.

Fischer assigned responsibility for planning and establishing the ghetto to Waldemar Schön, head of the department for the movement and evacuation of population in the district. Various possibilities were examined, such as the expulsion of Jews from the center of town and the creation of a ghetto in its more remote suburbs. But such proposals aroused Polish opposition. Poles did not take kindly to the fact that the Germans were doing what they pleased with the city and making complex changes. Other delays stemmed from the hope that a Jewish reservation would be set up in the neighborhood of Lublin, or that there would be a mass emigration to Madagascar, alternatives that would make the ghetto unnecessary.

At the end of August 1940, creation of a ghetto began in earnest. Transferring masses of Jews from outside the Jewish quarter would take months, so it was decided to turn the existing Jewish quarter into a ghetto. On Yom Kippur, October 12, 1940, the loudspeakers placed in the city's squares notified the Jews of Warsaw that a ghetto was being established and that movement to and from the ghetto area would continue only until the end of October. Czerniakow wrote in his diary with marked sarcasm, "Schön informed us that in the name of humanity, by order of the commander, the general commander, and according to instructions from above, a ghetto would be set up."

Entire streets and parts of streets were included in the ghetto. There was no uniformity. Until the day the decree was activated, no one knew its ultimate boundaries. The Germans were careful not to use the word *ghetto,* writing and speaking instead of the "Jewish Residential Quarter of Warsaw," and demanding that the Jews use the same term. Yet, except for official notices published by the Judenrat, this was never done. The announcement of the ghetto set off a whirlwind of activities; people seeking apartments, changing apartments, and making deals continued

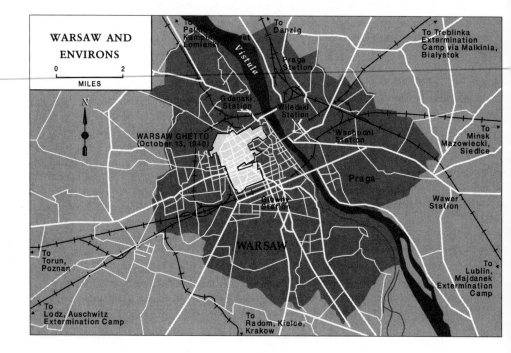

until the date the borders closed. Poles who lived on the edge of
the Jewish quarter had to move to other parts of Warsaw, while
the Jews who lived in other areas of the city had to move to the
intended ghetto area. For many, the move meant a significant
change in lifestyle. Wealthier and more assimilated Jews who
owned spacious apartments lived throughout the city. The Poles
forced to move from the Jewish quarter were the poorer elements
of the population. They left behind small and old apartments,
most of them lacking modern sanitary facilities.

The Judenrat acted as a clearing-house for those seeking new
homes, but most contacts were made independently amid great
confusion, with every interested party exploiting the situation.
Czerniakow noted in one characteristically terse sentence that he
had been left without an apartment, and Ludwik Landau wrote
on October 19, 1940, "Practically speaking, the transfer of busi-
neses or residences has only affected the more affluent inhabit-

ants . . . hence running after an apartment for days on end is so physically debilitating and nerve-wracking, that it does not help anything."

Polish residents objected to the establishment of the ghetto, but once the matter was settled, a number of Poles appealed to the Germans to adjust the ghetto's boundaries, according to their interests. Some families acquired a place to live after considerable effort, only to find that a change in the ghetto borders left them again without a roof over their heads.

On October 30, the date by which all moving had to be finalized, a diarist wrote:

> These are the last days for evacuating Jewish apartments in the Aryan quarters and finding a new one in the ghetto. The poor Jews are wandering about the outskirts of Warsaw. The wealthier did not wait until the last moment and managed in advance to find some hovel among their fellow sufferers, but the poor, who are thought to be gone, could not leave their homes for lack of means. They awaited some miracle, as the Jews are wont to do. In the face of such enormous troubles, all the energy they devote to earning a livelihood at which they excel, was paralyzed. Fatalism and submission to their fate has replaced these qualities.

Thus, October 31 found many without a place to live. The Germans announced that out of consideration for the Jews' desire to obey orders, the final date would be extended to November 15.

Jews were troubled by what character the ghetto would assume. Would it be an open ghetto or a closed one? Jews who had shops or small workshops still operating on the Polish side wondered whether to take their minimal goods and working tools to the ghetto in case it should be closed off, or to hope that the ghetto would remain open, making it possible to live inside the ghetto and still earn a livelihood elsewhere. During the final days, rumors spread about postponement of the ghetto plans or their abandonment altogether.

On November 16, 1940, the ghetto was sealed. Jews who arrived at the gates found them blocked by Polish and German police. Ringelblum observed that one could not compare this with the ghetto of medieval times. Then, the ghetto was closed only at night, if it was sealed at all, and while erected by hostile decree, it did help to maintain a Jewish way of life and added to the security of the Jews. Inside the ghetto, Jews were safe and secure. By contrast, the Warsaw ghetto was a cage isolating more than 400,000 people like lepers. Conditions were beyond the inhabitants' imagination. Masses of Warsaw Jews were pushed into these crowded quarters enclosed by a wall. Apart from a few who received permission for a limited span of a few hours or days, no Jew ever went outside the walls. The only way the Jews could leave the environs of the ghetto was on the closed and dim cattle cars going to the concentration and death camps or in a coffin en route to the cemetery. Only death released them from the ghetto. Only death led to deliverance from suffering and pain.

In the beginning, official estimates placed 380,740 people in the ghetto, including 1,718 Christians who were registered as Jews on the basis of Nazi legislation. In July 1940, the governor-general issued an order defining who was a Jew according to the Nuremberg racial laws of 1935, which stated that a person was a Jew if he was a believer in the Jewish faith, if he identified himself as a Jew, if he had three grandparents who were wholly Jewish, or if he or his parents had converted to Christianity and he was married to a Jew. Until then, whoever claimed to be Christian was not considered a Jew. Still, there were only a few instances of conversion among the Jews in order to avert their fate.

Yet, from the very beginning of the occupation in September 1939, the Germans issued racial decrees. For instance, when the order was issued that Jews wear a Star of David, Christians of Jewish origin were ordered to comply. Through the intercession of some of the leading converted individuals and their families, the heads of the senior welfare institution of the General Government asked German authorities to exempt Polish Christians of Jewish origin, who had social and cultural rights. The Germans asked for a list of the candidates to be released from this decree. This list was submitted, and then the request was turned down. With the establishment of the ghetto in October 1940, German trucks sought out those who appeared on the list and they were forced to move to the ghetto. Still, some Jews and scores of assimilated Jewish families managed to remain in the Polish sector disguised as Poles.

Explanations vary as to what motivated local German authorities to set up a sealed ghetto in Warsaw. The Germans themselves later said that the ghetto was a response to the threat of disease, especially the typhus epidemic. Ludwik Hirschfeld, an outstanding epidemiologist, responded by noting ironically that there was no surer way of spreading an epidemic than by confining masses of people together, adding that it was doubtful that one could stop an epidemic from spreading beyond the ghetto.

There is every reason to believe that the authorities exploited health warnings to carry out a plan. At any rate, when Fischer first referred to setting up a ghetto during his meeting with Frank, there were no signs of an epidemic and matters of health were not discussed as a possible reason. Nor was there any epidemic when Batz announced the implementation of the ghetto.

The Warsaw ghetto was not the first of its kind; it was merely the largest. The Lodz ghetto, established in May 1940, preceded the Warsaw ghetto. Lodz was not included in the General Government, but was the second largest city, and contained the second largest Jewish community, in interwar Poland. It is possible that the Germans did not consider it desirable that the closed ghetto in Lodz should be the only one in the annexed territories and the Warthegau region. However, the man who ordered the establishment of the Warsaw ghetto provided his own explanation. Governor Ludwig Fischer stated in a comprehensive bi-annual report dated September 1941, under the heading "The Jewish Quarter in Warsaw":

In view of the large number of Jews to be found in Warsaw, at the very beginning of German rule, thought was being given to concentrating the Jews in the Jewish quarter. The intention was, first and foremost, to separate the Jews from the Aryan surroundings and from general political considerations of our world-view [*Weltanschauung*]. There were in addition other important reasons, health-wise and economic . . . in general, 700 ethnic Germans [*Volksdeutsch*], 113,000 Poles and 138,000 Jews were evacuated, making 251,000 in all. In this fashion, 11,567 Jewish apartments in the Jewish quarter and some 13,800 Jewish apartments in other parts of the city were made available. The transfer was made in the course of some six weeks in a tremendous organizational undertaking. The quarter was an area of 403 hectares, with a population of 450,000 to 500,000 Jews living in an unusually crowded state. A calculation has been made that 108,000 Jews live in one square kilometer of the quarter, as compared with 38,000 per square kilometer in the residential area of Warsaw, which is also above average.

During the first months, life in the ghetto seemed like a form of imprisonment. Jews felt that the ghetto was a return to medieval times and an offense to the honor and person of the Jew. Ironically enough, some Jews believed at the beginning that the walls of the ghetto could create a form of Jewish immunity against attacks and robbery from outside. This naive expectation was revealed quickly as illusory. The ghetto was an enclave of fragmented streets inhabited by people whose lives had been shattered. After further retrenchment in the ghetto's layout, two masses of streets and houses were formed, linked by a narrow bridge. Chlodna Street was a strange mixture: the houses and the sidewalks were included in the ghetto, but the road itself and traffic traveling on it were considered "Aryan." The Aryan road and Jewish sidewalks were separated by wooden fences. The entire length of the ghetto could be passed through in forty minutes. The ghetto was encircled by a wall two and a half meters high, topped by barbed wire. The wall had twenty-two gates, reduced in the course of time to thirteen, and at the final stage of the ghetto's existence, to only four. At the gates stood the guards of three police forces: German, Polish, and Jewish. Every person, every wagon, and every vehicle that approached was thoroughly searched. Crowded in the narrow streets of the ghetto lived a population equal to that of a city in other parts of the world: 26,000 people lived in Pawia Street, 20,000 in Mila Street, and 20,000 in Gesia Street. The sidewalks were filled with masses of people whose threadbare clothing reeked with the smell of rotting foodstuffs and human sweat. The odor of waste and refuse filled the air. In the ghetto, it was said that a day felt like a month and that a month felt like years. Open spaces, freedom, the sight of a flower, greenery, of trees and the sound of birds, all were abstract ideas in another corner of the earth — far off and unattainable. In a contemporary memoir, one writer said:

Our ghetto was not an incarceration for a year or two, the ghetto is not an expiation for a crime. In the course of time, a sort of permanent reality has been woven whose very essence was the ghetto. In the ghetto, a mother is trying to explain to her child the concept of distance. Distance, she says, "is more than our Leszno Street. It is an open field, and a field is a large area on which the grass grows, or ears of corn, and when one is standing in its midst, one does not see its beginning or its end. Distance is so large and open and empty that the sky and the earth meet there." A child cannot imagine its wonderful description. "Distance," continues the mother, "is a long journey, a continuous journey for many hours and sometimes for days and nights, in a train or a car, or perhaps aboard an airplane which flies through the air like a bird and moves more swiftly than the eye can follow. The railway train breathes and puffs and swallows lots of coal, the same coal that we lack to heat our room. And a ship is a boat, like the ones pictured in your book, but is real and the sea is a huge and real bath where the waves rise and fall in an endless game. And these forests are trees, trees like those in Karmelicka Street and Nowolipie, so many trees that one cannot count them. No, the trees are not like the single trees here. They are strong and upright, with crowns of green leaves, and the forest is full of such trees as far as the eye can see and full of leaves and bushes and the song of the birds. No, even if we multiply the number of trees in Karmelicka by many thousands, we would still not have a forest. For a forest is something else and the trees here are like birds in a cage, while in the forest they breathe freely. Freedom, yes, what is freedom."

In 1941 an underground Polish paper printed an impression of the ghetto as seen from the outside:

> The ghetto was set up in the most crowded quarter. It was laid out in such a fashion that it has neither a park, nor does it touch on the Vistula at any point, and the only area covered with trees is the cemetery. The density cannot be described. The average occupancy of a room is six souls and sometimes the number reaches twenty. According to estimates of the population department, there are now living in Warsaw on every hectare, some 70 individuals, and in the ghetto — 1,100 . . . Since January 1941, Jews from the cities and villages in the Warsaw district have been evacuated to the densely populated and famished ghetto. The population of the ghetto reached 500,000. Due to the increasing crowdedness, such undescribably unhealthy conditions were created that cannot be put in writing, hunger and distress abound. The streets are full of masses of people moving about aimlessly, many are pale and feeble. Alongside the walls, many beggars are sitting or lying around and it is not an uncommon sight to witness people collapsing from starvation. Every day, the asylum gathers up dozens of abandoned babies. Some die in the streets. Contagious disease is rife, particularly tuberculosis.

The ghetto was frequently called "a coffin," but it also had a particular tempo of its own. It had its own culture and political underground. The well-known leader of the religious Zionists, Rabbi Yitzhak Nissenbaum, tried to provide a religious understanding of life and duty within the ghetto. He introduced the concept of *kiddush hahayim*, "the sanctity of life," in place of the more common *kiddush hashem*, the sanctification of God's name, the traditional term for martyrdom used by the Jewish community. Nissenbaum's justification: During the Middle Ages, the enemies of the Jews wanted to destroy their spiritual world, intending in the main to convert them to Christianity. The Nazis were trying to annihilate the Jewish people. Therefore, if in the past it was the Jews' primary duty to sacrifice their lives rather than renounce their beliefs, in the ghetto it was now their sacred obligation to struggle for their physical survival. Survival itself became a sanctified response to the Nazis. Jews within the ghetto were less philosophical, less religious. Nevertheless, they intuitively understood Nissenbaum's point. Survival was the common mission. Residents spoke of *überleben,* which could be translated as "to overcome and stay alive" and to arrive eventually at a release from sorrows.

Some Orthodox Jews continued to abide by the kosher dietary laws, and were not prepared to forgo praying in a minyan (a quorum of ten men) when praying together with a group of more than ten was prohibited. For all that, the wartime Jew of the ghetto was most unlike his forebears, as the conditions of the ghetto did little to strengthen his religious beliefs. Families struggled to maintain traditions even as scarcity and distress contributed to human frailty. In the history of the ghetto, however, there was but one instance of the murder of a man for his food or money. As long as there was a spark of normality hidden in the darkness of the ghetto, trust in the spiritual world endured.

Even at the height of Germany's military success, few Jews doubted that eventually the Nazis would be defeated. Jewish existence depended on this inner conviction. The ghetto's inhabitants believed deeply that a concept based on hatred, evil, and utter brutality could not dominate the world forever. Yet it was clear to the Jews that many would be sacrificed to the enemy. But they did not know the extent of that sacrifice, foretold in a statement by Frank on August 24, 1942:

> Concerning the fact that we are discussing, the death of 1.2 million Jews by starvation [in the General Government], there is no need to talk over any further. This is clear and if these Jews will not die by starvation, we shall have to speed up additional anti-Jewish decrees, and hope that this will actually happen.

In early August 1941, Frank alluded to the anticipated disappearance of Jews: "Shortly there would be no need to feed them at all, except for the 300,000 who were useful workers." One can assume that Frank was already aware of the planned annihilation of the Jews, which had begun weeks earlier in the German-controlled territories of the Soviet Union, and that he was revealing information that he had learned directly from the Führer. Until then, Frank and Fischer had spoken of the need to provide the Jews with a minimum of food and other basic necessities in order to exploit their working capacity. Similar statements were forthcoming from members of the police and the higher echelons of the local SS. Bruno Streckenbach, commander of the Security Police in the General Government, claimed in May 1940 that "the number of Jews in the General Government was likely to increase, and that it was impossible to starve them all in the long run." At that stage, the Nazis tended to provide workers with only the most essential necessities and ignore the fact that the fare allotted to nonworking Jews actually condemned them to death. From data acquired from a Polish underground source, the daily allocation of food to the various ethnic groups in 1941 assumed the following proportions: Germans, 2,613 calories; Poles, 669; Jews, 184. The same data also reveal the prices charged each group per caloric value. The Germans paid 0.3 zloty per calorie; the Poles, 2.6 zloty; and the Jews, 5.6 zloty for the same food value. Thus, even survival at a subsistence level was expensive for ghetto Jews. Under such circumstances, it is not surprising that anxiety over the acquisition of food took priority over all other concerns for the ghetto inhabitants. Yet even the minute quantities and the excessive prices do not adequately reflect the severity of the situation. Outside the ghetto, an open market offered basic foods, which, though expensive — the price of food in May 1940 was ten times greater than it was before the war — was nonetheless available. Food did not enter the ghetto by ordinary, legal means. What did reach ghetto residents distributed by the Judenrat was damaged and overpriced.

Work permitted one to obtain various kinds of food, but only a very small amount of simple foodstuffs — bread and potatoes. Families suffering from constant hunger gave up the food cards that allowed them some jam, sugar, and, at times, a tiny ration of meat in order to get more potatoes and bread.

Journalists, teachers, and other professionals had to find new careers, trying their luck, for example, at selling haberdashery on street corners. The Jewish community could be divided into three categories, according to their financial resources. According to one chronicler of the ghetto, some twenty thousand formed an elite, with money and valuable possessions that could be turned into money. In their homes, one could still find enough food on the table and more stored for future use. Such people were affluent before the war; others accumulated money by large-scale smuggling of goods into the ghetto. Still others owned enterprises that continued to operate in the ghetto, both legally and illegally, and were partners to all sorts of secret dealings with the Germans and the Poles. Ghetto wheeler-dealers, who had reached this status only during their stay in the ghetto, overindulged in a life of enjoyment and excess in a devil-may-care atmosphere of "eat and drink, for tomorrow we die."

Most of these families lived in comparatively spacious apartments in Chlodna Street. They wore clean clothes and were conscious of their appearance. They frequented a number of cafés, restaurants, and clubs in the ghetto. The striking gap between those who were more than sated, clean, and well dressed and those who lacked everything and went hungry was an element of ghetto reality. Two or three times a week, a newspaper called *The Jewish Paper* (*Gazeta Zydowska*) appeared in Polish in Cracow, addressed to the Jews of the General Government. This publication contained official announcements and cynical propaganda that the authorities wished to spread among the Jews. On the last page were advertisements for restaurants and amusement halls, while alongside these announcements, in smaller lettering, appeared the numbers of those who had died of hunger during that week. In similiar proximity, families lay near the entrances to these places of amusement, huddled together to ward off the cold, awaiting the tossing of a coin in their direction from passersby on their way to a café.

Alongside the well fed, who amounted to a small percent of the population, there were some 200,000 "in-betweens," including people who had retained some of their possessions, or who had some form of temporary work, maintained their own apartments, and had limited quantities of basic foods. The status of these "in-betweens" was measured in time. Some could hold their heads above water for many months, but eventually their possessions would dwindle and they would deteriorate to the status of the hungry masses.

The ravenous multitude numbered more than 200,000. For them, each day was a battle for a crust of bread. Every month, thousands lost their hope and strength in the struggle to survive. In appearance, they resembled human skeletons, with bones protruding in their gray and sunken faces. Spiritually, they were dead; their eyes had lost all expression or contact with reality. They were the living dead, indifferent to everything and succumbing to their fate. Many of them would sit or lie down, crowded and wrapped in rags, a silent protest against their Creator and Creation. Passersby turned away at the sight of these lost Jews because they could do nothing to help them. They may also have sensed that someday in the not so distant future they too might be in this hopeless situation. The German authorities did not consider helping them in any way but demanded that sidewalks be cleared of corpses lest they be disturbed by the sight. Actually, not a few German soldiers who visited the Jewish ghetto gazed at the bodies strewn about and viewed the horrors of the city gradually sinking into lifelessness and insensibility.

At first, the hungry and freezing cried out for help from their fellow human beings, but as their strength gave out and the uselessness of their pleas became evident, their voices slowly weakened until there was utter silence. The children were the last to quiet down, and the penetrating bitter weeping of babies and infants was like an innocent voice of accusation against the wicked and evil world. Ringelblum despairingly described his insomnia and the deafening crying of children which he could not shake.

The corpses that had been shorn of their remaining clothing were covered with paper. At dawn, the dead were loaded on wagons that brought them to mass graves on the outskirts of the large Jewish cemetery. These Jews had not only been deprived of their right to live as human beings but were even robbed of the right to die with human dignity. There was not a sign or gravestone marking their passing, no marker where the name of the departed was noted; no linkage between family members, between parents and their children. The memory of the individual was eradicated for eternity.

The major cause of these mass deaths was the typhus epidemic. Other factors, such as cold and frost, the suffocating crowdedness and melancholy, were secondary. The struggle against typhus occupied the Jews to the very limits of their strength. The many doctors in the ghetto worked in hurried succession at the sickbeds, trying to subdue the disease. Medication was not available, nor were such preventive treatments as food, warmth, and sanitary conditions. It would often occur that a doctor, instead of receiving payment for his visit, would secretly leave a coin beside the sickbed.

The Judenrat's sanitary crews, in which Jews worked under the supervision of non-Jews, battled the epidemic in their own fashion. The home of a typhus victim was shut down for a certain period while all the members of the household and their bedclothes were taken forcibly to be disinfected. In many cases, property from the home was stolen. It was doubtful whether this procedure helped to control the epidemic, and perhaps contributed to its spread. The Germans had their own way of fighting the disease. In his report of January 1941, Fischer, the governor of the Warsaw district, made the following statement:

The main purpose of the campaign to explain and demonstrate the dangers of typhus [flecken-typhus or spotted fever], executed in collaboration with the department of health, was to point out that the Jews are the disseminators of typhus. The principal slogan of the campaign is "The Jews — Lice — Typhus." The matter has been demonstrated and clarified to the [Polish] community with the help of 3,000 large posters, 7,000 smaller posters, and 500,000 pamphlets. The Polish press [under German patronage] and the radio have shared in the distribution of this information. In addition, the children in Polish schools have been warned of the danger every single day.

In the battle against hunger, food was smuggled into the ghetto from Polish sectors of the city via the wall or by more sophisticated methods. Through openings made in the wall, over the wall, by channels under the wall, or through hidden passages between the houses, smuggled goods streamed in, sometimes literally (in one instance, a stream of milk flowed through a pipe leading from the Polish side into a pitcher placed in a house within the ghetto). Not a day passed, even at the height of the expulsion, when food was not brought into the ghetto by secret means, often at the cost of many lives. Shots could be heard daily as troops fired on the smugglers, even the children. The daily loss of life did not stop the inhabitants from carrying on with their activities. They had few other choices if they were to survive. People caught in the act of smuggling were immediately replaced, much like soldiers shot during a battle.

Why did the Germans not put an end to the smuggling, which was surely in their power? In dealing with smugglers, they did not impose the usual collective punishments, nor did they murder large numbers of smugglers. Local officials may have acquiesced to the "clandestine importation of food" because, according to Czerniakow, smuggling brought in 80 percent of all the food in the ghetto. The Germans knew that cutting off the food supply completely would lead to starvation and the utter extinction of the ghetto within weeks, or at most a few months.

There were three types of smuggling. The first was well-organized wholesale smuggling, requiring cooperation between the Jews and the Poles, and an organization that employed hundreds in a disciplined and efficient hierarchical structure. Everyone knew his job; every aspect was carefully planned and carried out swiftly, from the moment that sacks of food were transferred through the wall and beyond, until the food was distributed to the consumer in the ghetto.

A second form of smuggling was carried out by some two thousand workers, who would leave the ghetto each morning in convoys to work in various places for Germans. These workers would usually smuggle items on their own person, in bags hanging from their shoulders. They would snatch small amounts of food for their families or for selling to neighbors. When such a petty smuggler was caught, what he had hidden was taken away from him and he could expect to be beaten.

The third form of smuggling was done individually, mainly by women and small children forced into smuggling by hunger and scarcity in their families. They managed to get through the gates or over the wall surreptitiously and begged on the Polish streets or tried some petty trading for a bit of food. In the writings of witnesses, considerable space is given to the description of these children who slipped over to the "other side," begged, and were given some bread by the Poles (according to some accounts, frequently by women who were known antisemites but who could not stand the sight of hungry children). Despite their own starving state, many of them did not eat the dry and tempting crusts they were given but brought them to their parents, or to their little brothers and sisters. The sacrifice of these children, many of whom were shot down like birds in flight, disturbed and moved the hearts of many of the ghetto's people. The Polish poet of Jewish origin, Henrika Lazowert, wrote this poem, "The Little Smuggler," in the ghetto:

> Through crack and crevice, over wire tight,
> With dawn, in daylight, and the dead of night,
> Hungry, daring, and brave of spirit,
> Sneaking, creeping shadow near it,
>
> And in amidst the game, the hand of fate
> touches me suddenly and I am too late,
> Know I am but a mortal.
> Don't wait in vain, mother,
> I'll not return, like another,
> To hear my voice no longer from afar,
> The street's dust my grave will mar
>
> For my fate is resolved.
> And on my face one care is etched,
> Who, my heart's own, has fetched
> Your bread for the morrow.

Leon Berenson, a gifted defense lawyer and activist in Poland between the wars, said that liberated Poland should erect a monument to honor the unknown child, the little smuggler from the Warsaw ghetto.

Polish publications referred at times to the smuggling of food that was so essential to the life of the ghetto and to Poles' intent to assist the Jews in their plight. While the highly organized smuggling involved collaboration between the two sides, it would be inaccurate to ascribe charity as the motive for this relationship. More precisely, both Polish and Jewish managers of the large-scale smuggling operations were mainly concerned with financial success. Quite a few people on both sides of the wall succeeded in accumulating substantial fortunes through smuggling. The food brought into the ghetto was sold at prices much higher than on the "Aryan side." The principal manipulators were the clients of cafés and restaurants in the ghetto who rarely shared their accumulated wealth with the starving masses. Moreover, heads of the smuggling network preferred to bring meats, fats, and even luxury items into the ghetto which only the rich could afford, rather than potatoes and bread, which took up too much space and were less profitable. As almost all the chroniclers of the ghetto have stressed, however, whatever their motives, the smugglers nonetheless contributed to the ghetto's glimmer of life and its strength to survive.

Smuggling was not a one-way proposition. Jews sold or traded their property, possessions, and clothing for food, and a steady stream of Jewish money, household goods, pianos, and other possessions poured into the Polish side. The Poles involved in the smuggling did so at risk to their own lives. Objectively speaking, their aid in a vital task should be praised.

As with smuggling, there were various manufacturing enterprises in the ghetto which emerged in response to the situation. The only legal commodities to enter the ghetto came through the *Transferstelle,* the German office responsible for the movement of goods and raw materials into and out from the ghetto. The *Transferstelle*'s compound, located on the Aryan side of the ghetto border, led to a sidetrack of the railway. This same compound would later be used as the point of departure for the death transports during the annihilation of the ghetto and the mass expulsion of July 1942. The name was then changed to the infamous *Umschlagplatz*, or "reloading or transport place."

In addition to the official economy focused in the *Transferstelle*, goods entered and left the ghetto illegally, including articles manufactured in secret — the "hidden commerce of the ghetto" — which employed skilled artisans and workers for illegal export. According to estimates in an economic study prepared for the underground archives in the ghetto, income from legally manufactured goods increased from more than 300,000 zloty in June 1941 to 1.2 million zloty in November of the same year, a growth of more than 400 percent in five months. During that period, the illegal production of the ghetto netted some 10 million zloty, an amount approximately three and a half times greater than that of the legal production.

One of the main customers for illegally produced goods, and also the supplier of the raw materials needed for this production, was the German army, which was in urgent need of brushes, beds, metalware, clothing, and other items. The army deliberately circumvented the civilian administration of the General Government to avoid the high duties normally paid to the transferring office. Moreover, the army, anxious for the prompt delivery of desperately needed material, was willing to buy directly from Jewish manufacturers, even when it meant paying higher prices, in order to avoid German manufacturers and the middlemen who were inclined to pocket some of the profits.

German businessmen who owned enterprises in the ghetto tried to get the ghetto Jews to work without pay. The Jews refused to work in these enterprises, and as a result, the German-owned factories produced poor-quality products. Therefore, the Wehrmacht preferred to work directly with Jewish manufacturers, whom they knew to be experienced, and willingly paid for that experience. Polish businessmen who had taken over for Jews in various national manufacturing markets also had difficulty obtaining manufactured goods, especially those produced by skilled and professional Jewish artisans. Polish merchants tried to acquire smuggled goods. Since Jews were the weaker partner in such deals, goods were more than occasionally extracted by exploitation or dishonest means. Nevertheless, Jewish manufacturers could keep their heads above water. The mere fact of their existence was proof that they did not forgo their share of the profit.

The Judenrat was under pressure to increase the German manufacturers' share of income from ghetto enterprises, and so an effort was made to attract Jewish workers to the German enterprises by providing them with larger rations of food. Jews refused to submit to slave labor, however, and the Judenrat refrained from forcing them to do so. According to official data, toward the end of its existence, there were some 70,000 workers in the ghetto. In the last months before the expulsion, when frightening rumors abounded, many applied for work at German enterprises because these were considered more secure in view of the dangers hovering over the ghetto.

Mutual help in the ghetto changed in the period from mid-1941 to mid-1942. In "The Social Welfare in Warsaw during the War," written in June 1942, Emanuel Ringelblum explained the changes and the difficulties. While acknowledging the positive contributions made by the Joint, including the assistance rendered to Jews by its various departments, he examined the negative aspects of their work. The Joint was inclined to give too much importance to the people "who form public opinion — the press, and leaders of political parties," rather than the public that depended on it. Ringelblum viewed this as a form of protectionism that affected and harmed its activities. Ringelblum also pointed to another weakness. In the first weeks of the war, when the Joint had enormous financial sums at its disposal, it generously helped many. The Jews of Warsaw assumed as a result that the impoverished and the refugees could depend on bounteous funds from the Joint. In the spring of 1940, with the Joint's funds declining rapidly, it took some time before the Jews realized that they themselves would have to shoulder the responsibility for the distress plaguing their community. By that spring, Ringelblum says, "it became clear that in this war, the Jews of the United States would not lend a hand as generously as they did in the first world war, but people continued to believe that American millions would still cover the aid expenses."

Why didn't American help arrive when Jews were being driven mad and dying from hunger? Ringelblum did not answer this question, stating only that the Jews of Warsaw eventually realized that they could not depend on others. He saw the apex of achievement and dedication of the people of the Joint in its proper place, in the self-contribution of the Jews of Warsaw who lent the Joint millions on the assumption that it would be returned after the war, despite a Nazi prohibition against such transactions. Managers of the Joint in Warsaw knew from the very outset that they were endangering their lives, and although they knew what awaited them if the matter was discovered they did not hesitate. It would remain forever one of the greatest open secrets of the ghetto — it was possible even in such a demoralized and corrupt social climate to keep this secret open to the Jews and closed to the Germans and the Poles, despite the presence of dozens of agents. All Warsaw Jews knew about these matters. The Germans did not.

Ringelblum did not differentiate between those matters concerning Jewish property and money, in which the Germans intervened as a matter of course, and other issues that interested them less, such as cultural or even underground political activities. For substantial sums donated by Jews of means to help the hungry was something that made the Germans anxious, and thus Ringelblum's amazement at the fact that they succeeded in hiding such a forbidden matter from the Germans.

Ringelblum recalls the scourge caused by German agents among the Jews of the ghetto. We do not know how many there were or who was behind them, but their existence was known to many since they operated as a network openly attached to the SD, the intelligence and surveillance organization of the SS. The head of this network was an interesting figure named Abraham Gancwajch, a native of Czestochowa. A Zionist in his youth, he had lived in various European countries, where his activities are a mystery. At the outbreak of the war, he was living in Lodz. He appeared in Warsaw at the beginning of 1940, where he attracted attention by preaching that one had to get used to the German regime and accept it. Gancwajch clearly believed that the Germans would win the war. Beginning in early 1941, Gancwajch acquired a reputation as someone willing to use connections among the German authorities to seek the release of prisoners or assistance for others in trouble. Among a helpless population, such rumors offered promise. In certain instances he did make use of his connections, but in most cases his efforts were fruitless.

Moreover, he was usually paid for his efforts. In time, he became a manager and rent-collector for the Germans, and soon he had agents in special uniforms, a counterforce to the Judenrat police, who acted under the peculiar and nonspecific guise of "the war against speculation and excessive prices." Like the Mafia, they forced ghetto businessmen to pay a form of protection against betrayal to the authorities. Later, Gancwajch set up a "first aid station," which had little to do with the sick or the injured but most probably ran ambulances to transport confiscated goods and materials.

Endowed with great rhetorical gifts, he made frequent use of them. Fluent in Hebrew, he introduced himself as a benefactor who would see to everything. He held receptions in his home and surrounded himself with both the naive and the less naive. At his peak in the ghetto, he strove to undermine the position of Czerniakow and the Judenrat in an effort to take over the management of the ghetto himself. Czerniakow speaks of him with ridicule and abhorrence, and he was one of the few men whom Czerniakow despised. His attempts to take over the ghetto eventually led to his downfall. Gancwajch was defeated in a quarrel between the German authorities.

On the bloody night of April 18, 1942, Gancwajch and his close assistant, Sternfeld, were sought by the Germans. He succeeded in evading them. There were unsubstantiated rumors that he was informing on Jews in hiding on the Polish side of town. Hillel Seidman, a senior official of the Judenrat and author of the book *The Diary of the Warsaw Ghetto*, claimed to have read reports in which Gancwajch would supply Germans with information about ghetto activities. According to Seidman, these reports did not contain ghetto secrets or reveal operations of the underground, nor were they written with malice.

The American scholar Christopher R. Browning, who researched in the archives of Yad Vashem, cited a collection of reports written by a German agent in the ghetto. We know that Ganwajch himself was not the informer who wrote those notes, but they may have been prepared by someone close to him. An examination of the material, which covers the period between March and May 1942, generally confirms Seidman's observations. The documents contain details of the mood and conditions in the ghetto, and report that rumors were rife about mass killing and the use of gas for this purpose. But the documents contain no information that would have been harmful to the ghetto and do not mention the political underground and its activities.

Why didn't the Jews revolt? How are we to understand the fact that masses of Warsaw Jews had reached the point of extreme starvation and weakness, yet they did not attack those well-fed Jews who publicly flaunted their affluence? The process of decline was gradual among the starving Jews. When it began, they were still hopeful, but when decline set in they were reduced to utter impotence. As long as people retained some hope and had the minimum requirements for living, they were not eager to revolt, while those close to death from hunger did not have the strength or will to organize or demonstrate violently.

Paradoxically, conditions improved in the ghetto in the last months before the mass expulsion. There was talk of a relative state of stabilization, a decline in the typhus epidemic, a reduction in the rate of death, an increase in the number of employers, and a minute increase in food rations. The weakest had died. Only the stronger and more vigorous remained alive. In January 1942 the death rate reached a figure of 5,123, or 1.5 percent of the population; by May the number had dropped to 3,363. In his March 1942 report, District Governor Fischer wrote of a decline in the incidence of typhus. In May he stressed the increasing number of Jewish workers and their greater role in various essential enterprises.

Clearly, the decision to deport and annihilate the Jews did not originate with the local German authorities and was not the result of a worsening situation in the ghetto. The directive to kill the Warsaw Jews came from higher sources. The deportation was preceded by a reign of absolute terror: killings of groups of people for crossing the ghetto borders, increasing rumors of "actions" and death camps, information about expulsions from many other ghettos, which had disappeared without a trace — and finally, on July 22, the terrible tragedy of the Jews of Warsaw.

5

THE TURNING POINT

THE LAUNCH OF Operation Barbarossa, the German assault on the Soviet Union, on June 22, 1941, was a watershed in the progress of the war. Germany's long-standing aspiration to dominate Eastern Europe was merged with its ideological and racial goals. In a briefing to his officers, Hitler described the war as the decisive confrontation between two completely opposing world-views, with mass annihilation necessary to prevent the recurrence of these ideologies. In an address to the troops Himmler was graphic:

> Here in this struggle stands National Socialism: an ideology based on the value of our Germanic, Nordic blood. Here stands a world as we have conceived it: beautiful, decent, socially equal . . . a happy beautiful world full of culture. That is what our Germany is like.
>
> On the other side stands a population of 180 million, a mixture of races whose very names are unpronounceable, and whose physique is such that one can shoot them down without

pity and compassion . . . These people have been welded by the Jews into one religion, one ideology that is called Bolshevism.

When you, my men, fight over there in the East, you are carrying on the same struggle against the same subhumanity, the same inferior races that at one time appeared under the name Huns, another time . . . under the name Magyars, another time under the name Tartars, and still another time under the name Genghis Khan and the Mongols.

Andreas Hillgruber, a scholar of German political history, identified four motives for Hitler's assault on the Soviets. The first was to exterminate "Jewish Bolshevik leadership," including its presumed source, the millions of Eastern European Jews. Hitler himself identified the three other motives in a speech to senior officers: to acquire land for German settlers, to impose German dominion over the Slavs, and to take over the rich sources of raw materials necessary to wage war against the Anglo-Saxon forces.

Indeed, from the very outset, the German occupying forces received instructions couched in ideological language. The murderous methods adopted were applied to entire sectors of humanity who were identified as the enemy. "Commissars Orders" were issued to wipe out the political commissars of the Red Army. Germany invaded the Soviet Union in group force. Its military might consisted of 121 divisions (including seventeen armored and twelve motorized divisions and three thousand planes). The army was accompanied by *Einsatzgruppen,* mobile killing units A, B, C, and D, which were deployed from the north to the south.

The *Einsatzgruppen* consisted of elements of various police forces that had been employed during the annexation of Austria in 1938 and Czechoslovakia in March 1939, as well as in the attack on Poland. Their role was to "purify" the area politically and to pinpoint potential and active opposition in the occupied territory. In 1939 the *Einsatzgruppen* had been under the authority of the army, which attempted to restrain its operations. By the time of the anti-Soviet campaign in 1941 however, the *Einsatzgruppen* were placed under the SS, and were thus independent of the army. Nevertheless, the army provided the *Einsatzgruppen* with all necessary services but did not interfere with their methods. The army reportedly took no direct responsibility for the mass killings undertaken by these murderous squads.

According to evidence from unit commanders, the *Einsatzgruppen* received verbal orders to annihilate all Jews in the territories occupied by the army from Reinhard Heydrich and Bruno Streckenbach (formerly commander of the Security Police in the General Government and later a department head in the central security office of the Reich). The written order issued by Heydrich in July 1941 specified that "Jews in the administration of the party and the state" were to be executed.

Within less than two years, by the spring of 1943, the *Einsatzgruppen* had murdered some 1,250,000 Jewish men, women and children. They were murdered in towns and villages, in cities and hamlets, one, by one, by one. In this homicidal campaign, hundreds of thousands of non-Jewish citizens of the Soviet Union also fell victim to the *Einsatzgruppen,* especially Soviet prisoners of war and officials of the Communist party.

However, if the killing of non-Jews was supposedly punishment meted out for their political and party affiliations, the methodical annihilation of Jews was carried out simply because they were Jews. Four *Einsatzgruppen,* numbering some six hundred to one thousand men, assisted by local forces and police in the Ukraine and the Baltic states, helped assemble Jews for their mass murder. The executions took place alongside pits in the ground. Families were ordered to remove their clothing, then were shot, falling or being thrown into the pit awaiting them.

Among the commanders of the *Einsatzgruppen* were well-educated men, including Otto Ohlendorf, who had finished his studies in law and economy and had begun a promising academic career. The mobile killing squad he commanded consisted of "ordinary men," a cross section of the German population. After the war, Ohlendorf was sentenced to death by the American court of justice that tried the *Einsatzgruppen.* He was convicted of the murder of some ninety thousand individuals, the majority of whom were Jews. In testimony before the international tribunal in the trial of the major war criminals in Nuremberg, Ohlendorf admitted that the instructions given him and his colleagues in the *Einsatzgruppen* stated that they were to "wipe out" all the Jews and other unwanted elements. When asked at the trial why it was necessary to kill children as well, he replied that the children would eventually grow up and then become dangerous as avengers of their parents' deaths.

Scholars' opinions differ as to when the order was given for the "final solution," who gave the order, and *whether* such an all-encompassing command had actually been issued. It is clear that the most senior leaders of the Nazi state and party were responsible for the employment of the killing units of the *Einsatzgruppen*. Hitler himself laid down their hierarchical responsibilities and received copies of their unit commanders' reports. The killing process began in the summer of 1941. Within six months, the Wannsee Conference took place in Berlin, and the "final solution of the Jewish problem," the murder of all Jews, became a coordinated plan operational on a European scale. Within less than a year, six killing centers complete with their gas chambers were in place and the deportations from the ghettos of Poland to the death camps had begun. One must view the first stage of the destruction of the Jews of Europe by the *Einsatzgruppen* as the transition from the system of terror, persecution, and severe oppression that preceded it to the indiscriminate all-inclusive murder from which only those who were needed for work in the concentration camps were exempted. The killing process was soon further refined by a natural evolution from mobile killing units, in which the killers were sent after the victims, to death camps, in which the victim was sent to the killer.

While full-scale systematic murder was proceeding in the Soviet Union, the unrestrained repression in Poland was taking a far more limited toll. The number of Jewish victims did not reach more than 6–8 percent until the spring of 1942, when the death camps became operational.

The city of Vilna was one of the places to suffer most from the *Einsatzgruppen*. Part of interwar Poland, Vilna was annexed by the Soviet Union in 1939, together with Lithuania. Today, it is the capital of the independent state of Lithuania. When the Germans conquered Vilna on June 24, 1941, they found some fifty-seven thousand Jews living in the city, composing a third of the local population. Six months later, only twenty thousand Jews survived; the remainder had been murdered, most in the woods of Ponar, some twelve kilometers from Vilna.

Information concerning the executions seeped into the sealed ghetto of Vilna when a few wounded survivors managed to escape and return to the ghetto. In a feverish discussion, members of the youth movement debated the need for an immediate reaction to the situation. Activists of Hashomer Hatzaír found temporary refuge in a Dominican nunnery in Vilna where they evaluated what could be done. On New Year's Eve, 1941, considered a safe time for holding such an assembly, a group of people from the youth movement gathered to hear a proclamation written by Abba Kovner, who later became a partisan fighter and then a well-known poet in Israel. Kovner wrote:

> Jewish youth, do not believe those that are trying to deceive you. . . . Before our eyes they took away our parents, our brothers and sisters. Where are the hundreds of men who were conscripted for labor? Where are the naked women and the children who were taken away from us on that dreadful night? Where are the Jews who were deported on Yom Kippur?
>
> And where are our own brethren from other ghettos?
>
> Of those taken through the gates of the ghetto not a single one has returned. All the Gestapo roads lead to Ponar, and Ponar means death.
>
> Ponar is not a concentration camp. They have all been shot there. Hitler plans to destroy all the Jews of Europe, and the Jews of Lithuania have been chosen as the first in line.
>
> We will not be led like sheep to the slaughter. True, we are weak and helpless, but the only response to the murderer is revolt!
>
> Brothers! it is better to die fighting like free men than to live at the mercy of the murderers. Arise! Arise with your last breath!

There were several striking parallels between what happened in Vilna and what was to happen in Warsaw. The call to arms in Vilna came after three-quarters of the city's pre-war Jewish population had been deported and murdered in Ponar. The call for armed resistance was made on January 1, 1942. It went unheeded until the ghetto was on the verge of extinction. Vilna was typical in that armed resistance gained mass support only when people understood that the Nazis planned to kill all Jews and that there was no way out of the ghetto: Ponar, where all the Gestapo roads led, was more than a metaphor for death.

But the decision to fight did not come easily to most ghetto inhabitants. Resistance meant rejecting the traditional authority of the leaders of the Jewish community: Kovner and other young fighters challenged the Judenrat when they urged that "it is better to die fighting like free men than to live at the mercy of the murderers."

Kovner was directly critical of the older generations who had submitted without a struggle: "We will not be led like sheep to the slaughter." Those who fought were clear eyed. Resistance was, at its essence, a choice between forms of death. Whatever Jews did, they would be killed. But one could die with honor by choosing "to defend oneself to the last breath."

Vilna was the first call to armed resistance by Jews in the occupied territories. While there had been proponents of resistance to the Nazis and their aspirations of territorial domination, this was the first Jewish call that acknowledged the impossibility of overcoming the Nazis or even contributing to their downfall, but demanded that Jews join a struggle to the death.

It was not surprising that this entreaty came from Vilna, one of the first sites of mass murder. What was surprising was the declaration's assertion at the end of 1941 before the killing centers were in place that the tragedy in Vilna was not a local wartime phenomenon but the first step in a comprehensive campaign to murder all the Jews of Europe. In this dreadfully precise forecast, Kovner and his friends had decoded the German plan. They understood the full implications of what was happening. With no obvious source of information, one can only assume that this knowledge was intuitive.

It was not happenstance that this public call to a final confrontation should come from the youth movements. The idea of resistance was adopted by the youth of Vilna representing different political persuasions. In January 1942 a Jewish resistance organization was established — the first of its kind in Nazi-occupied

Europe — called the United Partisan Organization, commonly known as the FPO. Within a short time, Communists, Bundists, and Zionists of various factions of the left and the right, such as Betar, the Zionist Youth, and Hashomer Hatzaír, all worked within the FPO. The willingness of many divergent organizations to work together indicated their awareness of the common danger.

Accord was not universal, however, and in various places, including Warsaw, rival organizations were set up. Differences of opinion in Vilna, though, had little to do with politics or ideology but related to where and how fighting would take place. Members of the Dror movement, headed by Mordecai Tennenbaum-Tamarof, a colorful, energetic, audacious young man, did not support the fighting organization in Vilna and moved to Bialystok. Tennenbaum's motivation is unknown. He may have considered Bialystok safer after the first murderous two weeks of German occupation, or he may have viewed Bialystok as more suitable for building the organization to meet the challenge to come. At any rate, Tennenbaum emerged as a leader of the struggle and commander of the Jewish fighting organization in Bialystok. He fell during the campaign of August 1943.

The Nazi invasion of the Soviet Union was a double blow to those Polish Jews who fled east to Soviet territory from Warsaw and other cities in central Poland. In cities such as Vilna, Kovno, and Bialystok Jews who had once escaped Nazi rule in 1939 were again under German domination. Yet the absence of a border permitted many to try to unite with their families and friends on the other side. As Jews were forbidden to move, others, especially the Poles, offered to help reunite families, or at least to do so for payment. There were also Poles who had different motivations.

In Warsaw before the war, a strong friendship had been formed between groups of Catholics and the Zionist-pioneering youth movement, Hashomer Hatzaír, based partly on the emphasis they both placed on the tradition of scouting. There were, however, basic differences between these two bodies. Polish Catholic scouts were very religious, the Jews were secular, radical socialist Zionists. Though some Catholic scouts were also liberal in their outlook, the dominant religious inclination led many toward a conservative non-Communist and nonsocialist position, while many of the Jewish youth movements were socialist. Still, the Catholic scouts who remained close to the Jewish youth movement were impressed by the strong comradeship that existed in the Jewish movement, by their free and frank expression in conversations and discussion, and in their songfests, hikes, and evening gatherings, even as their youthful joie de vivre was tempered by their unknown future.

The life of one young Catholic scout, Irena Adamowicz, was transformed by Jews. Throughout the existence of the ghetto, Adamowicz was a runner for the Jewish underground. She met with groups from Hashomer Hatzaír in the provinces and the sealed ghettos to pass on instructions and material. At these meetings, she also described to eager listeners the actions, decisions, and intelligence she picked up in her travels. She clearly felt a close affinity for the Jews and the underground. During the course of the war, Adamowicz widened her contacts with Jewish groups in the ghetto.

Another Catholic scout who remained loyal to his Jewish friends was Alexander Kaminski, a prominent figure in the Polish underground during the war and editor of the *Biuletyn Informacyjny* (Bulletin of Information), the central publication in occupied Poland of the AK, the military arm of the Polish government-in-exile. Under Kaminski's influence, the paper extensively covered the distress and fate of the Jews. On a number of occasions, Kaminski interceded with the Polish underground on behalf of the Jews. Later, he established ongoing contact between representatives of the Jewish Fighting Organization on the Polish side of Warsaw and the command of the AK.

Among the Catholic scouts who were friends of the Jews was a German youth who enlisted as a doctor in the German army during the war. This career move did not affect his warm relationship with both Poles and Jews. According to Ringelblum, Mordecai Anielewicz, who was later to lead the Warsaw Ghetto Uprising, reported that this German doctor used the army mailbag to pass greetings to the underground groups of Hashomer Hatzaír in Warsaw. When on leave, he would slip into the ghetto of Warsaw and spend days and nights in the company of his

Adam Czerniakow, leader of the Warsaw Judenrat, overseen by a German officer in his office. (Yad Vashem, Jerusalem, Israel)

The construction of the Warsaw ghetto wall.
(Main Crimes Commission, Warsaw, Poland)

An SS man publicly humiliates a religious Jew in Warsaw, 1939.
(Bildarchiv Preussischer Kulturbesitz, Berlin, Germany)

German soldiers oversee Jews forced to clear rubble, 1939.
(Bundesarchiv, Koblenz, Germany)

Jews taken from the Warsaw ghetto for forced labor.
(Bundesarchiv, Koblenz, Germany)

Street vendors selling household goods in the Warsaw ghetto, 1941–42. (Bundesarchiv, Koblenz, Germany)

Buying books in the Warsaw ghetto, February 1941. (Bildarchiv Preussischer Kulturbesitz, Berlin, Germany)

A German propaganda photograph of two Jewish policemen and a destitute Jew in the ghetto, 1941–42. (Bundesarchiv, Koblenz, Germany)

Janusz Korczak with children from his orphanage, Warsaw, 1940–42. (Beit Lochamei Haghetaot, Israel)

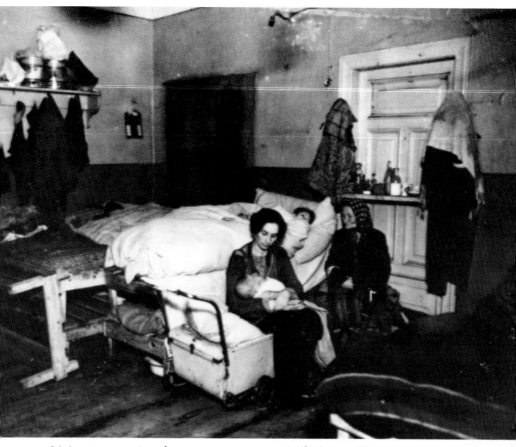

Living quarters in a former synagogue, 32 Mila Street, Warsaw,
Poland, 1940. Housing was so scarce that even sacred sites were used.
(Yad Vashem, Jerusalem, Israel)

Opposite, top: Jewish smugglers in the Warsaw ghetto, 1940.
(Archives of Mechanical Documentation, Warsaw, Poland)

Opposite, bottom: Jewish smugglers in the Warsaw ghetto, 1941.
(Z.I.H./Jewish Historical Institute, Warsaw, Poland)

Synagogue on 27 Nowolipki Street, Warsaw, Poland, used as a shelter by Jews expelled from Lodz, 1940. (Yad Vashem, Jerusalem, Israel)

Jewish friends of the youth movement. Hashomer Hatzaír youth found refuge at the nunnery in Vilna due to intervention by Polish Catholic scouts, which Ringelblum considered a rare example of a Polish organization consistently helping a Jewish organization.

Another Polish scout, Henryk Grabowski, was sent from Warsaw to Vilna to renew contact with members of the movement centered there. Grabowski returned with a description of the horrors in Vilna. In 1947 Yitzhak Zuckerman wrote that

> because of that autumn day in 1941, when Heniek [an endearment for *Henryk*], the Polish scout, returned from his mission in Vilna and brought with him the dire news of the annihiliation of the Jews, serious things began to happen in the movement . . . all educational work intended to preserve the human aspect of the younger generation and arouse their fighting spirit, would have had no meaning in those days, unless it was attended by the strength to create an armed Jewish defensive force.

Soon after Grabowski's departure, contacts from the youth movement arrived in Vilna, with Tosia Altman among them. Thus, the depressing news of the destruction in Vilna arrived in Warsaw along with a call to battle and insurgence. Yet the situation in Warsaw differed from that in Vilna. Vilna was introduced to the German invasion through the indiscriminate snatching of people, mass murder, and *selektsia* (selection of people for killing). While Warsaw had undergone considerable oppression and unruly behavior, it had not experienced the outright killing of tens of thousands of Jews. The Jews of Warsaw, including officials in the underground, considered Vilna unique because of its location near the Soviet front. They mistakenly reasoned that the chaos of Vilna did not foreshadow the beginning of a cataclysm for Jews throughout Europe.

The youth movements of Warsaw, however, correctly assessed the implications in the murder of Vilna's Jews. They began to prepare for the struggle to come. The news from Vilna signaled a change in the movement. The time had come to keep a watchful eye on events. Feelers were put out about joining with the Polish military underground, but for various reasons these efforts were not successful. Certainly the Jews locked in the ghetto could not prepare for military action without some assistance from the Polish underground. Intelligence, arms, military training, and contact with other countries were available to the Polish forces and could not be duplicated in the ghetto. Ringelblum wrote that in January 1942, while lecturing at a seminar for youth movement leaders at the Hashomer Hatzaír hostel at Nalewki 23, Anielewicz called him into one of the rooms and showed him two pistols. This is the first intimation we have of weapons in the ghetto.

At the instigation of the pioneering movement, a conference of all Jewish political underground bodies in Warsaw was called in March 1942. Yitzhak Zuckerman attended as a representative of Hehalutz. He described his proposal to set up a general fighting organization; to establish Jewish political representation in the underground; to conduct negotiations with Polish factions; and to appoint a delegation authorized to act on behalf of the fighting organization and the Polish Jewish underground on the Polish side of the city.

The conference reached no decisions and established no framework for active opposition. According to Zuckerman and others present at the meeting, mainly representatives of the Bund prevented the creation of a fighting unit. Consistent with their ideology, the Bund opposed a separate Jewish fighting force, arguing that the plight of the Jews was an integral concern to all of Poland. The Bund may have been reluctant to collaborate with Zionist and bourgeois elements. The pioneering youth movements favored including the Bund in any organization to be established. They needed the Bund because they rightly believed that it was the only faction in the Jewish camp with direct access to the Polish military underground.

Actually, in the early stages of the consultations, the Bund expressed ambivalence about cooperating with other Jewish youth groups. One veteran Bund leader was sharply opposed, while the representative of the younger generation indicated an inclination to collaborate with the Zionist youth. In addition to the significant objections of the Bund, various factions of the political underground were insufficiently prepared to act on the proposals of the pioneering youth movements. In view of the Bund's objections and the approaching danger and urgency of the situation, the Jewish bodies approached another element — the Communists.

Between the wars and during most of the independent Polish Republic's regime, the Communists were not a legal political party. Many veteran members had been imprisoned. The Polish Communist party, destroyed by the Soviet Comintern in 1938, was accused by the Communist International of straying from the party line and of being infiltrated by foreign agents. The "purification" begun by Stalin and his administration finished off party members or sent them into exile deep in the heart of the Soviet Union. The elite among the Party leadership were "called" to Moscow where they were judged and condemned at staged trials, and then disappeared. The surviving Polish Communists were left without power or significance while the Soviet Union signed a pact with the Nazis and contributed to the division of Poland among its major enemies.

At the height of the war against the Nazis, the Soviet Union enlisted the patriotism of the Poles and other peoples in their fateful struggle. In an agreement with the Polish government in exile in London, commanded by General Wladyslaw Sikorski, refugees and members of the Polish army imprisoned in Soviet camps were released and a Polish army was organized as a fighting unit in the Allied camp, subordinate in many respects to the Soviets. This army, known as "Anders' army" after its commander, General Wladyslaw Anders, had pro-Jewish and anti-Jewish factions. Owing to friction between this military force and the Soviets, Anders's army was evacuated from the Soviet Union to the Middle East and the western fronts. The army had only a small proportion of Jews despite the fact that many enlisted during the mobilization stage.

At the beginning of 1943, after Anders's army had left the Soviet Union, the Soviets initiated another Polish fighting force among Poles remaining in the Soviet Union. Modeled after the Red Army, it was integrated into the Red Army's structure. Jews composed a comparatively large portion of this army.

In January 1942 the Communist party in the Polish under-

ground was rehabilitated and renamed the Party of Polish Workers (Polska Partia Robotnicza, or the PPR). However, it was not
accepted into the broad political coalition. A military unit with
Communist inclinations known as the Popular Army (Armia Ludowa, the AL) was set up alongside the PPR.

The Red Army and the anti-Nazi struggle of the Soviet people
attracted much sympathetic support among the Jews in occupied
Poland, as this force appeared to wage a decisive battle against
the Nazis, and subsequently the advance of the Red Army opened
the visible chance for liberation and rescue for Polish Jews. The
pre-war Communist party had actually been the only political
body composed of both Poles and Jews. In the Jewish youth movements, especially Hashomer Hatzaír, but also to a certain extent
within the Dror and a part of the political Jewish underground,
admiration for the Soviets and their struggle was unbounded. But
in 1943 not all factions sought to link the leftist Jewish organizations with the Communists.

The Communists' basic strategic principles and the naiveté of
the Jewish factions proved decisive. The AK, the Polish military
underground, was content with sporadic attacks against the
Nazis. Their major aim was to gather strength and train their
fighters for a strong attack during the last stages of the war when
there was an opportunity to self-liberate Poland. The Jews could
not wait. Their end, sadly, would come well before the conclusion
of the war.

In contrast, the Communists sought to direct an immediate
guerrilla war against the Nazis. They saw their task as providing
constant support and assistance to the Soviet military campaign.
Jewish interests, or rather the Jewish need, paralleled the Communist concept at the time. They could not wait, particularly in
view of the fact that the AK did not show any active involvement
on behalf of the Jews.

In December 1941 the first death camp was established at
Chelmno, seventy kilometers west of Lodz, in the area annexed
by the German Reich and far from the military arena on the
Russian front. On December 8, the day the United States declared
war on Germany, the gassing began. Jews from the neighboring
villages of Kolo, Klodawa, Izbica Kujawska, Dombie, and others,

were brought to Chelmno. The victims were taken to an abandoned castle, then murdered in sealed gas chambers. Their corpses were placed in massive pits in a nearby forest.

The next month, in January 1942, two Jews who were forced to work burying the corpses managed to escape and reach Warsaw. The evidence of one man, Jacob Grojanowski, was taken by the people of "Ringelblum's archives" in the Warsaw underground and passed on to London via secret channels of the Polish underground. Thus in 1942 details of the camp became known in London as well as in Warsaw.

In the autumn of 1941, the Germans had begun their planned extermination of the Jews in the area of the General Government. The instructions to set up extermination squads and death camps were evidently passed by word of mouth from Himmler to Odilo Globocnik, a Nazi leader and one of the heads of the SS in Austria, who had commanded the SS and the police in the eastern district of Lublin since November 1939. Known for his extremism and close connections to Himmler, Globocnik was chosen to establish death camps in the area under his supervision. In order to exploit the Jewish work force, he also set up forced labor camps to be run by the SS.

The extermination campaign was known as *Aktion Reinhard,* after Reinhard Heydrich, who had been head of the Reich Security's main office (the RSHA), and also the acting governor of the Protectorate of Bohemia and Moravia, where he was assassinated by the Czech underground in May 1942. Hans Höfle, a major in the SS, was responsible for the operative unit of the "Reinhard Campaign." He headed a force of 450 SS members and police, among them dozens of functionaries who participated in the early "Euthanasia" campaign, the systematic murder of mentally retarded and physically handicapped Germans initiated in 1939. These SS men became experienced, hardened murderers; they had learned to deal with their guilt. Their strength was enhanced by supplementary forces from Ukraine and the Baltic states.

The first camp to be set up within the context of the Reinhard Campaign was Belzec. Situated in the district of Lublin, on the railway line from Lublin to Lwow, it began functioning in 1942. Two other camps were established in 1942: Sobibor, east of

Lublin, and Treblinka, west of Lublin, where exterminations began in July 1942 with the arrival of victims from the Warsaw ghetto.

The evacuation of the Jews of Lublin began in March 1942, and within two months thirty thousand Jews were sent to Belzec. Only four thousand Jews remained in Lublin, where they lived in camplike conditions. News of the evacuation of the Jews of Lublin reached Warsaw both via individuals who had managed to escape during the evacuation and through letters asking the Warsaw Jews if they knew where the Lublin Jews had been taken. The deportation was one more indication that the dreadful circle was closing around Warsaw. The Jewish underground press of Warsaw repeatedly warned readers that the "Jewish population is fated to physical extermination."

In March and April 1942, representatives of the Communist party branch in the Warsaw ghetto had talks with the Left Po'alei Zion, and also approached Hashomer Hatzaír and Dror. The negotiations led to the establishment of the "anti-fascist bloc" as a military fighting unit. As a result, members of the youth movements were motivated to join this body initiated by the Communists. Two Jewish Communists, Joseph Lewartowski-Finklestein and Pinkus Kartin, who had arrived in the Warsaw ghetto by the most dangerous channels, played key roles in the creation of the bloc and in organizing the fighting unit.

Lewartowski was one of the oldest Communists in the Bialystok ghetto when he was sent to lead the new branch being organized in the Warsaw ghetto, a city he knew well from his secret activities in the party. In his youth, Lewartowski had belonged to the Left Po'alei Zion and was acquainted with many of its activists. Lewartowski was a warm and popular man with deeply embedded Jewish roots. He did not succeed in establishing a wide base of Communist cells in the ghetto, but he did manage to create an intense and close relationship with the members of the Zionist youth movements.

Pinkus Kartin was quite different. He hailed from Luck in western Ukraine and had been a member of the Communist party since adolescence. Like many others, he paid for his beliefs and his attachment to the party with years of imprisonment in interwar Poland. He volunteered for the Dombrowski Brigade and fought on the Republican side in the Spanish Civil War. At the end of that war, he escaped to France, where he was active in the Party. He was eventually returned to the Soviet Union as part of an agreement between Germany and the Soviet Union to exchange civilians. There he joined the circles of Polish immigrants and went through a course for training cadres of Party activists, and in 1941 he was parachuted into Poland with the first group of activists to launch and lead the rehabilitated Communist party.

Kartin's obvious Jewish features prevented his fulfilling this role among the Polish public. For a considerable time, he was obliged to hide in the apartment of a Polish shoemaker until it was decided to send him to the Warsaw ghetto to organize a Communist branch inside the ghetto. His military past and lively personality charmed the members of the youth movements, who were sorely in need of military training and experience. This mature and experienced figure fired their imaginations and aroused their expectations.

The fighting unit of the anti-fascist bloc was divided into groups of five, composed mostly of members of the youth movements. A few candidates from outside the organized bodies were also enlisted after their background had been carefully checked and they had shown willingness to become part of a military organization. The groups met weekly in private dwellings to be trained in guerrilla tactics and later learned how to use the only available pistol, which the anti-fascist bloc had smuggled into the ghetto.

The organization was at best amateurish. The "army trainers" were youth movement veterans whose military knowledge was acquired from books or learned from Kartin. During a secret parade of the groups in Leszno Street, the organization's men were ordered to march up and down the street in pairs or trios at a certain hour. This exercise by a force of about five hundred was evidently intended to display its strength to the bloc commanders, but group members discovered friends and acquaintances and kept signaling to each other in an undisciplined and unprofessional manner.

The youth movements mistakenly assumed that the tremendous power of the Red Army stood behind the Communists. But it soon became clear that the PPR had no direct contact with the Soviet Union and the Red Army, nor could it expect any support from these sources. Moreover, the newly formed Communist party was received with little approval and explicit antagonism by many in the Polish community, who were in no hurry to pardon the betrayal they had suffered in the campaign of September 1939. Hence only small groups of loyal Communists and radical leftists responded to the proposal for a leftist alliance to support the struggling Soviet Union. As a result, the Communists were less than able to assist the Jews in the ghetto.

The aims of the military struggle were also in doubt. The Communists intended to prepare the young people to enter the forests to support the partisan forces. Members of the youth movements, however, viewed as paramount the need for defensive action and preparation for the struggle within the ghetto. Nothing came of the promises of materiel and training made to the youth leaders. As a result, the Communists had no young partisans in the forests, nor did they have bases ready to absorb the Jewish fighters. In May 1942 the groups of five were informed that the time had arrived to set up the first company of fighters and to leave the ghetto for the forests. A date was set for leaving, but the event, intended to be the first real military action, was canceled at the last moment, helping to bring an end to the antifascist bloc itself.

On May 30 three outstanding Communist activists of the ghetto, including Pinkus Kartin, were arrested. The arrests aroused fear that the Germans had tracked down the bloc, which could lead to the complete collapse of the ghetto underground. But it was subsequently learned that the arrests were linked to a wave of Communist arrests on the Polish side of Warsaw. The arrests came when ghetto activists were to meet their Polish comrades outside the ghetto. It is likely that those arrested were severely tortured before they were killed, but they betrayed no one and no further arrests were made. Yet the incident was not without its ramifications. The shock of the arrests left its mark on the ghetto underground. The bloc ceased to exist, and the Communist underground suffered a serious setback from which it never recovered.

In postwar Poland, Communist historians claimed that the Jewish Fighting Organization established during the expulsion was an extension of the Anti-fascist Bloc. But there is no basis for this assumption and its intent to give Communists the credit of having been the first to found a fighting organization. Nor did Communists actually figure in the founding of the Jewish Fighting Organization. The significance of the bloc lay in the fact that it was the first to organize a fighting body in the ghetto which united a variety of political underground groups.

Another event that alarmed the ghetto was the wave of terror in April 1942 and the ensuing murder of prominent Jews. On Friday evening, the eighteenth, which the Jews called "the bloody night," trucks filled with German soldiers and SS men entered the ghetto. The soldiers went into houses and apartments, taking some sixty men, whom they shot and left lying in the streets. Fifty-two were dead, others wounded. Some Jews had been warned in advance of imminent danger (including Yitzhak Zuckerman) and went into hiding.

During the following days, many frightened inhabitants tried to find out who the Germans sought and why. The answers, however, were not so simple. Among those on the wanted list were agents, including Abraham Gancwajch and his close partner Sternfeld, who managed to escape, due to advance warning. Among those killed was Menahem Linder, a Jewish sociologist and demographer involved in the underground archives, who was close to Emanuel Ringelblum, the political underground of the Zionist left, and a number of activists in the Bund.

It was difficult to point to any common political characteristics shared by the various people who were murdered or wanted. The official explanation was that the killings were an act of retaliation. This was confirmed by Brandt of the Gestapo, who said "that the reason for the night's act of retaliation was the appearance of secret publications in the ghetto and that more stringent means would be taken if they continued to appear."

Adam Czerniakow and other members of the Judenrat passed

on this message and tried to stop publication of these journals, but the underground did not accept the explanation. Not only did the publications continue, but many took a sharper line. The underground was convinced that the killings were intended to rid the ghetto of people whom the Nazis considered individuals of initiative and influence, who could take the lead against them personally or through a resistance organization. Similar "clearing" operations were carried out in other ghettos before the beginning of the deportations to the death camps.

At the same time, the underground bore some responsibility for publishing the journals used as a pretext for the Nazi's actions. Ringelblum took the underground to task for neglecting the rules of secrecy. As a result secrecy became more stringent, and the publications went into "deep underground."

Another result was the dispersal of the groups of young people who had been recruited and organized at the height of the war for underground work. Only a hard core of experienced members remained in the underground. It became clear that a stage of comparative stability had ended in the ghetto and that the future called for greater preparedness.

After "the bloody night," there were other incidents in which individuals were murdered. Orders and "sanctions" increased against those Jews who lived outside the ghetto without permission. Previously, those who were not shot on the spot had been imprisoned in the ghetto and released on completion of their sentence. In June 1942, 110 Jews were killed, including women and young children from among the inmates of the ghetto prison. This aroused anger against Hans Auerswald, commissar of the ghetto, who previously had been considered a moderate.

Officially, the murders were characterized as retribution for the growing opposition that police encountered outside the ghetto. Whatever the rationale, it was a step in the process of evacuating the Warsaw ghetto.

Anxiety was rife during the weeks preceding the expulsion. Frightening rumors were afloat, creating a dense cloud of unease that hovered over the ghetto. The underground archives published a bulletin providing information on the expulsion and the mass killings in the death camps, but it reached only the inner circles of the underground. The situation resembled the awful days preceding the pogroms endured by the Jews in the 1880s in the towns and villages of southwestern Russia. But under the Nazi regime the Jews in the ghetto had no means to repel an attack. Millions, actually the whole Jewish population, were condemned to death in a sealed cell. The Jews of the ghetto were not told what crime they had committed or what was required of them.

The youth movements expressed their challenge to the public. In *Jutrznia* (Dawn), the underground journal of Hashomer Hatzaír, the following appeared on March 28, 1942:

> We know that Hitler's system of murder, slaughter and robbery leads steadily to a dead end and the destruction of the Jews. The fate of the Jews in the Soviet Russian areas occupied by the Germans, and in the Warthegau marks a new period in the total annihilation of the Jewish population. For the Jewish masses, this will be a period of greater bloodshed . . . than any in their history. There is no doubt that when Hitler feels the end of his rule approaching, he will seek to drown the Jews in a sea of blood. There must therefore be a start to the recruiting of all creative forces among the Jews. Despite the destruction, many such forces still remain, for generation after generation, passivity and lack of faith in our own strength pressed upon us; but our history also boasts of pages glowing with heroism and struggle. *It is our duty to join this period of heroism . . .*

These determined statements reveal the blindness and frustration of the Judenrat. Czerniakow makes a number of references in his diary to rumors concerning the dangers attached to expulsion. We know that members of the underground who occupied public positions tried to convince him of the gravity of the situation. David Wdowinski, a senior activist of the Revisionist movement in the ghetto, brought refugees from Lublin to Czerniakow in order make him realize what fate lay in store for the entire ghetto.

In the last days preceding the expulsion there was confusion and chaos in the ghetto. Terror stood at the locked gates, and the masses of Jews were helpless.

And the Judenrat?

On July 20, 1942, two days before the deportation action began, Czerniakow finally decided to shake off his crippling inactivity. He wrote in his diary:

> At 7:30 in the morning I asked Mende [of the Gestapo] how much truth there was in the rumors. He replied that he had heard nothing. When asked whether it could happen, he replied that he knew of no such scheme. Uncertain, I left his office. I proceeded to his chief, Kommissar Bohm. He told me that this was not his department but Hoehmann [Hohmann] might say something about the rumors. I mentioned that according to rumor, the deportation is to start tonight at 7:30. He replied that he would be bound to know something if it were about to happen. Not seeing any other way out, I went to the Deputy Chief of Sector III, Scheerer. He expressed his surprise on hearing the rumors and informed me that he too knew nothing about it. Finally I asked whether I could tell the population that their fears were groundless. He replied that I could and that all the talk was utter nonsense.

The manner in which the head of the Judenrat was sent from room to room, the way everyone lied to him even as the expulsion plan was drawn up and readied, and the way the *Einsatzgruppe* units of the Reinhard Campaign were prepared to spring on their prey are but other evident indications of the Nazis' cynical methods.

On that wearying day of rounds, Czerniakow was still not satisfied, and he approached Auerswald, the commissar of the ghetto, who had recently been called to Berlin and had undoubtedly been instructed as to how he was to act in preparation for the deportation. Auerswald had worked with Czerniakow for some time, and despite the fact that they were on different sides of the barricade, the two had had frank and open discussions from time to time. Yet on the eve of the deportation and slaughter of tens of thousands of Warsaw Jews, this German did not offer a single personal word to a man he had known well and whose integrity he could not question.

Not only had the verdict condemning the Jews of Warsaw already been decided when Czerniakow hurried from official to official, but on the previous day, July 19, 1942, Himmler had dispatched an order to the supreme commander of the SS and the police, Friedrich Wilhelm Krüger, which stated:

> I order that the resettlement of the entire Jewish population of the General Government be carried out and completed by December 31, 1942. From December 31, 1942, no persons of Jewish origin may remain within the General Government, unless they are in the collection camps in Warsaw, Cracow, Czestochowa, Radom and Lublin . . . These measures are required with a view to the necessary ethnic division of races and peoples for the new order in Europe, and also in the interests of the security and cleanliness of the German Reich and its sphere of interest.

6

POLITICAL PARTIES AND YOUTH MOVEMENTS

A JEWISH UNDERGROUND was established in Warsaw at the very onset of the occupation and was active until the end of the Jewish community's existence in the city. The existence of such an underground was unknown to the Poles, at least at the beginning. In his book *He Who Saves His Life*, Kazimierz Iranek-Osmecki dealt with Polish assistance to the Jews during World War II. He wrote:

> During the early years of the occupation, no official link existed between the Polish underground and the Jews, because the Jews at that time had still not evolved an underground organization of their own and the Polish underground authorities had to contact Jews unofficially.

The fact that the Polish underground, which supposedly represented all Polish citizens, did not include Jewish representatives or establish contact with the Jewish underground is further evidence of the estrangement between the Poles and the Jews.

Youth movements and political parties struggled to define

their roles during the Nazi occupation. One activist group argued that political activity should be abandoned in order to work for social welfare and mutual assistance for party members and the Jewish community. Others claimed that a political party should confine itself to political action and leave social welfare to experienced groups. Eventually, a consensus was reached that the parties must include both political activities and social services.

Given ghetto conditions, parties could not advance their political aims as in the past, but they continued to provide information and political interpretation of unfolding events for their members. Such issues as the Ribbentrop-Molotov nonaggression pact between the Soviet Union and Germany in 1939, which divided Poland into German and Soviet sectors, and the plot that led to the fourth division of Poland, fomented sharp dissension among the parties and their subgroups.

Political parties were engaged in public activities, and they sought to attract many members. Underground work was by its very nature limited to small cadres. While groups still gathered to sing hymns and renew their faith on days dedicated to the memory of certain leaders, national holidays, and celebrations marking past political events, such occasions were more ceremonies of comradeship than political events.

Party meetings were generally held in soup kitchens, which concretely symbolized the link between politics and the reality of daily assistance represented by the kitchens. The parties lacked the opportunity for large public demonstrations, so their activities were only a shadow of their former presence. Fear and anxiety over Hitler's regime also caused many ghetto inhabitants to abandon political action.

Of all underground parties, the socialist Bund displayed the greatest vitality, both in its organization and in its activities. As the only party to maintain contact with a faction of the Polish socialist movement — and thus a part of the Polish underground — the Bund succeeded in 1942 in passing through Polish underground channels news of the mass murders of Polish Jews to representatives in London.

Among the Zionist parties, the Po'alei Zion, which had not had much influence in the period between the wars, displayed an ability to unite the rank and file and preserve friendships. Other Zionist parties invested a great deal of effort in creating contacts with countries outside Poland, and especially with the Jewish Agency, the World Jewish Congress, and the Hehalutz movement, all of which were able to continue their work thanks to dedicated activists in neutral Switzerland.

A modest stream of food packages and money from Switzerland, Portugal, and other points managed to reach the ghetto prior to the outbreak of the German-Soviet war in 1941. The packages from neutral European countries were an important source of help — and encouragement — for starving Jews. Such items as coffee, cocoa, or tins of meat were rare and in great demand within a smaller group in the ghetto and, thus, could be used to barter for large quantities of basic foods. The packages, however, were usually addressed to the same people; therefore only a small number of individuals could enjoy this nourishment, and they were not necessarily most in need of help.

Youth movements flourished alongside the political parties as a kind of preparation for adult activism. Some organizations, primarily the Zionist youth movements, promoted emigration to Palestine and helped prepare young people for life in kibbutzim and other communal groups. The younger generation adapted more easily to the underground than did the political parties. Enthusiastic, daring, and rebellious, these young people were not weighed down by responsibility for families or children. As in the past, they constituted an intimate and united group.

Between the two world wars, such youth organizations as Dror, Hashomer Hatzaír, Gordonia, and Akiva prepared for life in Palestine. Some organizations forbade their members to participate in "current affairs" in the Diaspora, preferring them to concentrate their efforts exclusively on the aim of *aliyah* (emigration to Palestine) and the life there. They did not want their members to get involved in Jewish life in Poland for fear that they would be reluctant to leave. Still, the process of emigration was slow. Entry into Palestine was restricted because of Britain's policy of limiting Jewish immigration. With the onset of war and the indefinite postponement of emigration possibilities, Zionist youth adapted to the new reality. They began training Jewish young people for the physical and spiritual difficulties that loomed.

Another difference between the parties and the youth movements was, in the long run, very significant. With the German occupation, leading figures of the political parties fled Poland and Polish territory, and were replaced by a secondary tier of leadership whose inexperience or limited abilities made them unable to decide on a course of action at the critical moment. The absence of well-known leaders deepened the divisions between the Poles and the Jews, and without a doubt weakened the Jewish community in Warsaw.

Leaders of the youth movements who moved east to Soviet-held territories were the oldest of the members, the guides and teachers. There is no way to know what might have happened if the younger members had been left without any leadership. At the beginning of 1940 some twenty outstanding activists from Hashomer Hatzaír and Dror returned from Soviet-occupied territory to the area under German rule in order to rehabilitate and stabilize the movements. One of these returned leaders, Mordecai Anielewicz, became commander of the Jewish Fighting Organization and led the Warsaw Ghetto Uprising three years later. Other returned activists included Yitzhak Zuckerman, Zivia Lubetkin, and Joseph Kaplan, who became architects of an important element in the underground of the Warsaw ghetto.

The youth movements created strong bonds of comradeship among their members. Literary and philosophical discussions provided a momentary respite from the stresses of life in the ghetto. Moral and ideological opposition to Nazi racism and evil became their motivating credo.

In an otherwise bitter and angry farewell to life, *A Surplus of Memory*, Yitzhak Zuckerman, one of the founders of Kibbutz Lochamei Hagetaot and Beit Lochamei Hagetaot (the House of Ghetto Fighters), a museum of the Holocaust and a memorial to its fighters in Israel, looked back warmly on the ghetto years in the movement:

And if I am questioned about the state of our movement — I can say that there was never a movement so lovely as it was before its demise. Even from the human aspect, it flourished later on, when everyone in the ghetto was seeking somewhere to hide and or simply manage, while between ourselves, we awaited orders and initiative. There was a common responsibility, not concern for ourselves . . . the possibility that one of us would abandon the other and get along somehow — something that sometimes even happened within families — did not exist within our circles.

During the Nazi occupation and the existence of the ghetto, the world of the Jewish youngster obviously became constricted. School, family, home, and the company of adults disappeared or lost their authority. The trust and logic of the adult world was undermined. Fears, frustration, and helplessness affected adults more profoundly than it did the adolescents and placed the head of the family in a humiliating and vulnerable situation. Fathers could not protect their children. Mothers could not feed their young. Hence, the youth movement with its friendly alliances frequently provided important moral and material support. Of necessity and by choice, young people turned to each other.

As a consequence of ghetto conditions, youth movements were kept intact, relationships were nurtured. Matters that were not their concern in ordinary times, such as the family's economic situation, became subjects for discussion. Groups functioned in many ways like communes. All members contributed what they had, whether money or food, to a common coffer, and everyone was allotted the minimum needed to survive.

Kitchens in the urban clubs and communes also served the public under the supervision of the Self-Help organization. They were actually run by women living in the movement's hostels. The hostels of Dror in Dzielna Street and Hashomer Hatzaír in Nalewki Street "were open to any hungry person." While youth members did die from starvation or illness, such deaths were relatively rare given the hunger and typhoid rampant in the ghetto.

Amid the tumult of life focused on daily needs, the movements continued to pursue literature and culture, as well as ideological and political thought. Hidden behind a wall in one youth hostel in a bare room furnished with simple tables and benches were shelves of books in various languages, including hundreds of volumes of belles-lettres and theoretical works, among them the forbidden literature of Thomas and Heinrich Mann, Franz Werfel, Theodore Dreiser, and Sinclair Lewis, as well as the writings of Karl Marx, Sigmund Freud, Theodore Herzl, Ben Borochov, Max Nordau, and others.

In the twilight hours, the dining tables would be moved, the benches arranged to form a square, and the room turned into a forum for discussions on fascism, capitalism, the Soviet Union, or questions of evil and human nature. Members spoke of antisemitism and racism, of a world that had lost its sense of direction. They returned again and again to the problem of educating young people as to the reality of the ghetto: Should those once considered too young to be included in the movement now be accepted? Would it be possible to impart to these young people the spiritual dedication that had been characteristic of the movement?

Despite the horrors of the ghetto, the force of youth could not be contained: teenagers concealed their first poetic expressions of love, and young girls wrote their intimate secrets in diaries. In the hostels one heard the hushed singing of beloved tunes and words calling for daring action, hours of merrymaking, laughter, and boisterousness.

In one underground publication, a young girl described her peers walking merrily arm-in-arm in a ghetto street, only to be severely criticized by an older person who asks whether they are not ashamed to be cheerful and full of laughter in the ghetto. The girl pondered the question and wondered whether it was permissible for youngsters to experience the rustles of spring and express their natural joy amid the darkness and mourning veiling the ghetto.

Young people tried to evade or oppose edicts imposed by the Nazis. For instance, when Jews were asked to doff their hats before a German in uniform, Mordecai Anielewicz decided to go bare-headed in the freezing cold of winter. Even though their bodies were enfeebled by lack of food and acutely sensitive to cold, many imitated Mordecai's hatlessness and manner of dress, which became emblematic of the movement.

In the world of the underground, the Zionist and Bund youth

movements differed from the structure of pre-war organizations. Two channels of activity granted young people positions of power. The first was their work on a comprehensive national level. The political movements in Warsaw maintained connections with countries abroad but almost entirely neglected the network of contacts with Jewish communities and organizations throughout the occupied area. In effect, they acquiesced to the Nazi ruling that divided the Jewish public into separate communities and denied the sealed ghettos a common leadership.

The youth movements, however, adopted a countrywide scope. Conferences and seminars were held in the Warsaw ghetto with representatives from the provinces who arrived in secret to participate in discussions, plans, and the lines of actions. Messengers, particularly female messengers, or "runners" (*mekashroth*), set out from Warsaw, regularly visiting towns and villages of the General Government and districts occupied by the German Reich. These young women carried false identity papers, an act that endangered their lives. They traveled the railways and crossed borders without permission, acts that were dangerous for ordinary Poles and fatal to Jews if they were caught. Ringelblum described them as "girl-heroines" who undertook dangerous missions under the threat of death. As a result, they were better informed than their adult counterparts and could piece together fragments of information into a more cohesive picture.

Mordecai Tennenbaum-Tamarof, commander of the Jewish fighting organization in Bialystok, described, in a final letter that he left for his sister in Palestine in July 1943, the conduct of his girlfriend, Tama Schneiderman, who was caught and disappeared during one of her missions:

> After contact between Warsaw and the movement was severed . . . it was again renewed and remained intact without interruptions since then. She crossed the border into Ostland — formerly Lithuania — a number of times, into White Russia, and into the Reich in Bendzin, to the Ukraine (Kowel and Luck), the district of Bialystok (more than a dozen times!). She was familiar with every ghetto in Poland (wall and barbed wire), every Judenrat. She was the real center of the Joint, of all the Zionist and

public federations. She absorbed all the scenes of tragedy, sorrow, and suffering. Whenever she came our way, on every occasion, she would bring with her enough material for our publications [the underground press] to last for months and for our archives as well. She was a living encyclopedia of the catastrophe and martyrdom of the Jews of Poland. Wherever there was an "action" [expulsion of the Jews to the death camps], she had to be there at once. Whenever someone was caught in the camps — they had to be rescued! At the station, when a railway carriage is being suspiciously prepared, it was necessary to find out why, and where it was headed, and warn others to be careful. A fire in a village — money was needed there. Seek out partisans in the forest. Buy arms. Everything.

Tama Schneiderman was one of many young men and women who, according to Tennenbaum, did "everything." Dozens were caught and fell in the course of their missions, but none betrayed their connections. Among the few who miraculously survived were Haike Grossman, who later became a member of the Israeli Knesset, Vladka Peltel Meed, who lives in the United States and is active in survivors' and cultural organizations, and Hela Schipper-Rufeisen, who lives on an agricultural settlement in Israel. Unlike Jewish men, whose identity could be revealed by forcing them to drop their pants, no physical examination could reveal a girl's Jewish identity. Yet their blonde hair, natural or dyed, could not conceal the sad expression in their eyes and their restless movements.

Maria Hochberg-Marianska Peleg, who was active in the rescue of people in Cracow, wrote in her memoirs that almost no one in the Polish underground in which she was active knew that she was Jewish. On one occasion, when she visited a church with an underground group, the pastor preached a sermon about the suffering of innocent people. Peleg, like many of the congregation, could not hold back the tears. When they were leaving the church, a friend said to her, "You have to be careful, you cry like a Jewess."

Runners undertook different activities. At first, they delivered information, published material, and letters to the branches and cells of youth movements throughout occupied Poland. Later, the runners passed on information, money, and personal regards as well as warnings to the Judenrat and the public. On their return, they brought accounts of the places they had visited and were thus an important source of information. Their most significant role began during the period of mass murders and the wholesale annihilation of the Jews, when they would race from one center of tragedy in order to warn another likely to be visited by disaster and to gather information about what was happening. They served as the living links connecting the cells of the youth movements and communes during the last months of the ghetto's existence. They acted as the lifesavers and couriers of the Jewish Fighting Organization.

The second area of prominent activity by the youth movements was in the underground press in Warsaw. We tend to imagine an underground press as made up of conspirators illegally expressing their opinions and disseminating propaganda, or trying to recruit supporters and allies. But the underground newspapers in the Warsaw ghetto played quite a different role. These publications contained the opinions and political attitudes of various factions, and dealt critically with the Judenrat's responsibilities in the ghetto and the likely fate of the Jews in the occupied territory, in Palestine, and in the rest of the world. Some fifty titles in many different languages appeared, mostly in Yiddish and Polish. Printed on thick, crude paper and folded by worn-out machines, the newspapers included illustrations that emphasized their particular fashion, political doctrines, and ideologies. Many of these newsheets and journals were preserved in Ringelblum's archives and were buried beneath the ghetto rubble to be dug up after the war.

Of paramount importance, these publications served as a window to the world, which somewhat diminished the isolation and loneliness of the Jews while providing reliable political and war information. Cut off and thirsty for information, ghetto residents found in the underground press encouragement, information, and their only contact with the world at large. The youth movement was the most decisive factor in publishing these papers. At first, the publications were intended only for members of the movement, written in a typical slang and concentrated on the internal life of the movement. With time, the journals addressed the wider public, providing information and spiritual nourishment. Their importance grew as ghetto conditions deteriorated. During the final stage of the ghetto, the underground press became the clarion call of opposition and prepared the ground for the struggle to come.

The youth movements, and to a lesser extent the remnants of political organizations, attempted to preserve the image of the Jew as open to and involved in what was occurring in the world. The youth movements aspired to mold and prepare the young people for their postwar future, when they assumed it would fall to them to lead their people.

The youth movements worked in comparatively comfortable circumstances. Until the spring of 1942, Nazi authorities did not aim their cruelty against the Jewish underground in the ghetto. Until the implementation of the final solution began, the Nazi goal was to isolate Jews, plunder their property, force them into slave labor, and actually starve them gradually to death. They did not concern themselves with the internal life of those they deemed to be subhuman. Politically, the Nazis directed their wrath against the Poles. Ringelblum summed up the Jewish conspiratorial activities during the first stage of the ghetto as follows:

> Justified conspiracy can be the term applied to the period leading up to the infamous 18th of April [1942]. All the political parties carried on more or less legal activities. Publications appeared on the scene like mushrooms after the rain. When one appeared once a month, another would appear twice a month. A certain political movement brought out a paper twice a month, then another would appear once a week, until it reached the point in which the bulletin appearing on behalf of a certain stream, would appear twice a week. These papers were commonly read in offices, workshops, etc.
>
> There were even festive public gatherings. In one such assembly, the speaker addressed a public of some 150 people on the subject of active opposition. I was present at a festivity of 500 young people of one movement. As the authors of the articles

published in the underground press were known, things came to a head in polemics between the various sides and finally to mutual recriminations, like in the best of times before the war.

Everyone imagined that everything was permissible. Even illegal Polish journals, such as *Barykada Wolnosci* [The Barricades of Freedom] (so I heard but could not verify its authenticity), were printed and appeared in the ghetto. The public believed that the Germans were only remotely concerned with Jewish opinion. They were convinced that they were only interested in uncovering stores of Jewish goods, money, or foreign currency held by the Jews. But apparently this was an error. Friday, the bloody day [referring to April 18, 1942], when the publishers and distributors of various papers were shot, gave evidence that they were not indifferent to their image as depicted by the Jews, especially their political image.

Characteristically, Ringelblum was correct in this analysis. The Germans were not interested in the beliefs and opinions of the Jews on political and social matters. This contrasted with their attitude toward the Poles, whose patriotism and national aspirations they attempted to ascertain in order to reach those who were prepared to accept German superiority and domination. As to the Jews, they were all condemned to a common fate regardless of their opinions or behavior. Many Poles, perhaps hundreds of thousands, signed, voluntarily or not, the *Volkslisten*, declaring themselves Germans in order to be received into the bosom of the German people. For the Jews, this was not a possibility.

The Germans dealt a cruel blow to the Jews when they thought that the Jews were working with the Poles in their underground activities. For instance, in 1940 a young man of Jewish origin, Andrezej Kazimierz Kot, an organizer of an underground political cell, escaped from prison and was subsequently caught. Kot, who had converted to Christianity years ago, had no connection with the Jews and the Jews had no part in his organization, but the Germans directed most of their anger and punishment at the Jewish public. In an instance of collective responsibility, 255 Jews, mostly members of the intelligentsia, paid for this incident with their lives.

Another affair involved the distribution of underground publications and proved a calamity for branches of the Bund in the General Government. All the movements and political factions sought to reach members in the provinces, yet the papers were bulky and not easy to hide inside runners' clothing. The Hashomer Hatzaír movement prepared a special volume with selected articles from a number of papers and gave the volume a fictitious name, *Przeglad Rolniczy* (The Agricultural Review), and a fake cover, with 1930 indicated as its publication date. Thus disguised, the material reached the provinces. This trick succeeded as long as runners were only superficially searched and the book was not opened.

The Bund had two advantages over other parties in the ghetto underground: it maintained branches in villages and ghettos outside Warsaw, and it had connections with the Polish socialist underground and therefore could ask for their assistance. Hence the Polish socialists responded to the Bund's request to loan a runner to deliver their publications, on the assumption that a true Pole, having no need to hide his or her identity, had a greater likelihood of success.

According to a Polish source, after some hesitation, the socialists decided to lend the services of Jadwiga Wyszinska, an actress whose days were numbered because of a critical illness. Wyszinska left Warsaw with a heavy load of papers as her first mission. In the course of a search, the names and addresses of those for whom the papers were intended were discovered. As a result, eleven leading members of the Bund in the town of Piotrkow Trybunalski were arrested in September 1941 and sent to Auschwitz, where they were killed. To an extent, this catastrophe led to the decline of the Bund's underground power in this town.

In other cities, such as Cracow, Czestochowa, or Tomaszow Mazowiecki, prominent figures in the Bund were arrested and some lost their lives. This blow to the Bund brought about the almost complete erosion of communication between the Bund in Warsaw and its branches in the provinces. Wyszinska, it was said, was sent to a concentration camp, and her stay there worked miraculously in her favor, for her disease was arrested and she returned home after the war.

In the early days, both the youth movements and the political parties had reservations about taking militant action. They directed their efforts instead toward preserving the essence of Jewish life in the ghetto. However, the two had differences. While political parties focused on current affairs rather than on the future, the youth movements tensely anticipated the future. They felt that the war would force the Jews to change tactics.

7

DEPORTATION TO DEATH

THE MASS DEPORTATION of Jews from the Warsaw ghetto began on July 22, 1942, the eve of the ninth of Av, according to the Hebrew calendar — the day on which Jews mourn the destruction of the first and second temples in Jerusalem and the end of their political independence in ancient times. The expulsion continued with only short interruptions for fifty-two days, until September 12. During the seven weeks of the great deportation, some 300,000 Jews were expelled or murdered; 265,000 of them were taken from the assembly point (*Umschlagplatz*) and sent in sealed and overcrowded freight trains to the Treblinka death camp, some sixty kilometers (forty miles) away. Another 11,580 Jews were sent to forced-labor camps. It is estimated that approximately 8,000 others managed to reach the Polish side of the city at the height of the deportations. More than 10,000 Jews were murdered in the streets of the ghetto during the forced evacuation. Perhaps as many as 55,000–60,000 Jews remained in the ghetto. Within a short time, the large Jewish community of Warsaw no longer existed.

The arrival of Warsaw's Jews in the summer of 1942 inaugurated the gas chambers of Treblinka. Like Belzec and Sobibor, the other *Aktion Reinhard* death camps, Treblinka was designed for one purpose alone, mass murder. The deportations from Warsaw and other ghettos of Poland could not have taken place until the infrastructure for mass murder was in place — death camps, gas chambers, and the railway transports.

On July 22, members of the Judenrat were taken as hostages. Adam Czerniakow commented in his diary on July 22:

> We were informed that apart from certain exceptions, the Jews, regardless of age or sex, would have to be evacuated eastward. Today, until 4 P.M., 6,000 people will have to be supplied. And this will be the case at the minimum every day . . . Sturmbannführer Major Höfle [the officer in charge of the evacuation] invited me to his office and informed me that my wife is free for the time being, but if the evacuation should fail, she will be the first to be shot as a hostage.

On the same day, large posters relating to the deportation appeared on the walls of the ghetto. Unlike other public announcements for which the Judenrat was responsible, these orders did not appear with the signature of Adam Czerniakow. They began with these words: "The Judenrat has been informed of the following: All Jewish persons living in Warsaw, regardless of age and sex, will be resettled in the East." The poster was unsigned.

The ghetto's inhabitants crowded round the posters, reading them again and again. The text of the posters also contained a long list of the categories of people exempt from the evacuation order. Those who were seemingly safe for the moment included employees and officers of private German enterprises; persons working for the Judenrat; all those who were fit for work and still not involved in essential work; police, hospital, and sanitary workers; the families of all those in exempt categories; and hospital patients not well enough to be released. Jews tried to figure out who was not included in the lists and arrived at the conclusion that some 60,000–70,000 were condemned to expulsion, most of them refugees, the elderly, and those unable to work. Many interpreted this Nazi move as an attempt to turn the ghetto into a slave-labor camp/working ghetto, similar to the one in Lodz, and to do away with the relative freedom enjoyed by the Jews of Warsaw.

The response was immediate. People streamed to the factories, especially the "workshops" owned by Germans, and these managed to employ some tens of thousands in the course of a few days. The would-be employees brought with them their own sewing machines and the equipment needed to work in these enterprises, and this ensured their acceptance for work. Others dug out their last savings to purchase employment in the German factories, which were considered preferable and a means of protection against the dreaded decree. Workers of every kind were given working permits. A permit with the SS stamp was considered the best safeguard against deportation. The Germans were "generous" in their distribution of these permits to workers and their families.

Czerniakow wrote in his diary on the first day of the expulsion that the problem that worried him the most was the fate of the children in the orphanages. The orphans seemed to him the most difficult and painful problem. Too young to work, they were also without the protection of families. While the entire ghetto was occupied in the feverish pursuit of work or a permit that would, it was hoped, prevent deportation, the orphans were left to fend for themselves, and Czerniakow was unable to protect them.

The division of the ghetto into many units and the illusions of security provided by the signed permits and "good" employment were undoubtedly well-planned steps in the German tactics for executing the deportation. Communal life ended and everyone was alone. At most, the family unit remained intact. Instead of viewing the tragic situation as a general catastrophe affecting the entire community, each family, and often each person, was taken up with the feverish and exhausting effort of acquiring the protective piece of paper as a way of saving themselves and their close relatives. The Nazis cynically created a mass panic, verging on madness, among the hundreds of thousands of Warsaw ghetto residents. Starving and psychologically exhausted, the Jews were entrapped with no hope of escape; they clung to false hopes to the bitter end.

Only a few dozen SS men and German police stood guard during the first days of the ghetto's evacuation. A supplementary unit of black-uniformed police — composed of Ukrainians and other men from the Baltic states — was brought into the action. But the greater part of the work during the first days was done by the Jewish Police, who from the very beginning acted independently of internal ghetto controls.

On July 23, Czerniakow wrote in his diary, "The hour is three in the afternoon. At the moment, there are 4,000 ready to leave. By four, according to the order, there must be 9,000." At 4:00 P.M., he swallowed a dose of potassium cyanide while sitting at his desk. Alongside his body, a short letter to his wife, Dr. Felicia Czerniakow, was found containing the following words: "The SS wants me to kill children with my own hands. There is no other way out and I must die."

Even in death Czerniakow was a controversial figure. Some saw his suicide as an act of personal integrity, a defining example of his well-intended but failed efforts. Once the Judenrat leader understood that he could no longer protect the ghetto's inhabitants and that all his work had been in vain, Czerniakow took personal responsibility. Others, especially those active in the underground, were less charitable. Ringelblum wrote: "Suicide of Czerniakow — too late, a sign of weakness — should have called for resistance — a weak man."

The deportations began despite Czerniakow's gesture. The first to be taken were inhabitants of the poorhouses and refugees, people on the verge of dying who were found in the streets. They were joined by refugees from Germany who had arrived in Warsaw two months earlier. The refugees marched in orderly lines in clean clothing, saying that any place would be better than the ghetto. When this "easy" march was concluded, other houses were approached, whole streets and finally entire enterprises were emptied. One diarist described the first days of deportations:

The day has passed, the fifth day of the expulsion. On the first day, the hungry, the refugees, and the beggars went. The more solid inhabitants still did not feel the act of expulsion. The matter touched mainly those who had no home, lacked food, or did not have the proper cover. The Germans imposed a quota of thousands which had to appear at the *Umschlagplatz*. The Jewish police emptied the refugee stations, rid the streets of the dying and covered the centers of filth and squalor in order to produce the required numbers, as there were no more pitiful, indifferent or apathetic volunteers and the quotas of victims had to be filled.

The Nazis were evidently very angry. In the afternoon an agitated police squad hurriedly went out into the streets of the ghetto and gathered whoever they could find . . . it seems to me that no one any longer thinks of his neighbor. Tension and anxiety focus on only one point: what will happen to me, how can I save my life and escape from this drowning ship?

After the first few days, German tactics changed. Police came to an apartment house, surrounded it, and demanded that all its tenants come down and appear before them with their permits. Nearby, one or two shouting Germans stood firing shots over the heads of the tenants and supervising the roundup. Though violence was kept at a distance, its threat was ever-present. Supplementary Ukrainian and Latvian police took part in the actual execution of the operation. After permits were examined, the Jews were divided into two groups: those who were released and those who were forced to leave.

Following the selection, the police spread through the apartments that had been left open. If homes were locked, the police simply opened them by force. They seized the people — mainly the elderly and relatives who were not included in the protective permits — as they hid in cellars, in attics, and chimney nooks. Police openly stole valuables from the empty apartments. Brutality, arrests, and beatings were ordinary, everyday occurrences.

This first stage of the "blockade and search of houses" took between a week and ten days. In the second stage, the Germans were not satisfied with supervising the seizures from the sidelines.

An enlarged force of German police and supplementary forces, together with the SS, took the "action" into their own hands. Permits were now only partially honored, but if the required quota was not met, families of those with permits were seized or permits were ignored and the deportation continued. Whole streets were surrounded, not just single houses. This second stage lasted for two weeks.

With every stage, the methods grew more extreme and violent, and the circle of deportees became wider. Permits no longer had any real value. People were seized not only from their homes and streets but from work places and workshops. People who were supposed to be at work were afraid to leave their signed permits with their wives, children, or parents at home, and took the permits to work with them. The SS and their helpers first took the women and children and the parents of the workers. Then they finally demanded of the employers managing the enterprises that they make do with a smaller number of workers essential to the production process and hand over the remaining workers to them. The following notes from August were found:

The permits no longer have any value. Some time has passed since the Germans themselves spread out in the ghetto; one cannot rely on any sort of papers. At times, they release the holders of permits and then there are times when they do not take the signatures into consideration at all and gather the victims indiscriminately. It all depends on the pace of the deportation. When the shipment train is full and the *Umschlagplatz* is full, the snatchers permit themselves a certain degree of generosity and pass over the young and holders of permits. This is not so when the raging fury of lagging behind in their quota takes over, when the railway carriages are empty and they are waiting to fill their quota of victims in the *Umschlagplatz*, in which case, the papers have no validity and there are only blows, kicks and shouting, which is an endless nightmare. Are these people not familiar with the normal language of human beings?

And these observations:

A new poster appeared in the ghetto: Everyone who volunteers to appear in the *Umschlagplatz* [this already happened during the first week of the expulsion] would receive three kilos of bread and a kilo of jam. And today it was quiet in the streets — no siege and no persecution. Thousands of volunteers came to the *Umschlagplatz*. In answer to the question as to what drives them to do so of their own accord, they answer that they do not have the strength to watch their little ones go hungry. The ploy succeeded. The temptation of sufficient bread is stronger than the possibility of losing one's life.

I saw a man with a boy on his shoulders. He stood out among the others going in that direction, for he did not carry large bundles but merely a small suitcase. The child on his shoulders was about five, shrunken, and evidently unable to walk on his own feet. His features were lovely and his large eyes stood out against his parchment-colored skin. Without meaning to, I overheard the conversation between the father and the toddler:

"Father, will we meet mother and be together again?"

"Of course, my child. She is already awaiting us there."

"And when will we be given bread, father?"

"Soon, it is already very, very near."

The appearance and features of people changed during the expulsion. It was not only the growing hunger and the impossibility of maintaining personal cleanliness that had brought this about. Anxiety and desperation had taken their toll.

On August 6, the Nazis attacked the children's institutions in the ghetto, including the Jewish orphanage run by Dr. Janusz Korczak, the famed Jewish-Polish educator who was something of a cross between Mr. Rogers and Dr. Benjamin Spock in his native land. Korczak lined his children up in rows of four. The orphans were clutching flasks of water and their favorite books and toys. They were in their best clothes. Korczak stood at the head of his 192 children, holding a child with each hand. One child carried the flag of King Matt with a Star of David set against the white field on the other side. They marched through the ghetto to the *Umschlagplatz* where they joined thousands of people waiting without shade, water, or shelter in the hot August sun. The children did not cry out. They walked quietly in forty-eight rows of four. One eyewitness recalled, "This was no march to the train cars but rather a mute protest against the murderous regime . . . a process the like of which no human eye has witnessed."

Between July 23 and September 6, some 230,000–240,000 people had been expelled or killed, while a few thousand escaped from the ghetto. On the night of September 6, the last massive selection began. The police announced by loud cries in the streets that on the following day all the Jews, regardless of age, sex, or place of work, had to leave their dwellings and meet in the area defined by Mila, Lubecki, Smocza, and Niska streets, the traditionally poor and densely populated heart of the Jewish quarter. No one knew the reason for this order. Rumors were rife that the expulsion had ended. Instead, the worst phase of the deportation was about to begin.

All the Jews had to go through the process of selection and to leave through a narrow passage with armed Germans standing on either side equipped with whips and bayonets. Every Jew had to have a number — to receive confirmation from his employer that he was one of the workers allotted to that specific factory. In all, thirty-five thousand numbers had been issued — only a tenth of the entire population of the ghetto at the beginning of the expulsion. The "cauldron" decree, as the order was later called — because the Jews were placed in an area the size of a cauldron — continued from September 6 to 10.

Many Jews had not received numbers. Despondent, they marched along the general line, passed through the selection process, accepted their fate, and were immediately taken aside to the site leading to the *Umschlagplatz*. Others hid. Those who were found were killed on the spot or had to join the line leading to the railway carriages.

Perhaps the most difficult experiences of all were suffered by many of the "lucky" ones who had numbers. Witnesses have told of babies crying when they went through the narrow passage of the "cauldron" carried by their mothers or fathers, and of SS soldiers sticking their bayonets into them or into the packs and bundles their parents were carrying on the suspicion that an infant was hidden.

Did the Jews of Warsaw know, with any certainty, what was awaiting them? Did they understand that going to the *Umschlagplatz* meant never returning, and that those who were pushed into the railway carriage were actually departing from this world? There were some people in the ghetto who had a more or less precise knowledge of what was going on. The truth spread in the form of rumors and a few short words spoken to a neighbor or friend. But in addition to the accurate information and the reliable facts, there were doubts, considerable difficulties believing that all this was possible.

By the second week of the deportation, there were some who returned to the ghetto in the railway carriages or trains carrying freight taken from the slaughtered in Treblinka. Some people managed to escape from the death camp and sneak back into the ghetto. Among the latter was David Nowodworski, an older member of the youth movement and the underground. Abraham Levin, a teacher and historian who worked in the underground archives in the ghetto, described his meeting with Nowodworski on August 28, more than a month after the deportations began:

Today we had a long talk with David Nowodworski, who returned from Treblinka. He told us in detail the whole story of his ordeal, from the moment he was taken until he managed to escape from the slaughter site and reach Warsaw. From his account, it is once again confirmed in no uncertain terms that all the transports, whether they were made up of people who were snatched or whether they went of their own accord, are all put to death and no one is saved. This is the naked truth and it is terrible to think that during the last few weeks, at least some 300,000 individuals from Warsaw and other cities such as Radom, Siedlce, and others, have been murdered.

The written evidence recorded from his words is so painful that it cannot be grasped in so many words. This is undoubtedly the greatest crime in the history of mankind.

The next day, Saturday, the twenty-ninth of August, Levin ended his diary entries with the following story:

> Moshe Lewite or Levitas, of 40 Twarda Street, went to look for his wife three weeks ago [who was taken] to the *Umschlag[platz]*. He was also caught and sent to Kosow. Two days ago, he returned, for the Germans had released him because he was a carpenter. He says that Kosow has been emptied and all its Jews expelled. People with money buy food from the farmers and share it with those who have no money. At any rate, this must be investigated. This was a sign that not all the expelled were slaughtered.

Even a sophisticated person like Abraham Levin, who had heard firsthand reports of Treblinka, could not withstand the suggestive power of the rumors and their illusory contents.

The truth of the death camp was not conveyed in a vacuum. There were also rumors of greetings, letters, and people who allegedly returned from the deportation. The Germans and their agents deliberately spread these false stories in order to create confusion and disinformation. Poles in the underworld promised that in exchange for large sums of money they would look for and find loved ones who had been deported. Every sign of hope was welcomed. People repressed knowledge of their doom. They desperately, even self-destructively, clung to illusions.

Historians have struggled to understand how this knowledge could be supressed by the victims, who, after all, had everything at stake in understanding what was happening to them. The answer may be found in the psychology of people who subconsciously refuse to believe the worst; the woman who ignores the lump in her breast or the person who dismisses chest pains as indigestion, the spouse who represses compelling evidence of infidelity.

The Polish underground was well aware of what was happening to the Jews of Warsaw, for in the very first days of the expulsion, they had already passed on to their contacts news of the awful secret of the railway station branching out from the out-of-the-way village of Treblinka. The Bund sent one of its

Polish-looking members to follow the path taken by the expelled Jews and investigate the place to which they were taken. The emissary, Zalman Friedrich, contacted a Polish socialist railway worker. With his help, Friedrich managed to reach the railway route taken by the evacuees to Sokolow and discovered the branch line leading to Treblinka. From people in the vicinity, he learned details about the place that endlessly swallowed up trainloads of living people.

An issue of the Bundist underground paper *On the Watch,* which appeared September 20, a few days after the end of the expulsion, described the route of the shipments that left Warsaw and the deceitful methods used by the Nazis even at death's door, even at Treblinka. Arriving Jews were addressed on the subject of work and the anticipated future. They were directed to a building marked BATHHOUSE, and until the very last minute it was not clear to the victims that beyond these buildings with their innocent signs, death awaited them.

The Jewish Police took an active part in all the phases of the expulsion. During the initial phases, the Jewish Police directed the seizures. Later on, they played secondary but supportive roles. The Jewish police were perceived as hostile, and after the expulsion ended, they were the target of anger and revulsion — traitors to their people. The writers of the diaries condemn the Jewish police in the sharpest terms. The poet Itzhak Katznelson viewed them as "the scum of the earth," "filthy souls," and "the so-called 'Jewish' policeman, who has nothing of the Jew and nothing of the human-being."

Emanuel Ringelblum wrote a note under the heading "Hatred Towards the Police," stating that when the expulsion ended, frustration and guilt were directed toward the police. Earlier in his chronicles, he had been more supportive of the police. Ringelblum commented that the newly established police displayed a positive approach to the people of the ghetto. In his notes on the involvement of the police at the height of the expulsion, however, Ringelblum does not hesitate to discuss the "cruelty of the Jewish Police, which at times was greater than that of the Germans, the Ukrainians and the Latvians."

At the beginning of the deportations the police adopted the

attitude taken again and again throughout the Holocaust. It was preferable, they argued, for representatives of the victims to do the work of rooting out people because they would show more consideration for their own kind and might reduce the number of victims and save the people who could be saved. Yet as the expulsions continued, police commanders ignored moral discipline and evaded responsibility for what was happening. Some of them aproached their role during the expulsion as a task that exhausted almost all their energy and capacities. Some rank-and-file police avoided participating in the actual expulsion or left the force and gave up their uniform and the protection it generally afforded them. The Jewish Police brutally executed their destructive and sickening tasks. After the expulsion, there was an overall loathing for the Jewish Police, who then tried to hide their identity or deny their actions. While the anger is understandable, the role of the Jewish Police must be kept in context. They were following orders, not initiating them. Their role was considerably exaggerated by ghetto chroniclers who reflect the outrage of ghetto residents. The police became an immediate target for rage. The accusations against them evade the issue of who activated the system and who was its driving force.

Even before the expulsion, the Germans succeeded in investing the Jewish police with a sense of imperiousness and power. They felt aloof, a notch above the rest of the Jews in the ghetto. The Jewish Police force was composed mainly of assimilated Jews and Christians who were the descendants of three Jewish grandparents and were defined as Jews by the race categories. Ringelblum and Katznelson maintained that the estrangement felt by these people toward the Jewish public and its masses was one of the reasons for the alienation and distance that as a rule existed between the police and the ghetto Jew, a situation that reached its peak during the expulsion. Several police officers were highly educated. There was a marked percentage of lawyers among them. As a rule, they were not ordinary inhabitants of the ghetto.

When, with the passing of time, filling the daily quota became problematic, the SS personnel blamed the police and intensified the pressure on them. They used threats and demanded that each policeman supply them with five "heads" per day. They warned that if the police did not fulfill this obligation, their relatives would be taken to make up the missing number. At this critical stage, the policemen themselves became hostages.

Events in the area known as the "cauldron" were not the last acts of the deportation. In typical Nazi fashion, the Jewish Police received their reward for a job well done: they were the last to be expelled. On September 12, the last selection was conducted in the apartment block of the Jewish Police.

By fall, only 35,000 Jews, or 10 percent of the 350,000 Jews who had inhabited the ghetto on the eve of the expulsion, received permission from the authorities to remain as essential workers. The people with special rights passed through a process of careful selection and were placed in dwellings allotted to the enterprises and workplaces, where they were forced to live in work camp–like conditions. Some 20,000–25,000 of those who remained in the ghetto after the expulsion could be termed "illegal." They had succeeded in hiding or evading the searches that continued throughout the entire period of the deportations, and they remained in the limited area of the ghetto and were included in the estimate of the ghetto workers.

Both legal residents and those who had hidden lived with the knowledge that their days were numbered. There was no future to Jewish life in Warsaw — or in occupied Poland.

8

THE ESTABLISHMENT OF THE
JEWISH FIGHTING ORGANIZATION

A s THE EXPULSIONS ENDED, Jews were exhausted, shocked, astounded, and angry. There was a time of reckoning and inner revulsion. Tough questions were asked and remained unanswered: Why had Jews made no effort to defend themselves? Why had there been no organized or spontaneous Jewish opposition on a serious scale? Why didn't Jews retaliate against the hated Jewish Police, especially since the police were not armed with deadly weapons?

The chroniclers' complaints were a form of moral stock-taking *after* the deportation; these charges were not made during the events themselves. Emanuel Ringelblum was especially harsh. In his article entitled "Why?" he asks again and again, "Why did they not resist when 300,000 Jews were being evacuated from Warsaw? . . . Why was it made so simple and easy for this enemy? . . . Why was there not a single victim among the hangmen?"

How could fifty SS men, assisted by two hundred Ukrainians and a similar number of Latvians, deport so many without encountering obstacles? Ringelblum raises disturbing questions without offering a compelling answer.

He understands some of the elements that led to so passive a response. Ringelblum details "the German strategies in preparation for the expulsion," and the element of surprise contained in the onset of the evacuation. In addition, he stresses the impermeability of the ghetto during the expulsion and the impossibility of getting even a small amount of food into the area. The use of the Jews themselves as accessories was a deterrent factor to resistance. The employment of a gradual but ever intensifying selection process masked the full intent of the near total expulsion. It led to the breakdown of community and the war of all against all for survival.

These factors all had their effect. However, two other causes lay behind the victims' lack of reaction. First, the ghetto disintegrated from within. One could compare the days of the expulsion to a closed-off and well-guarded hunting field, with excited hunters shooting and killing indiscriminately, pursuing their unarmed and unprotected victims. Furthermore, there is a pattern to the Jewish response to the expulsion order. Under totalitarian regimes, a persecuted person, who has no chance or likelihood of being saved or of saving himself by fighting back, is also isolated even if he or she is among many who share the same fate. Such a person can offer no self-defense. Only two responses are possible: attempts to escape, or self-deception by grasping at illusions. For the ghetto's inhabitants, the entire world was reduced to Nazis and their helpers on the one hand, and their seemingly isolated Jewish prey on the other. The outside world neither reacted nor helped. No encouragement or assistance in any form was forthcoming from the Polish side or from the free world.

There were instances of individual rebellion. Thousands were murdered in the ghetto when they tried to escape or hide from the convoys, or when they failed to obey the snatchers' orders. The fact that some 20,000–25,000 people remained in the ghetto by illegal means — hiding despite the determined searches — can be seen as the primary form of opposition under the circumstances.

The Poles denounced the Jewish passivity, and not without

some justification, according to Ringelblum. But, he adds, the Poles ignored their own responsibility for the Jewish failure to respond. In his essay "Polish-Jewish Relations During the Second World War," Ringelblum wrote:

> The evacuation campaign lasted forty-four days, and there was no reaction from the Aryan side [the Polish side of Warsaw]. On the Aryan side, there was utter silence while this drama was being enacted in view of hundreds of thousands of Poles. There was no outcry from the government [meaning the Polish government in exile], not a single word of encouragement, no promise of help, or even moral support.

Only on the seventeenth of September, after the expulsion ended, did the "leaders of the Civilian Struggle," the civilian arm of the political underground subordinate to the London-based government-in-exile, address the expulsion. In a proclamation to the Polish population, they stated:

> Without being able to actively oppose what is being done, the leadership of the Civilian Struggle in the name of the entire Polish people protests against the crimes which are being committed against the Jews. All the political and social organizations in Poland are united in this protest.

There was nothing in this declaration of protest regarding the adoption of any action or the Polish underground's stated intention of taking such steps. Moreover, there was no call to the Polish public in the declaration to render help to Jews fleeing from the ghetto, and not a word of encouragement to the Jews to abandon the ghetto and seek shelter among the Poles.

Plans for active Jewish resistance during the expulsion fell apart. The reasons why reveal the complete powerlessness of the Jews. On July 23, the second day of the expulsion, the activists of the underground in the ghetto called an emergency meeting to discuss what was happening and to decide on the steps to be taken. Representatives of the pioneering Zionist youth movements and others from political parties favored taking an active

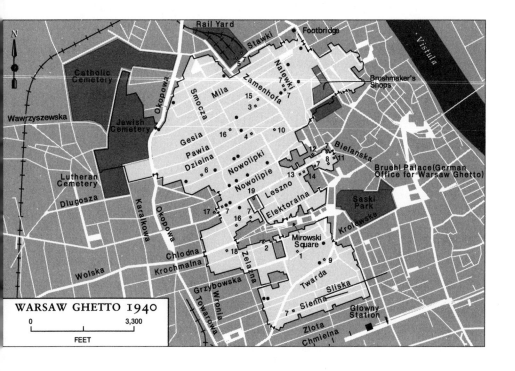

WARSAW GHETTO 1940

0 — 3,300

FEET

LEGEND

— Ghetto Boundary, November
15, 1940; Wall with
Barbed Wire on Top
⊷ Entrances, Gates to Ghetto
• Selected Ghetto Factories
▪ Selected Features (Ghetto
Public Institutions)

1 Jewish Council (Judenrat)
2 Jewish Police
3 Gesiowka (Jewish Prison)
4 Pawiak Prison
5 *Umschlagplatz* (Assembly
Point and Transfer Office)
6 Hiding Place of Ringelblum
Archives
7 Hospitals
8 The Great Synagogue

9 Nozjik Synagogue
10 Moriah Synagogue
11 ZTOS (Jewish Mutual Aid
Society)
12 CENTOS (Association for
the Care of Jewish
Orphans)
13 Office for Combatting Usury
and Profiteering
14 ORT (Organization for
Rehabilitation through
Training)
15 Post Office
16 Center for Vocational
Training
17 Labor Bureau (*Arbeitsamt*)
18 Korczak Orphanage
19 Courthouse (Tribunals)

stand. The outcome of the meeting, however, was determined by two well-known and respected personalities: the historian Yitzhak Schiper and Alexander Zisha Friedman, one of the leaders of the Orthodox Agudath Israel. A young Zionist leader summarized the debate:

> The conference was impressed by the remarks of Zisha Friedman and Schiper. Fridman put his trust in God: "I believe in the Almighty and a miracle. He will not allow his people to be destroyed. We must be patient and a miracle will occur. Fighting against the enemy makes no sense. . . ." Schiper does not hold with self-defense. "Defense means the utter destruction of the Warsaw ghetto! I believe we can hold together the core of the Warsaw ghetto. We are in the midst of a war. Every nation sacrifices victims. We are also paying with victims in order to save the core of the people. If I were convinced that we could not manage to save the core, I would arrive at a different conclusion."

Schiper's reasoning seemed compelling. Active resistance would trigger collective retaliation, and while there was some hope for a majority or a part of the ghetto to survive, such actions were tantamount to collective suicide and would not garner widespread support. *Only when all hope for survival was abandoned did armed resistance begin within the ghetto. Only then could resistance enjoy widespread support.*

The assembly dispersed without making any decisions but with the intention of meeting again. But the course of the events put an end to any further gathering. There was another attempt to set up a committee of representatives from those underground bodies that had agreed to undertake armed resistance. But this group also failed to organize and could by no means take any active steps. According to Yitzhak Zuckerman, the frequent snatchings in the streets prevented the members of this committee from moving about freely. Hence, the deportations that placed every individual in danger also prevented the organization of an opposition.

At a meeting of a few activists during the first days of the expulsion, the leader of the Left Po'alei Zion, Shachna Zagan, took on the task of formulating a manifesto. But before he had time to finish it, he was caught and taken to the *Umschlagplatz;* every attempt to extricate him was unsuccessful.

From the onset of the expulsion, the youth movements were faced with two contradictory challenges: ensuring the security of their members and preparing for active resistance. Each of them required initiative and constant unfamiliar activities. Members of the Dror movement had a group working on a farm in Czerniakow, not far from Warsaw. A trusting relationship had grown up between the group of Jewish workers and the owners of the farm, and for some time, it had been used as a meeting place and refuge for runners en route. Because of the expulsion, Dror established a larger unit of its members on the farm. It was situated outside the ghetto and therefore outside the area where there was the danger of being liquidated.

Members of the Gordonia movement, mostly refugees from towns and villages throughout the country, decided to leave the ghetto several days before the expulsion. They transferred their members in small groups to ghettos in such towns as Opoczno and Czestochowa, which were still not experiencing deportations. Heads of Hashomer Hatzaír instructed their members on the first or second day of the expulsion to leave their parents' homes and take temporary refuge in a hostel in Nalewki Street. Youngsters were required to abandon their families at the height of the deportations, at the very moment when the threat of being uprooted and separated was affecting everyone around them.

Members of this movement subsequently found a haven in a Jewish-owned carpentry workshop that came under German management on the eve of the expulsion. The Jewish owners were still permitted to run the place, and as experts supervising the production they were afforded preferential treatment. The owners were two brothers named Landau. One of them, Alexander, was involved with the underground in the ghetto, and from the beginning of the expulsion he opened the doors of his enterprise to many of the activists of the political underground.

At this workshop, known as OBW (or the *Ostdeutsche Bauwerkstätte*), a number of people from the underground archives and the Left Po'alei Zion were also to be found, as well as the Communist leader Joseph Lewartowski-Finklestein. Eighteen-year-old Margalit Landau, the only daughter of Alexander Landau, was a dedicated member of Hashomer Hatzaír, and through her good offices a singularly close relationship developed between her father and the heads of the movement. The group of buildings allotted to house the workers of the OBW was the hub of activity of the Jewish Fighting Organization.

In addition to this workshop, the Halmann carpentry factory on Nowolipki Street was also one of the focal centers of the underground members and a place where they found refuge as supposed artisans. One of the former owners of this enterprise, named Arbuz, was also connected with underground circles through his son, who was a member of a youth movement. Emanuel Ringelblum stayed for a time in the Halmann carpentry shop. The cover offered by these workshops to those who were involved in secret activities became known to the regular workers, and they complained that people who were not professional carpenters were taken into these workshops and could endanger the enterprise's existence and the security of its employees. As we shall see, the OBW suffered quite considerably from the underground members who were taken into the workshop.

On July 28, a week after the start of the deportations, representatives of the pioneering youth movements, Hashomer Hatzaír, Dror, and Akiva, met at the Dror hostel on Dzielna Street and decided to create the Jewish Fighting Organization (*Zydowska Organizacja Bojowa,* or ZOB). This step was an indication that the youth movements had given up the idea that there was any likelihood of establishing a wider framework of fighting organizations that would include a variety of different parties. They were determined, therefore, to set up such an organization independently, within the limited framework of the youth movements.

Important figures from the underground participated in the founding session, including Yitzhak Zuckerman (who was known as "Antek"), Joseph Kaplan, and Mordecai Tennenbaum-Tamarof (who was later moved to Bialystok). But Mordecai Anielewicz was not present. He was on a mission to the Zaglembie area on the eve of the deportation. At this meeting, an executive committee of the new organization was chosen, and it was decided to send Arieh Wilner (Jurek) to the Polish side of the city in order to contact the underground there and obtain urgent assistance, arms, and guidance.

Once created, the organization had no weapons, no plan of action, and no contact with the outside world — neither with the Allies fighting on the war fronts, nor with the Polish underground beyond the ghetto walls.

The first activities of the new organization did not augur well for the future. A manifesto was prepared in which the true intentions of the Germans were described and the fate of Jews after deportation was outlined. Jews were called on to oppose and evade their pursuers. This manifesto was received by ghetto inhabitants with distrust if not actual antagonism. Readers of the manifesto feared that the publication itself was an act of provocation, and that any attempt at opposition might serve the Germans as a pretext to expel all the Jews from the ghetto. Again, despair, not hope, was a prerequisite for resistance.

Without firearms, the fighting organization explored the possibilities of using small arms and poisonous acids. The latter were obtained from factories that produced honey substitutes, but experiments with this liquid demonstrated that it appeared to have no effect on the human body. Its impotence became a source of bitter humor among the rank and file of the organization. Zuckerman wrote in his memoirs:

> It was the Jewish police who caught and expelled masses of Jews. They were armed with sticks; we could also use sticks and knives against them . . . talk or threats would not do. One had to become cruel and use violent methods. Unfortunately, we did not adopt these ways although they were morally justified.

In his memoirs, Zuckerman repeatedly asked "what if": "If we had done," and "If we had decided in good time, things would have been different." In most cases, it seems unlikely that anything could have been done to change the course of events. There is a note of regret and hesitation in the words of this man who was responsible for the direction taken by the underground and who, after the event, tried in his depressing and revealing criticism to examine the insoluble dilemmas of that time.

Opposition to the police was a possibility. If this option had been acted on, it might have deterred the Germans by forcing them to employ more of their forces. We do not have any details relating to the strength and size of the ZOB in its early days, but one can assume that it was composed of some two hundred members. In one area, at least, their directives proved effective to a large extent. Members of the organization generally managed to evade the selection process and also did not rely on the permits to save themselves. Many members of the youth movement were caught and sent to Treblinka, but the percentage of organization members was comparatively small.

If deported, members were instructed to jump off the moving train. Some of these escapes succeeded, and there were those who jumped from a train in motion more than once. Organization members were equipped with tools for cutting the barbed wire stretched across the hatches of the freight trains. Those who left the trains in this manner and succeeded in landing without incident turned to those units or groups beyond the cemetery in Powazki, which bordered the Jewish cemetery.

Workers from the OBW workshop grew vegetables on the grounds of the Jewish cemetery, and a notable portion of these workers were also members of the organization. The escapees had to cross the fence at a suitable time and hide among the gravestones. With the end of the working day, or on the following day, they frequently succeeded in returning to the ghetto with a group of workers. During the deportations, small groups also managed to leave the ghetto for the forests, where partisan units had been organized. They sent members or groups to various localities, such as Tarnow, places where they could strengthen the nucleus of a fighting organization in the making.

As Zuckerman pointed out, when the organization was first established in Warsaw it was not merely a local structure but an organization that hoped to multiply and create cells and groups in ghettos throughout the occupied lands. One may assume that was the case during the different stages of development of the political underground. Warsaw was also the center that activated and guided branches in the provinces as the Jewish fighting force was being organized. For some time prior to the force's creation, the leadership of the youth movement in Warsaw tried to propagate the idea of a militant opposition and assist in creating fighting forces in many ghettos.

In the first week of August, the first shipment of weapons reached the ghetto from the Polish side. It included five pistols and six hand grenades, which were obtained via the Gwardia Ludowa (formerly Armia Ludowa), the fighting unit of the Polish Communist underground. During the same week, the organization executed its first operation — carrying out a sentence against the Jewish Police commander in the ghetto, Jozef Szerynski. The man responsible was Israel Kanal, a member of the small group of Akiva members which was then concentrated in the OBW on Mila Street. Kanal had been a policeman in the ghetto for some time and served together with other members as an arm of the underground within the police force. With the onset of the expulsion, he refused to continue serving with the police. On the day he had to attack Szerynski, however, he once again donned his policeman's cap and insignia. Szerynski was wounded in the neck but did not die.

Nonetheless, the sound of the shot echoed throughout the ghetto. Many thought that the Poles were behind the operation. Abraham Levin wrote as much in his diary, despite the fact that he worked in Oneg Shabbos, the underground archives, which was located in the OBW area and was close to the underground. The Jews could not imagine that an organization that had adopted methods of armed opposition had arisen within their midst and was responsible for the assault. Moreover, the fighting organization was highly secretive, and even members of the political underground were not aware of its existence.

Even after its operations increased and notices of these operations were posted on the walls of the ghetto, only a few conspirators knew the names of the members of the organization, its commanders, and methods. Familiarity between members of the organization was also constrained, and even the commanders were only acquainted with those members who came from their own movements and did not know the names and features of many others.

Although the organization had been rather restrained in the early stages of its existence, its actions had included demolishing construction materials and burning finished products of some workshops. These operations made a serious impression on the ghetto. Nevertheless, the debacle experienced by the organization on September 3 cast its shadow over everything and caused profound frustration.

A group of eighteen members of the pioneering movement, mostly members of Dror, left Warsaw for the region of Hrubieszow in the Lublin district at the height of the deportation in August. A Jewish partisan cell in the forest of the area was being organized, and its members were to join with the group that had left Warsaw. The Warsaw group made its way by train, bearing documents that had been prepared for them by Joseph Kaplan using official paper and insignia at his disposal at the office of the OBW.

At a small station near their destination, the travelers were arrested by the Germans, their documents were discovered to be false, and they were all tortured and put to death, except for one, who succeeded in evading the Germans and returning to Warsaw. Then, on September 3, a police car pulled up outside the little office of the OBW enterprise, and an unknown German got out and asked to see Joseph Kaplan. This did not arouse suspicion, for Kaplan actually worked in the office and was familiar with its affairs. Only later did observers notice that there was another person seated in the German car, Israel Zelzer, one of the few members of Gordonia who had remained in Warsaw and had been one of the group destined for Hrubieszow.

Kaplan, one of the outstanding figures in the underground and a founder of the fighting organization, was arrested and taken into the police car. Efforts were immediately made to follow the men and discover their whereabouts in order to try to save them. Shmuel Breslaw, one of the leaders of Hashomer Hatzaír in Warsaw, was assigned the task. He was soon detected because it was forbidden to be in the streets during the working day. Without having time to evade the German car that had stopped alongside the pavement, Breslaw was asked to identify himself. He pulled out a knife and attacked the uniformed German sitting in the car. He was shot on the spot.

In the confusion that followed, a member of the organization, Reginka Justman, was instructed to transfer the organization's cache of weapons from the store in Mila Street to the Dror hostel in Dzielna Street. She left after working hours, when it was possible to move about and there were quite a few people in the streets. But she too was caught. The weapons were confiscated, and she was then taken to the *Umschlagplatz.*

The organization lost two of its leaders and its store of arms on the same day. Kaplan was taken to the Pawiak Prison, situated on the border of the ghetto. A policeman connected to the underground, Arieh Grzybowski, was instructed to stand near the gates of the prison to observe whether Kaplan would be moved. Indeed, a few days later, Kaplan and Zelzer, together with a small group of Jews, were taken from the prison to the *Umschlagplatz.* The Jewish policeman Engelman followed the convoy in the hope that he would be able to free Kaplan. But during the march, one of the German policemen separated Kaplan and Zelzer from the rest, pushed them into the entranceway of a house, and shot them. Only Reginka Justman escaped the mayhem. After the store of weapons had been found, she was taken to the assembly point and at that juncture saved by members of the organization.

One of those present at the funeral of Shmuel Breslaw in the Jewish cemetery in Gesia Street described the scene:

We escorted Shmuel on his last journey and said farewell to Joseph in our hearts. . . . We stood on the edge of the open grave. Scenes flickered by like a film. Burning memories. Chapters from the past as painful as blows. Joseph and Shmuel — all the stages of war behind them. Until the end — nameless and cruel. They were weary, left only with the strength of stubbornness which does not succumb, without finishing their life's mission. And who will take up their flag?

Soon it will be our turn. And those of Joseph and Shmuel's friends outside the walls, and those who had never heard of them — will they be given any sign or indication of what is happening here? A small group of youngsters at the far end of a large Jewish cemetery in a city where Jewish life is ebbing. . . . We stand in frozen silence, bending over the grave. The lament — they are eulogizing the dead. In strong and harsh words directed mainly to those who have survived, and someone quietly begins to sing: "Strengthen the hands of our brothers" [*Techezakna yedei kol acheinu*] . . . Everyone quietly joins in.

And Abraham Levin, whose daughter Ora worked with the OBW group in the cemetery and took part in Shmuel's funeral, wrote in his diary on Thursday, September 3, "Shmuel's funeral, which took place in the presence of the guards who worked in the cemetery . . . is our tragedy according to Ora's story. God Almighty!" Under the heading "Opposition," Ringelblum wrote a hurried comment: "The role of the youth, the only ones to remain on the battlefield. People with imagination. Shmuel would not get through the tragedy of the ghetto alive."

The deaths and loss of the arms cache were direct strikes at the heart of the fighting organization. Brave efforts and endless devotion had been invested until the few could find their way and a nucleus was established from which action could be expected. And then, without warning, on a day during the expulsion that was actually easier than many others, a series of incidents — neither planned nor intentional on the part of the enemy — left everyone feeling absolutely helpless. In this way the impulsive acts of a group of young people were rendered powerless by the enemy's omnipotent strength.

The young organization was suffering from shock and despair. Zuckerman, in an unrelenting chapter of his memoirs, describes the atmosphere of "the days of September 1942," when members of the organization spent the time of the catastrophic "cauldron" in hiding in Mila Street. On September 12, when the deportation was showing signs of ending, a group of veteran members of the organization met. They spoke of Joseph with sadness, full of secret longings and a sense of finality. Zuckerman continued:

The words were bitter, heavy and determined. There would be no Jewish opposition. We were too late. The people are gone.

When there were hundreds of thousands in Warsaw, we could not manage to organize a Jewish striking force — how could we succeed in doing so now when there are only tens of thousands left. We did not manage to train the masses. We have no weapons, and it is unlikely that we will get any. There is no strength to begin anew. The people are destroyed, our honor crushed.

This small group still has the strength to restore our honor. Let us go out into the streets tomorrow, burn down the ghetto and attack the Germans. We will be killed. It is fitting that we should be killed. But our honor will be victorious. There will be a day when we are remembered: the youth of this helpless people have risen and saved our honor with everything they had.

Zuckerman described his reaction to these remarks:

The failure and shame is great. The acts that are being proposed are acts of desperation. They will vanish without a trace. The harm done to the enemy will be insignificant, and the youth will die. Until now, we have suffered endless failures, and we will experience further defeats. We must start anew. For the time being, the action is at an end. Possibly, there will be a comparative standstill, for weeks and perhaps months. Every day is a windfall . . . perhaps we will succeed after all.

Zuckerman's comments accurately reflect the disappointment and hopelessness of those days. Members no longer relied on their leaders, no longer blindly believed in their understanding and resourcefulness. The certainty that their leaders could help the group through the obstacles and act promptly at the right time was undermined. The feelings of the rank and file, which were sometimes accompanied by ridicule and outbursts, was that members should go out immediately, without delay, and even with empty hands, with clenched fists, take vengeance on those Jews who took part in uprooting the Jews and kill every German who appeared in the streets of the ghetto. The determination was simple: no more delays, no grandiose plans that would never be realized.

Arieh Wilner, who since the loss of Kaplan and Breslaw had not moved from the ghetto to his post on the Aryan side, claimed that he knew from a reliable source that there was to be an interval in the deportation. His advice: They must stop the grumbling and fatalistic moods and find the strength during the interval of time available to prepare for the inevitable struggle. The organization would fight when the last of the Jews were being taken from the ghetto. It was possible to obtain weapons and to prepare and strengthen themselves. Impatience was an act of despair and disintegration, which not only would not affect the murderers and those responsible, but also would not earn the agreement and support of the remaining Jews of the ghetto.

Wilner's statement was made in the same spirit as Zuckerman's assumptions, but his approach was accepted unwillingly and with some hesitation. From the point of view of the Jewish Fighting Organization, which had no sooner begun when it suffered heavy losses, this marked the conclusion of the expulsion.

9

BETWEEN THE EXPULSION
AND JANUARY 1943

THE GHETTO WAS never the same again. What remained was merely a sort of temporary working camp. Most of the ghetto was empty. Building after building, street after street was abandoned. Their Jews had been deported and the streets resembled a ghost town. Only four enclaves — groups of buildings, entire streets, and parts of streets adjoining various enterprises — were set aside as housing for the remaining Jews. Each enclave was separated from the others. Traffic was forbidden in the no man's land that divided these quarters, and all communication between sectors was banned.

The largest and most populated enclave was the "central ghetto," which encompassed some of the major streets of Jewish Warsaw, such as Nalewki, Gesia, Mila, Muranowska, and others. In its structure and arrangement, it resembled the old ghetto more than did any of the other enclaves. The Judenrat, headed by Czerniakow's former deputy, Marc Lichtenbaum, was located there, as were the remnants of the Jewish Police. This Judenrat bore no resemblance to the institution that formerly bore the name. Its responsibilities were curtailed and its existence mainly served as a cover for the employment of the many administrative officials.

Many of the "illegals" found refuge in the central ghetto, where they could slip into empty houses and occupy apartments. This ghetto was also the site of some workshops, including what was left of the OBW. Many of those who were employed, however, worked in the *Werterfassung,* a workers' unit owned by the SS which collected objects and property left behind by the expelled population. The Germans even permitted the "illegals" to perform this type of work and by doing so provided them with de facto recognition and the right to stay in the ghetto.

The three other enclaves were actually nuclei of workshops and isolated shops, with adjacent residential housing. The largest of these centers was the enclave that occupied a major portion of Leszno Street, Nowolipie, and several other lanes. Two large workshops were situated in this center: Walter C. Többens and K. G. Schultz. In the two other centers, brushmakers were situated in parts of streets near the "central ghetto" and in the small enclave that included a branch of the Többens enterprise in Prosta Street. This enclave was in an area comparatively distant from the other quarters of the ghetto.

The municipal doctor of the Warsaw ghetto, M. Lensky, described the ghetto as he remembered it:

> Traffic in the streets was limited from 5 to 7:30 in the morning and from 4 to 8 in the evening. It was only during these hours that food and provisions could be bought, people could obtain necessities or visit one another. But during the day, the Jews lived in fear . . . when I looked out of the window of my room, I could see three streets: Gesia, Nalewki, Franciszkanska. The appearance of the streets during the hours between 8 and 4 aroused in me a feeling of horror, and the slightest knock at the door instilled fear.
>
> Are there no signs of renewed action? There was not a sound in the streets. From time to time, one got a glimpse of a bent-over Jew clinging to the wall and scurrying from entrance to entrance like a mouse, until he was swallowed up by an open entranceway and disappeared. Most entrance gates were closed, for there were

workshops in the houses, and alongside the entrance gates stood Jewish guards from among the working personnel who permitted no one to enter. It was only possible to enter houses that had no institutions or factories. Even the gates of the hospital were closed from 8 to 3. Entering and leaving was forbidden.

As in the past, the ghetto's food, which had been drastically reduced, was generally brought into the ghetto by smuggling. Professional smuggling was almost nonexistent, but the activities of worker-smugglers increased when they would leave in the morning to work in various services for the Germans and return to the ghetto in the evening.

Ironically enough, life became easier at this final stage of the ghetto's existence; hunger abated significantly and the death rate declined. The deported had left their possessions behind, and these could be traded for food by those who had remained. The elderly, the children, the weak, and the poor had been deported. Those who remained were for the most part stronger young men and women who could withstand more successfully the illnesses that had swept the ghetto and led to the high death rate among the enfeebled inhabitants.

The Jewish population after the expulsion consisted of a lonely and isolated remnant of the once vast and varied Jewish population of Warsaw. Most of the 55,000–60,000 who remained were workers. Frequently, only one person remained out of whole families, and it often occurred that in the short time the ghetto was to exist, single men and women lived together, often more out of loneliness than love. They were motivated by the powerful desire to escape the loneliness and suffering, the urge to enjoy life while it was still possible. Signs of disintegration and the neglect of accepted moral norms were also evident in other aspects of life. However, only a few instances of violent crimes were recorded, and not even one case of murder among the last Jews of the Warsaw ghetto.

Prior to the expulsion, the German ruling authority consisted of the civilian commissar and the *Transferstelle,* the police, and the SS. After the expulsion, the only decision-making power was embodied in the police network and the Gestapo. These institutions tried to make it appear as if everything had returned to normal and the remaining population was in no imminent danger. Jews were expected to work and those who worked were told that they would not be harmed.

Moreover, the Germans used a series of ploys to create a calm atmosphere. For instance, the Jewish authorities were ordered to collect the aimless children wandering about and establish a children's home. This task, cynically enough, was assigned to the Jewish police. Mende, of the Gestapo, who was one of the cruelest hunters during the expulsion, addressed the Judenrat in a speech: "The children are the future of the people and therefore everything must be done for the children of the ghetto."

But the remnant of Jews who remained were not given to illusion. They had nothing but mistrust and deep hatred for the Germans. Jews lived in pain and isolation. Of one thing alone were they certain: that ghetto existence was temporary; it would not take long before the last Jews would be expelled and ghetto life concluded.

Consciences weighed heavily on the Jews; many were guilt-ridden. As long as the expulsion was going on, the struggle for survival consumed all of one's energy. When the tension had subsided, there was time for bitter and disturbing moral re-examination. Men and women mourned their families, who had been uprooted without any attempt at defense or opposition. Writing about the ghetto's mood after the expulsion, Emanuel Ringelblum said:

> Most of the population supports opposition. It appears to me that no longer would they go to the slaughter like sheep. The public wants the enemy to pay heavily for life, they will attack them with knives, sticks, acids. No longer will they allow themselves to be expelled by means of a siege. No longer will they allow themselves to be caught in the streets.

Many years later, Dr. Lensky wrote in his memoirs:

> Reality was so bitter, that it was difficult to believe that the remaining survivors were to be given a breathing spell for a

while. Everyone felt in his heart that the actions could start anew any day, and the question kept cropping up as to what was to be done in order to defend ourselves effectively. If the Jews would receive a sufficient number of weapons, we could easily organize armed units of defense. But to our sorrow, we could not obtain weapons. The underground itself was lacking people, and its equipment was poor. It is therefore impossible for the underground to propose the idea of armed opposition, although from a psychological standpoint, the Jewish community was ready to carry out this mission.

Throughout the Polish ghettos, hopelessness was a prerequisite for resistance. As long as the ghetto's population could be deceived by reassurances from those in authority — Germans or Jews — they were prepared to carry out German orders and treat the Jewish Fighting Organization as provocateurs endangering the entire ghetto. In this new climate, however, the Judenrat and the police could no longer dominate public life. Public opinion no longer regarded the Jewish Fighting Organization as an irresponsible element that could bring catastrophe to the ghetto. They had already experienced catastrophe.

The return of some of the outstanding figures of the underground who had not been present during the expulsion also added to the internal strength of the organization. Foremost among the returnees was Mordecai Anielewicz, who had been staying in Zaglembie. After he learned of the mass expulsion, he immediately set out for Warsaw. Anielewicz had earned a reputation as a forceful and gifted leader during the period preceding the establishment of the fighting organization. He had considerable influence with his comrades in Hashomer Hatzaír, and because he had been outside the ghetto during the expulsion, he was not weighed down by a sense of personal failure for not resisting. He was prepared to act decisively. He cleared away any doubts regarding internal affairs and restored discipline and inner confidence. He then proceeded to establish contact with those groups he considered allies or natural partners of the fighting organization.

Eliezer Geller, who had led the Gordonia movement, together

with a group of friends, also returned to Warsaw. Geller and his people had left Warsaw on the assumption that it was still possible to find places where Jews lived in comparatively peaceful conditions. He had not fully realized that the murder campaign was an overall decree that would apply to the Jews wherever they lived. When he returned, he regretted that his movement had not been involved in the founding of the Jewish Fighting Organization from its outset, and he immediately got involved in the organization's work.

The changed atmosphere in the ghetto made possible a renewed understanding between the groups that had founded the organization. Those segments of the underground who had formerly objected to the use of force during the expulsion changed their minds. At the end of October there were deliberations in Mila Street between Mordecai Anielewicz and Yitzhak Zuckerman, and members of the Po'alei Zion. At this meeting, they agreed to join the Jewish Fighting Organization, whose dual task was defending the Jews of Warsaw and punishing the police and other Jews who had participated in the expulsion.

Still, certain differences of opinion remained. The members of the Left Po'alei Zion emphatically insisted that the structure of the fighting organization should be based on two authoritative organs: one political, and one military. Representatives of the youth movements claimed that this dual focus would lead to differences and arguments, which in the end would paralyze their defensive actions. Leaders of the political parties were hesitant to establish a framework in which the youth movements dominated and had the right to make decisions; they were reluctant to turn over to young people the right to decide on matters of life and death.

The youth movements finally yielded to the pressure of the parties. The acceptance of two organs of authority did not only stem from a strong desire to widen the framework of the fighting organization and give it increasing influence over the ghetto. To a large extent, the concept of two authorities was insisted on by the Polish underground, which was composed of two such authorities — political and military — with the former holding the power to make decisions on critical issues.

The Poles specifically demanded that negotiations with them on behalf of the Jews should be made by a body that incorporated all the various Jewish political forces. They were uninformed about the youth movements and did not consider them to have the requisite responsibility and status for negotiations. Consequently, the heads of the organization saw the two authoritative arms not only as the answer to internal differences but also as a way to participate in negotiations with the Polish underground.

The Jewish National Committee, which included representatives of the political Zionist forces in addition to those of the youth movements, was established as the political framework for the ghetto underground. But at no point did this committee become a decisive factor in the ghetto. Actually, this committee merely lent public support and help to the Jewish Fighting Organization.

Later on, the Zionist socialist Po'alei Zion, the Communists, and the Bund joined the fighting organization. In negotiations with the Bund, a further difficulty arose. Bund members were prepared to participate in the Jewish Fighting Organization, but they refused to be partners in the national committee because of its Zionist-political cast. Consequently, a third framework was established in the form of the Coordinating Committee, in which representatives of the national committee and the Bund participated. The Coordinating Committee spoke for the Jewish underground and the Jewish Fighting Organization in negotiations with the Polish underground authorities.

The enlarged Jewish Fighting Organization (ZOB), which had already established its major functions and institutions at the end of October 1942, was the continuation of the fighting body of the youth movements founded at the height of the expulsion. But in its institutions and the composition of its leadership, this was a new organization. According to Yitzhak Zuckerman's report, delivered in London in 1944, the "new" organization appointed a staff composed of Mordecai Anielewicz, commander, organization department; Zuckerman, deputy commander, arms and munitions; Marek Edelman and Jochanan Morgenstern, intelligence; Hirsch Berlinski, planning; and Michael Rosenfeld.

The Coordinating Committee and the Jewish Fighting Organization achieved an impressive degree of solidarity among the various political and ideological streams of Jewish society which previously had been unable in the interwar period to work together as a united body. Still, political and religious differences prevented a wall-to-wall coalition of Jewish factions. Even when faced with a Nazi enemy who did not distinguish among them, the Jews could not come together. Two prominent forces on the Jewish political scene between the wars remained outside: religious Jews (the Hasidic Orthodox camp and the religious Zionist movement), and the Revisionist party's Betar youth movement.

Little reliable data has been found on the secret activities of these bodies during the war and the ghetto period. We know that a group of the Betar people spent time at a farm in the vicinity of Hrubieszow and that certain members of this group returned to Warsaw at the height of the expulsion or toward its conclusion. David Wdowinski, the senior Revisionist leader in the Warsaw ghetto, presented himself in his postwar memoirs as also heading the Revisionist fighting organization. According to Wdowinski, the organization of fighting forces occurred after the expulsion, and

> the youth decided that Jewish life would be paid for very dearly in the event of a new transfer action. They would not be led to Treblinka like sheep. That is how the Jewish fighting groups — the Jewish Fighting Organization and the Jewish Military Organization — were created.

From Wdowinski's statement, it appears that he did not know — or did not think it necessary to describe — the true order in which these two organizations were founded and acted during the last months of the ghetto. It is clear that the organization founded by a nucleus of the Betar youth movement's members began to organize *after* the expulsion. With regard to the disturbing question of why this organization was established separately and was not included in the wider framework of the Jewish Fighting Organization — in which so many different and divided political orientations were represented — reports diverge. The divisions are political and make the writing of history more difficult.

According to circles close to the Revisionists, the heads of the Jewish Fighting Organization refused to accept into their ranks members of Betar as an organized movement similar to the other youth movements, but insisted that they join the organization solely as individuals. Zuckerman claimed that there were negotiations with the Betar people and that for a time they were considered members of the general organization, but they disagreed over tactics and Betar insisted on maintaining its exclusive connections with the Polish forces. Both sides agree that Betar members demanded that the command be handed over to them because they had members with previous military experience. This was unacceptable to the leadership of the overall fighting organization.

Whatever the case, the Betar members founded a separate organization that included unattached individuals as well as people from other movements, among them the Communists. The second organization founded was called the Jewish Fighting Union (ZZW). The heads of this organization were Pavel Frenkel, Nathan Shultz, S. Hasensprung, Leon (Arieh) Rodal, Eliahu Alberstein, and Yitzhak Bilawski. We do not know how functions were divided among them. We do know, however, that the ZZW succeeded in establishing stable contacts with one of the secondary military branches of the Polish underground.

Some of the Polish people were genuinely motivated and did a great deal to help the organization. Henry Iwanski, an officer of the AK, the Polish military underground, was especially effective. On the other hand, there were those who were motivated by material benefits. It was because of these connections that the organization obtained large quantities of weapons. According to Wdowinski, the ZZW was made up of some 300 fighters, while Polish sources reported it had "150 young Jews, well-armed and ready for anything."

The first missions of the Jewish Fighting Organization (ZOB) were directed against those members of the Jewish police force and Judenrat officials who carried out the Germans' orders. Revenge was exacted from Jacob Lejkin, a deputy commander in the police force who acted as police commander during the expulsion. The actual commander, Szerynski, had been charged by the Germans with dishonest dealings in confiscated furs and was only released on the eve of the expulsion. Lejkin, a lawyer by profession, had been a functionary in student circles in Warsaw in the past. He rushed about like a man possessed, driving his police force to ever more feverish action, and his name came to symbolize the faithful servant who obeys the enemy's orders.

The organization imposed the death sentence on Lejkin and assigned responsibility for his execution to a group of fighters, who appointed Eliahu Rozanski, Margalit Landau, and Mordecai Grobas to carry it out. The group followed Lejkin's movements, staying in an apartment along his daily route. On the evening of October 29, Rozanski killed Lejkin; his adjutant was wounded during the incident.

The following day, small notices signed by the ZOB were posted around the ghetto stating:

> We would like to inform the public that as a consequence of the sentence imposed on the high command, officers, and personnel of the Jewish service which maintains order in Warsaw [the police] . . . the judgment against Jacob Lejkin, deputy commander of the Jewish servicemen, was executed on the 29th of October, at 6 P.M.

The notice also stated that severe retaliation would be taken against those who assisted and served the enemy.

Shortly after Lejkin's execution, an employee of the Judenrat, Yisrael First, was also punished in the same manner. First had been a confidant of the German police in the ghetto and in the ranks of the Judenrat. The execution made a strong impression in the ghetto and demonstrated to the public that there was an avenging force within its confines. In response, police personnel, who had previously been haughty and arrogant, tried to hide their identity by setting aside their insignia and caps.

The Jewish Fighting Organization had started the campaign of punishment to get back at those who actively and brutally as-

Street scene in the Warsaw ghetto, September 19, 1941.
(Heinz Joest photographer, Gunther Schwarberg Collection)

A destitute Jewish woman lying in a Warsaw ghetto
street surrounded by observers, 1941.
(Bundesarchiv, Koblenz, Germany)

The Warsaw ghetto wall in January 1941. (*New York Times* Archives)

A woman escaping from the flames during the Warsaw Ghetto
Uprising, only to be caught later by the Germans.
(Myron and Ally Friedman/United States Holocaust Memorial Museum)

Zivia Lubetkin and Yitzhak (Antek) Zuckerman, founders and
leaders of the Jewish Fighting Organization, ZOB.
(Yad Vashem, Jerusalem, Israel)

General Jürgen Stroop (third from left) and his soldiers view the burning Warsaw ghetto. *(Stroop Report,* National Archives, Washington, D.C.)

SS troops burn the Warsaw ghetto during the Warsaw Ghetto Uprising.
(Bildarchiv Preussischer Kulturbesitz, Berlin, Germany)

Arrest of Jewish workers at the Brauer firm during the Warsaw Ghetto Uprising. *(Stroop Report,* National Archives, Washington, D.C.)

Jewish resistance fighters captured by SS troops during the Warsaw Ghetto Uprising. *(Stroop Report,* National Archives, Washington, D.C.)

sisted the Nazis during the deportation. But after their first en-
counters, it became clear that the results went much further.
There was considerable discomfort and anxiety among others
who had carried out German orders. Members of the Jewish
Fighting Organization soon understood that it would not be difficult for them to impose their authority on the various branches
of Jewish administrative personnel in the ghetto.

While the organization was establishing itself in the ghetto, its
representatives were contacting factions in the Polish underground attached to the London-based Polish government-in-exile
on the Polish side of the city. From February 1, 1942, a department for Jewish affairs was active within the framework of the
Polish military underground, the AK. Henryk Wolinski, a Polish
lawyer whose nickname in the underground was Waclaw, headed
this department. He was a sensitive man who understood the
distress and tragedy being suffered by the Jews.

It was only at the end of the great deportation that the first
contact between the ghetto and the armed forces of the Polish
underground was made. The mediator for the Jewish side was
Leon Feiner (known as Mikolaj in the underground), a Bund
member from the Polish side of the city. He requested that information be passed on to Shmuel Zygelbojm, a member of the
National Polish Council in London on behalf of the Bund. From
Wolinski's report, it was clear that during the expulsion there was
no regular contact with the ghetto and that nothing was done by
the Polish military underground to come to the Jews' aid. These
facts were in complete contradiction to the story invented by
General Tadeusz Komorowski ("Bor"), deputy commander of the
AK and later its chief commander. Komorowski claimed in the
book he published after the war that the AK approached the
Jewish leaders of the Warsaw ghetto through the person responsible for the Jewish department in the AK, offering their help in
operating a campaign of resistance. But the Jews rejected the
offer, and not having any alternative, the people of the AK then
decided to carry out actions affecting the progress of the expulsion on their own. Komorowski's account contradicted documented facts. It is not supported by Wolinski, and there is no hint

of any move of this kind or the planning of such an action connected with the deportation of the Jews from Warsaw or anywhere else in occupied Poland.

Moreover, in the report on his department's activities, Wolinski states that in October 1942 he met, through the members of the Polish scout movement, with Jurek (Arieh Wilner), representing the Jewish Fighting Organization in the ghetto. Wolinski points out that in their first conversation, Jurek mentioned that he had tried to reach the circles of the Polish military underground, and that at the height of the expulsion in August he met with an AK man on behalf of the fighting organization in the ghetto and asked them for assistance, but his request was turned down. Wolinski adds that he checked the facts presented to him by Jurek and found that Jurek's complaints were well founded, but that the person with whom he was in contact gave him a negative answer on his own and did not pass the matter on for an official decision.

Wolinski made sincere efforts to advance the recognition of the Jewish Fighting Organization and to obtain arms. On December 3, 1942, he submitted a memorandum to his superiors informing them that a representative of the Jewish Fighting Committee, Wilner, and a representative of the Bund, Feiner, coordinated their positions and both of them were presenting the Jewish matter to the underground authorities. The two stressed the necessity of supplying arms to the Jewish Fighting Organization *without delay,* for they were in no doubt that the destruction of the ghetto had not come to an end and would be renewed at any moment.

The code of the Jewish Fighting Organization in which its principal aims were laid down was also submitted through Wolinski — that is, the organization of the Jewish public in preparation for the anticipated annihilation of all remaining Jews and the elimination of German agents from within. The names of the parties and movements united within the fighting organization were also included. Wolinski stresses that the document handed over by the organization was passed on to the chief commander of the AK, Stefan Rowecki — "Grot" — who confirmed that he had received it and praised the Jewish will to fight.

According to Wolinski, as a result of the urgent requests of the ZOB, ten pistols and a small quantity of ammunition were given them by the high command of the AK in December 1942. Wolinski claims that "these weapons were in a very poor condition and were only partially usable." The ZOB viewed this gesture as far from satisfying their most basic needs and continued to demand increasing help in the way of arms. Their requests led to the receipt of ten additional pistols and a small quantity of explosives.

The connections with the Polish underground raise a number of questions. Why did AK recognition and assistance to the Jewish Fighting Organization encounter so many obstacles, and why was the assistance so limited? The AK was constantly concerned with increasing its arms stocks, but the quantities agreed upon were minuscule compared to the reserves of arms at its disposal. Undoubtedly, its stinginess stemmed from other sources. One of them was that the officers of the AK did not consider the Jews capable of preparing themselves for armed resistance. Another reason was the suspicious attitude that Jews were potential Communists, and still another reason was the fact that the AK's political and strategic aims were mainly directed toward activating the Polish forces at the end of the war, and not toward stirring up the atmosphere in Warsaw or encouraging the creation of another focus of fighting in the city.

These two arguments are contradictory, however, for if the Jews were not thought highly of as fighters, there was no reason to believe that their resistance would actually take place or have any effect.

More than anything else, however, the AK decision reflects the alienation between Poles and Jews and the indifference of the Polish forces toward the Jews. As we have seen, Polish society was not identical to the Polish state. Although Jews were citizens of the Polish state and had lived in Poland for centuries, they were social outsiders. They did not belong to the national-ethnic-religious partnership encompassing the Polish nation, and therefore underground institutions did not feel the need to accept responsibility for their fate. They did not belong to what sociologist Helen Fein has called the "universe of common obligation."

This attitude was not common to *all* Poles. Quite a few were deeply affected by the catastrophe endured by the Jews and wanted to help them for purely humanistic reasons and also because they considered the Jews part of Polish society. In general, many saw the fate of the Jews under the Nazi regime as a warning. They feared — and not without reason — that after the Germans completed their annihilation of the Jews, the Poles would be next.

One can understand General Stefan Rowecki's own attitude from a broadcast sent to London in 1943, which contained this passage relating to the Jews:

> After all, Jews from all sorts of organizations, including the Communists, approach us and ask for arms, as if we had arsenals full of weapons. As an experiment, I gave them some pistols. I'm not certain they will use these weapons at all. I shall not give them additional weapons for you know that we ourselves have none. I am awaiting a new shipment. Please inform me what connections the Jews have with London.

In one of his orders, Rowecki explained that if the Germans take steps against the Poles in order to annihilate them en masse — which does not really fit in with their basic proclivities but is not exactly out of the question — then without taking into consideration that the hour for the Polish uprising was not ripe as yet, the forces of the underground army should begin a massive resistance action "to defend the lives of our people." This decisive stand was expressed in regard to Poles, but did not include Jewish citizens.

Wolinski's department was involved with the establishment of a cell called Zegota whose purpose was to save Jews who lived among the Poles. In his book on rescuing Jews, Wladyslaw Bartoszewski, who participated in Zegota, mentions a number of individuals who were its founders, among them Wolinski. This group earned much credit for aiding persecuted Jews existing in the Polish underground in Warsaw and some other cities. Zegota was an enterprise set up by various organizations and members of Polish Catholic and democratic circles in the autumn of 1942.

Only at the beginning of 1943 did the underground take the group under its aegis for political motives.

The organization of Zegota was unique, but the underground leadership limited Zegota's field of action solely to rescue. It did not permit the group to deal with aspects of political opposition and aid to the Jews in their anticipated defensive campaign.

In the autumn of 1942, Jan Karski was secretly sent to London as an emissary of the Polish underground. Before leaving, he met with two representatives of the Jewish underground: Leon Feiner, of the Bund, and a second man, who, though not specified, was evidently Arieh Wilner, a spokesman for the Zionists. In London, Karski also acted as a faithful emissary of the Polish Jews as well. He met with public figures, statesmen, and the Jewish leadership in Britain, and afterward left for the United States. There he contacted and informed many leaders of the situation in Poland and was received by President Franklin Delano Roosevelt. Karski visited many cities and appeared at meetings throughout the country, repeating again and again his description of the situation in occupied Poland and the destruction of the Jews.

In his book *The Story of a Secret State*, published in 1944, this emissary, or "courier," as he was then termed, described his visit to the ghetto and what he was told there. The Bund representative told Karski:

Our entire people will be destroyed. Perhaps a few may be saved, but three million Polish Jews are doomed. This cannot be prevented by any force in Poland, neither by the Polish nor the Jewish underground. Responsibility lies on the shoulders of the Allies. Let not a single leader of the United Nations be able to say that they did not know that we were being murdered in Poland and could not be helped, except from the outside. . . .

Tell the Jewish leaders that this is no case for politics or tactics. Tell them that the earth must be shaken to its very foundations. The world must be aroused. Perhaps, then it will wake up, understand, perceive. Tell them that they must find the strength and courage to make sacrifices no other statesmen have ever had to make. Sacrifices as painful as the fate of my dying people, and as unique . . . We are organizing a defense of the ghetto not because we think it can be defended but to let the world see the hopelessness of our battle — as a demonstration and a reproach. We are even now negotiating with your commander for the arms we need. If we get them, then one of these days, the deportation squad is going to get a bloody surprise.

Half a year after the mass deportations from Warsaw, the Jewish Fighting Organization decided to organize a public demonstration in the streets of the central ghetto, to take place on January 22, 1943, to arrest policemen and express their condemnation of these individuals for their part in the expulsion of Jews from Warsaw. Close to the event, placards were posted on the walls which stated, among other things:

Jewish Masses! The hour is close. You must be ready to resist. Do not go to your slaughter as sheep. Not even one Jew is to go to the train. Those who cannot resist actively, should display passive resistance. That is, they should hide. Our slogan should be: We should all be ready to die as human beings.

But there was no public demonstration by the Jewish Fighting Organization, and there was no sorrow and fury at the beginning of the expulsion. Just before the intended demonstration, the Germans began the second expulsion from the Warsaw ghetto, known as the January "action." Instead of a demonstration in the ghetto, the fighting organization plunged into its first street battle, which again became the *via dolorosa* to the *Umschlagplatz*.

10

JANUARY 1943: THE FIRST
INSTANCE OF RESISTANCE

THE SECOND EXPULSION, or "action," against the Jews of the Warsaw ghetto began on Monday, January 18, 1943, and lasted four days. It was not entirely unexpected. Those Jews who remained from the mass expulsion could no longer delude themselves. They knew that they were not to enjoy a prolonged or stable existence. The Germans would soon end the ghetto.

Information about the deportations and the complete liquidation of ghettos throughout Poland continued to come in from far and wide. Rumors concerning actions that were soon to take place in Warsaw spread rapidly throughout the ghetto. On Monday, January 11, Abraham Levin recorded in his diary:

> Our mood is very gloomy and depressed. News which reached us from various places indicates that the Germans intend to finish off the Jews completely. They will not leave a single Jew alive. This was the fate of Radomsko, and other places. This news is unbearably depressing. We fear that the new "action" here within our midst will be the last for all of us.

On Friday, January 15, Levin wrote, "As I have already mentioned an 'action' had been predicted for the 15th of this month . . . we can be content that the night passed peacefully, and today there is no news of evil or tragic events. We cannot but be in constant fear, since we are unable to help ourselves and to rescue the few remaining survivors when the day of destruction comes." The last entry in Abraham Levin's diary was dated January 16; with that entry, the diary and its author were silenced forever.

Units of the Jewish Fighting Organization and the remaining Jews in general began to prepare themselves to maintain a permanent state of readiness. Groups of workers and skilled artisans were taken out of the workshops to unknown destinations. Every report of movements by the German police on the Polish side of Warsaw, or a suspicious German move near the gates of the central ghetto, only intensified the nervousness. Mondays were the days that had to be watched, for this was the day on which the expulsions usually began or were renewed.

Nevertheless, the expulsion on Monday, January 18, was something of a surprise. The Germans had been occupied with snatching Poles and sending them off to Germany for forced labor, and it was assumed that with their resources stretched, the Germans would not be free to deal with the Jews. Ludwik Landau, in his daily notes, wrote at the beginning of his entry for the eighteenth:

> Warsaw [Polish Warsaw] passed through a horrible day. The snatches reached unheard of proportions. The pursuit went on in the street, the municipal trams, the intercity lines, the railway stations, in the railways and the churches . . . it is not surprising that the city was empty yesterday: There is not a soul in the streets, and the trams are empty . . . today the city was quiet. But rumor has it that the Germans are not stopping their efforts and that they are ordering cars for today and went off. That they are seen around town is explained by the fact that they have moved on to the ghetto. And indeed they have begun the uprooting again.

The action began when convoys of Jews from the Placowka outpost outside the ghetto were stopped at the exit gates and not permitted to leave the closed-off area. This was taken as a bad omen, and information concerning the barred gates and concentrations of Germans who were preparing to execute the action quickly spread throughout the ghetto.

At 6:00 A.M. the expulsions began. Armed Germans and Ukrainians, who were certain that it would be an easy job, tried to repeat the system they had used in the previous expulsion: they called out for Jews to come out of their houses and concentrate in the courtyards. But they soon learned that the ruse would not work. Jews were not prepared to obey their orders as in the past, and many work places were unoccupied.

The expulsion started in the central ghetto. Among those who were killed by indiscriminate and random shooting on the first day was Yitzhak Gitterman, one of the heads of the Joint Distribution Committee in Poland, a leading figure in the public underground and an active member of the Jewish National Committee.

Bernard Goldstein, an activist of the Bund in the underground, described the first moves of the January action in his memoir, *Five Years in the Warsaw Ghetto*:

> Suddenly, on the 18th of January, 1943, at 6 A.M., some of the streets in which the forced laborers of the workshops and factories still lived were filled with the sound of vile shouting, bursts of gunfire, and the noise of motorcycles and trucks. The wild beasts thrust their way into the courtyards and began to drag out, to brutally maul and fire on anyone who would not hurry to obey the order to go out into the street and form lines leading to the *Umschlagplatz*.
>
> The workers who were gathered at the assembly points in order to go out to workshops and factories were also taken to the *Umschlagplatz*, accompanied by shouting, blows and a rain of bullets. Neither documents nor permits were acknowledged.

Among those who turned up for work that day were members of the Judenrat, and some of them were also taken to the transports together with their families.

Some pursuers managed to surprise inhabitants of the houses and lay their hands on workers. Most of the people of the ghetto, however, escaped to hiding places that they had prepared in advance. Some were in improvised corners of their cellars, in attics, and in rooms disguised by cupboards or wooden walls.

Dr. Lensky wrote in his memoirs that

> on the days of the expulsion, the 18th to the 21st of January, 1943, a group of Jewish doctors from the hospital, together with their families, sat hidden in a room behind a clothes closet. Thirty people were in that room. It was in a part of the hospital situated at Gesia Street 6–8. Ukrainians entered the place. Their colleagues had already taken the sick and some of the staff to Treblinka. When they saw that there was no one in the place, the Ukrainians hurried to fill their pockets with whatever they could lay their hands on. They sought watches, jewelry, gold and similar items. Approaching the closet behind which the people were hidden, they extracted drawers and took various items away with them.
>
> The people in hiding behind the closet could hear the Ukrainians' voices and their every movement during their search. Fear penetrated deeply into the hearts of individuals hiding there, for there were some old people and little children in the place. The slightest movement, sneeze or cough could have given them away. But the Ukrainians who were busy plundering the place did not suspect that in the hideaway behind the closet the hearts of 30 Jews were beating madly. . . . Of course, camouflage of this kind was inadequate and insecure.

The surprise German move against the ghetto had prevented the national committee from meeting and discussing whether the time was ripe for resistance action. Armed companies could not coordinate their steps. So they sprang into action independently.

The first shot was fired by Arieh Wilner when the pursuers penetrated a dwelling of members of the Jewish Fighting Organization in the vicinity of the OBW on Mila Street; the first battle in the ghetto was led by Mordecai Anielewicz. His plan was a simple one. Anielewicz chose a dozen fighters with pistols and stood prepared for the struggle. The fighters were to join the lines going to the *Umschlagplatz*, and at a certain point on the way

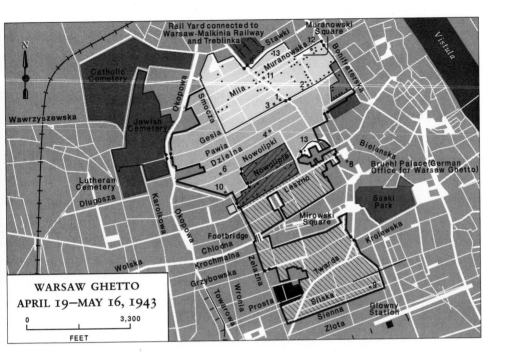

WARSAW GHETTO
APRIL 19–MAY 16, 1943

0   3,300

FEET

LEGEND

——	Ghetto Boundary July 22, 1942	1 Jewish Council (Judenrat)
——	Reduced Ghetto	2 Jewish Police
▦	Main Ghetto	3 Gesiowka-Jewish Prison
▨	Area Unoccupied, Jews in Hiding	4 Pawiak Prison
▨	Area Resettled by Poles	5 *Umschlagplatz* (Assembly Point and Transfer Office)
■	Brushmakers' Shops	6 Hiding Place of Ringelblum Archives
■	Ghetto Factory Area: Többens, K. G. Schultz, Rorich, Hoffmann, Schilling	7 Czyste Hospital, Deportation Center
■	Central Ghetto Factory Area, Többens	8 The Great Synagogue
□	January 1943 Revolt	9 Korczak Orphanage
•	Bunkers & Fighting Points April–May 1943 Revolt	10 Deportation Office (*Befehlsstelle*)
↔	Entrances, Gates to Ghetto	11 ZOB Headquarters
■	Selected Features (Ghetto Public Institutions)	12 ZZW Headquarters
		13 SS *Werterfassung*

and at a given signal, they were to burst out of the lines and attack the German guards escorting the queue.

Thus, members of the group entered the long line of hundreds concentrated on Mila Street, and at the corner of Zamenhof and Niska, near the transports, the signal was given and the battle began. Each Jewish fighter assaulted the nearest German. Even on a one-to-one basis, this was not a battle between equals. The Jews were armed with a few pistols and limited ammunition, while the Germans had semiautomatic rifles and ample ammunition.

The Jews had the momentary advantage of surprise and exploited it fully. After a few minutes, the Germans recovered from the shock of being attacked, and the initial forces were soon augmented by reserves. Most of the Jewish fighters fell in battle.

The battle was a decisive one. The hundreds of Jews who had been standing in the lines dispersed; the Germans saw that they were facing Jewish resistance, and the first Germans fell in the streets of the ghetto. At the same time, the Jews drew encouragement from the dust of the battle, and many ghetto dwellers adopted whatever means of passive resistance possible in the circumstances — that is, not to obey the German orders, to hide, and to evade deportation.

Two days after the battle, Berlinski wrote a few brief sentences on his meeting with Anielewicz in Mila Street:

> Today I am again with the people of Hashomer. Mordecai showed me the weapons that were taken. . . . They had disarmed the Germans, taken their weapons, and already know how to use them. Mordecai described the battle on the corner of Zamenhof and Niska, when he and a group of those who were being pursued initiated the struggle. Some of the SS members were killed and wounded; others fled, leaving behind their caps and some weapons. Then the Germans set fire to the building where Mordecai and his group were concentrated. He managed to escape. I congratulate him on his victory.

Another group led by Yitzhak Zuckerman defended themselves from a house in Zamenhof Street. They had entrenched themselves in an apartment, and when the Germans entered to search, the fighters opened fire. The bravery of Zechariah Art-stein and Hanoch Gutman in this attack was particularly not-able. According to some of the participants, two Germans were wounded. At the end of this defensive action, in which a Jewish fighter was killed, the group retreated to a house on Muranowska Street. A conflict on a smaller scale also took place in the work-shop district.

January 18 marked a turning point in the existence of the Jewish Fighting Organization. The Germans had anticipated a smooth and simple process, but they encountered opposition and paid for it with casualties. For the first time, the Jew was no longer seen as a submissive victim.

Moreover, from that day onward, the Germans refrained from searching the dwellings and from climbing up to attics and down to cellars. The ease with which they had taken Jews was a thing of the past, and as they witnessed, to their amazement, one could lose one's life not only on the battlefield at the front but also in the narrow lanes of the Warsaw ghetto.

One cannot wholly understand the change that took place in the Jewish public's attitude without appreciating the impression made by the events of January 1943. Jews were no longer passive; they could fight back. Yitzhak Zuckerman concluded that "the revolt in January is what made possible the April rebellion." Without the initiative taken in January, the subsequent wide-spread revolt three months later would not have occurred. The mute acceptance of their fate and the sense of hopelessness that accompanied the mass expulsions in the summer of 1942 gave way to more defiant attitudes. Evading the Germans proved possible. The crisis and frustration experienced by the fighters in September finally disappeared. When a company of fighters met in Mila Street after the battle, mourning for fallen friends did not diminish the sense of excitement and achievement in bat-tle. They realized that their mission was no longer an impossible dream.

The Jewish Fighting Organization now appeared openly in the streets of the ghetto in January and freed those who were being led to the railway carriages, thus proving that its struggle was directed toward aiding all the persecuted Jews. On that day, the

Jews in the ghetto and the Jewish Fighting Organization became blood brothers.

A Jewish poet living in the ghetto, who had previously contributed light verse for public entertainment in clubs and cafés, wrote a poem entitled "Counterattack" about the impact of the events of January. The following are a few lines from the poem:

> Let us see, before the throat
> Stifles the last cry of woe.
> Their arrogant hands, their whip-holding fists
> Hold our tense fear — fear of man.
> From Niska, Mila and Muranow,
> Like a bouquet of blood-flowers
> The heart cries out from the gun-barrels
> This is our spring — our counterattack.

The second expulsion, the January action, was over in four days. From the second day, the Germans were obliged to invest enormous effort in catching the Jews. They succeeded only in catching the sick and the feeble, or those they happened upon accidentally. During those four days, some 5,000–6,500 people were taken from the ghetto or murdered. Taking part in the action were some two hundred German police and eight hundred auxiliaries from the Ukraine and the Baltic states.

On the last day, there was mass slaughter. In a hail of bullets the Nazis murdered a thousand Jews in the streets of the ghetto in apparent retaliation for the fact that the ghetto was no longer silent and submissive. SS Senior Colonel Ferdinand von Sammern–Frankenegg, police commandant of the Warsaw district, evidently did not report to his superiors on the dead and wounded among his soldiers resulting from the resistance in the Warsaw ghetto.

There is no precise information on the German casualties during the January resistance. The Poles spoke of dozens, but this is certainly an exaggeration. At any rate, ambulances were heard racing in and out of the ghetto. One can assume that on the eve of the last action in April von Sammern did not dare to enlighten his superiors as to the true situation in the ghetto and was not eager to reveal the events of January and the existence of the armed Jewish force in the area under his supervision. The mere fact that the Jews were capable of fighting and that the Jewish people could be considered an active enemy rather than a subhuman group ready for extermination was perhaps beyond the Nazis' comprehension.

Notwithstanding the mass murders and the thousands hunted down in January, the Jews assumed that the Germans were deflected from carrying out their plans and forced to stop the action midway. Jewish resistance, they felt, had led to the failure of the mass expulsion and the withdrawal of German troops from the ghetto. This perception was also shared by the members of the military forces of the Polish underground. Neither Jews nor Poles had any reliable information stemming from German or other sources. The Jews responded to what was happening around them, and thus they assumed that the second expulsion would be total. After the Germans managed to uproot some 300,000 people in one concentrated sweep, it followed that during the second round they would complete the process by removing all the Jews of Warsaw.

Zivia Lubetkin, one of the veterans of the fighting organization, wrote in her memoirs:

> The action in January continued only for four days. The Germans intended to do away with the entire Jewish population of Warsaw this time, but when they were confronted with armed and unexpected opposition, they stopped the "action." Evidently it did not seem to them befitting for Germans to pay with their lives for the death of the Jews of the ghetto.
>
> Now they decided to gain time to achieve this end by finding a new method of annihilation. They did not know that time was also working to our advantage, that in our second confrontation they would have to pay a heavier price.

The Jews assumed that the resistance had revealed the Achilles' heel of the German military machine. They also believed that the

Germans had been forced to recruit considerable forces for this action. From the German point of view, an outburst of street fighting could incite the Poles, who were thought to be waiting to get into the fray, and news of the resistance in Warsaw could not be hidden from the rest of the world, and would attract attention to their plight.

The Germans determined that the mass slaughter would continue as long as it proceeded smoothly. But when confronted by Jewish resistance, the Germans were halted. Filled with renewed confidence, the fighters mistakenly thought that the Nazis might stop the annihilation of the remaining Jews altogether.

The Poles were amazed at this manifestation of Jewish resistance, and the Polish underground press contained considerable praise for the Jews, discussing the difference between the lack of opposition of July–September 1942 and the events of January 1943. The central publication of the AK wrote that

> the brave stand of these people, at the saddest moments of the Jewish experience, who had not lost their sense of honor, merited appreciation of what was one of the most brilliant chapters in the annals of the Jews of Poland.

Moreover, it was not only the Polish underground press that had warm words of praise. In the eyes of the Poles, it was assumed that the killing of the Jews was carried out because the Jews did not display any opposition. The Poles did not fathom the significance of the "final solution" as a German plan to physically exterminate the Jews of Europe on the basis of allegedly ideological principles and political purposes.

A secret Polish periodical of Polish farmers, *Through Conflict to Victory*, claimed in its issue of February 28, 1943, that

> after the campaign of punishment, contrary to expectations, there came a momentary calm. The blockades and transports ceased. There is the general assumption that the reason for this stems from the armed resistance shown by the Jews, which made a deep and widespread impression.

Waclaw Zagorski, a prominent activist in Polish socialist circles and a friend of the Jews, pointed out in his notes from January 1943:

Opinions are increasingly confirmed that this form of Jewish self-defense is likely to bring about results. This is retaliation and armed resistance. For the first time, the Jews responded to the attempt to renew the shipments to the gas chambers in Treblinka with shooting. After three days the Germans withdrew their forces from the ghetto.

At the beginning of the first action, the resistance had appeared to many — including the "reasonable" circles of the underground — as a dangerous game that might hasten the deaths of those who could be rescued. Now, ironically, after a few months the resistance was viewed as a means of saving the remainder of the Jews. Thus, those who resisted were no longer seen as adventurous fighters who endangered the rest of the public but as faithful pathfinders whose bravery was the only possible response to an insoluble and utterly lost situation.

Only in Warsaw did the Uprising enjoy widespread mass support. In other ghettos where Jewish underground organizations had been active, such as Vilna and Bialystok, the masses had not taken to the idea of fighting and did not join the fighters during their uprisings. Many were impressed by the young people who were prepared to enter the fray, knowing that this battle could be their last and could end in utter disaster and death. Naturally, this manner of fighting — in which all those who participate are prepared to die fighting — attracted only the remarkable few, mostly young people who were responsible for neither their parents nor their children. Parents with children consistently clung to any solution or glimmer of hope, and when in the end they were without hope, they accepted their fate. In Warsaw, in the time between the first mass expulsions and the final destruction of the ghetto, the resolve of the fighters and the distrust of other ghetto residents hardened. The Jewish masses saw no grounds for hope except through fighting. Even if their perceptions were misleading, many were provoked to strong-willed actions.

Why did the Germans withdraw? Were the assumptions of the ghetto fighters correct? The weight of historical evidence contradicts the conclusion arrived at by Jews and non-Jews during January 1943. Some days before January 18, Himmler was in Warsaw and visited the ghetto. He issued a series of orders relating to the Jews. The head of the SS surveyed the town from his armored car, angered that the eradication of the ghetto had not been carried out as he had ordered. On the eleventh of the month, he wrote to Wilhelm Krüger, who headed the SS and the police in Cracow, complaining that forty thousand Jews remained in Warsaw, and revealing his decision that within a few days some eight thousand Jews would be "erased."

The local authorities had evidently chosen not to inform their commander that more than fifty-five thousand Jews remained in Warsaw, in order to limit his anger. They had not executed his expulsion plan in full, leaving far more Jews than the 10 percent he had permitted to remain.

Himmler was also displeased with the many workshops privately owned by Germans, which he saw as attempts to profit under the guise of exploiting Jewish labor. He was especially vexed by the example of the large Többens workshop. In a letter Himmler wrote:

> If I am not mistaken, this is a case of a person who had nothing, becoming tremendously wealthy, if not a millionaire, within three years and this was made possible simply because we, the state, placed cheap Jewish labor at his disposal.

Himmler recommended transferring the sixteen thousand Jews occupied in the production of munitions to the vicinity of Lublin.

Thus, from its inception the second expulsion was not planned as a campaign of total annihilation of the ghetto, as the Jews had assumed, but as a correction and completion of the first expulsion. The Germans prepared themselves for a partial evacuation, which was also not executed in its entirety. It is indeed possible that the Jewish resistance played a part in this failure to fulfill the German plan. It is not known whether Himmler was informed of the armed struggles during the second action, or whether the decision to wipe out Jewish existence in Warsaw completely was conceived during his visit without any connection to the January expulsion and the incidents of resistance.

But on February 16, Himmler sent an order to Krüger from his field headquarters which stated:

> For reasons of security, I am ordering you to destroy the Warsaw ghetto after transferring the concentration camp from there. At the same time, all building parts and materials of any kind which can still be used are to be preserved.
>
> The destruction of the ghetto and the transfer of the concentration camp is essential, otherwise we shall not succeed in getting Warsaw into a calm state and as long as the ghetto is standing, it will be impossible to wipe out the crime. A general plan for the destruction of the ghetto should be submitted to me, and in any case, we must arrive at the stage in which the residential area, which exists at present for 500,000 sub-humans [*Untermenschen*], and which had never been suitable for the Germans, will disappear from the face of the area, and the city of Warsaw, with its million inhabitants, which has always been a center of agitation and rebellion, should be reduced in size.

In the not quite three months between the January and April expulsions, when the remaining Jews of Warsaw were to be uprooted and the ghetto erased from the face of the earth, preparations were well under way for the approaching resistance and final struggle — the Warsaw Ghetto Uprising.

The German authorities faced a very complex task in the utter annihilation ordered by Himmler. Jews in the ghetto were completely unaware of the bureaucratic struggles among German authorities. The SS was intent on pursuing the war against the Jews. The Wehrmacht was interested in the task of conducting World War II. While the SS was intensely ideological, the army was far more pragmatic. There were sharp differences between the commanding forces of the Wehrmacht in the General Government and the heads of the SS. The Wehrmacht had been promised a substantial number of Jewish workers. In addition, Jewish workers were employed in the munitions factories and other enterprises supplying such necessities as clothing, shoes, beds, and other items to the German armies. As a result of the murder of the Jews, the Jewish work force was gradually reduced, which led the Wehrmacht to complain that more and more Jews were being taken and that the production lines were being halted.

At the outset of the annihilation process, the Wehrmacht command in the General Government was not aware of the extent and substance of this manufacturing process. Still, in May 1942 the branch of the Wehrmacht responsible for munitions planned to replace the skilled Polish and Ukrainian workers with one hundred thousand Jews. Moreover, the munitions department intended to expand the manufacture of clothing and shoes within the General Government and thus relieve the burden of production in the Third Reich. Jewish workers were essential to this reconfiguration of the labor force.

On July 17, 1942, some days before the mass expulsion from Warsaw, Krüger had informed the Wehrmacht of the policy regarding the annihilation of the ghettos, a situation that would not permit any Jewish work force. At the same time, the SS asked the railway management to arrange for a sufficient number of freight trains.

On July 28, Albert Ganzenmüller, who ran the German railways, confirmed that "from 22 of July, there is a daily train carrying some 5,000 Jews from Warsaw through Malkinia to Treblinka." From the width and breadth of the General Government, reports reached the munitions department that the Jews were being taken away from the production process without any prior warning, and as a result the factories could not fulfill their obligations. The munitions branch tried to make certain that the Jews most needed in the production lines would not be expelled, and in Warsaw the agreement of the SS was obtained to the effect that the Jews employed in production for the war effort would be concentrated in a workers' ghetto, separated from the rest of the Jews.

It was evidently on the basis of this obligation to provide materiel to the Wehrmacht that after the mass expulsion the Germans concentrated the workshops and large enterprises in smaller ghettos, but, nevertheless, the uprooting of the Jews, including those defined as necessary workers, continued. Some six thousand Jewish workers in Warsaw were considered essential and were employed under the aegis of the munitions branch. In September 1942 the general field marshal and chief of staff of the high command of the armed forces, Wilhelm Keitel, ordered that the Jews be replaced by Polish workers. But this order could not alleviate the labor shortage because the Poles who could be recruited for this purpose, either voluntarily or otherwise, had been sent to Germany as forced laborers to work on farms or in German industry.

During the second half of September, the commander of the Wehrmacht forces in the General Government, General Curt Ludwig von Gienanth, sent a sharply worded letter to the high command of the Wehrmacht in which he pointed out the repudiation of their promises about the Jewish workers. He stated that the evacuation of the Jews caused difficulties and delays in the orderly production of munitions, preventing the most urgent work from being executed in time. Gienanth also noted that it was particularly difficult to replace skilled workers, given problems and the loss of time in training new workers. According to information from reliable sources in the SS, the Jews constituted three hundred thousand of the one million skilled workers in the General Government, including one hundred thousand experienced workers. In fact, the workers making winter clothing in the textile factories were all Jews. Gienanth claimed that as a result of the expulsion of the Jews, "the heavy pressure on the military potential of the Reich would immediately reduce the supplies to the front and the forces in the General Government."

We have no information as to what happened after this letter was delivered to Himmler, but three weeks later General Gienanth was dismissed from his position. There were no protests or complaints from the Wehrmacht on humanistic, ideological, or political grounds. Complaints were purely pragmatic, centering on the Wehrmacht's needs and the difficulties that the expulsion of the Jews caused to the production process.

Friction on these issues was discussed at high levels. In December 1942 Hans Frank, head of the General Government, decided at a meeting of his "government" that "clearly the situation in the labor field was aggravated, if at the height of the war effort, an order is issued to prepare the annihilation." Friedrich Wilhelm Krüger, SS general and chief commander of the SS and the police in the General Government, and Himmler's confidant in the Frank government, went even further in expressing his opinion.

On May 31, 1943, after the rebellion and the destruction of the ghetto, a conference on matters of security took place in Cracow, attended by Frank, Krüger, and Ernst Kaltenbrunner, the general in the SS who had replaced Heydrich in the Reich Main Security Office (RSHA). Krüger began by emphasizing the advantages and benefits derived from clearing the area of Jews. He then said:

> Recently we received a repetition of the order to carry out the clearance of Jews within the shortest possible time. Therefore, the Jews must also be taken out of the munitions industry and related economic enterprises. Until now, only Jews working for the war effort were left. These Jews were concentrated in large camps and were daily taken to work in the above-mentioned enterprises. But the wishes of the SS Reichsführer [Himmler] is that these Jews should stop working . . . I have studied the matter thoroughly with Lieutenant-General Schindler [responsible for armaments in the General Government] and it appears that [despite the wishes of Himmler] this is not possible because there are experts among the Jewish workers, skilled mechanics and experienced artisans in the various branches and it is difficult to find replacements for them among the Poles. [I] therefore address the Obergruppenführer, to kindly ask him to change his decision regarding the evacuation of the Jewish work force.

Shortly thereafter, Krüger was ousted from his position. It is uncertain whether the general decline of security in the General Government was the cause of his departure or whether his statement played a part in his dismissal.

In September 1942, the matter was argued in Hitler's presence by Himmler and the man responsible for the Reich's labor concerns, Fritz Sauckel. Hitler himself decided that, for the time being, the skilled Jewish workers should remain in the General Government. This situation undoubtedly forced Himmler, who had given the order to destroy the Warsaw ghetto, to maintain temporarily the Jews occupied in the munitions factories and to transfer them to camps set up for this purpose.

In addition, Himmler and the SS made every effort to establish their hold on the economy, especially in the field of munitions. If Jewish workers were to continue for the time being, Himmler saw to it that the workers, the factories, and the workshops were brought under the supervision or ownership of the SS. It was decided to transfer the factories and the large workshops to camps in Poniatowa and Trawniki in the Lublin region, which was the power center of the SS and of the executor of the death camps, Odilo Globocnik.

The task assigned to the SS and the police in Warsaw was not easy in light of the changes in the ghetto following the bloody conflict with the Jewish Fighting Organization. The Germans were obliged to separate the inhabitants of the ghetto from the workers in the factories designated for transfer to the work camps and convince them to move to the new location. The SS also had to see that equipment and materials in the ghetto were transferred to work camps.

To execute this plan, they behaved with comparative restraint toward the Jews, making promises and offering concessions. Walter Többens, the owner of the largest factory in the ghetto and the target of Himmler's sharp criticism and suspicion, was appointed commissar of the transfer action. He had to persuade the Jews that this was a transfer to another working location and not an expulsion to a death camp.

Some twenty thousand Jewish workers were to be transferred

to the work camps and Többens signed a contract under which the factories would be evacuated and supervised by the SS, while production supervision would remain in the hands of the former owners.

One doubts whether the German entrepreneurs trusted the SS assurances that these newly located enterprises were ensured a certain permanence. More likely, this proposal seemed desirable from their point of view and provided some confidence that they would retain the enormous capital they had accumulated through the exploitation of Jews.

At the beginning of March 1943, Többens announced the departure of two clothing workshops, but of 1,600 workers only 280 appeared for transport, and some of them escaped while still in the transport queues. The Germans pursued and detained them under the supervision of the workshop guards, but members of the ZOB managed to extricate 60 of the detainees. The plan for transferring workers from the area of the brush workshops ended in failure. Out of 3,600 workers, only 30 turned up.

In the second half of March, two transports of workers from the workshop area of the ghetto were transferred to the camps in Poniatowa and Trawniki. Jewish foremen returned to the ghetto and confirmed that indeed this was not an expulsion but a move to a working camp. Többens claimed that the new location would enable the Jews to live with their families, that the children would have proper schools, and that he personally guaranteed the safety of "his" Jews and of those who would agree to move. Despite his coaxing, after the first wave of evacuees, the Jews became more obstinate and would not volunteer.

The Jewish Fighting Organization addressed the workshop employees in a proclamation warning them that volunteering to move meant the destruction of the ghetto and the annihilation of the evacuees. On March 20, Többens entered the battle of proclamations, retaliating with a proclamation of his own. In this manner, the German responsible for the transfer conducted an open controversy with the Jewish Fighting Organization on the walls of the ghetto. Többens declared:

The last transport was not put to death . . . Jewish munitions workers! Do not listen to those who wish to mislead you. They want to incite you into actions which may have unavoidable results.

Többens claimed that there was no security in the "shelters" or hiding places and no safe refuge among the Poles on the Aryan side. It was a fact, he added, that the Jews with money returned from the Aryan side because they could not abide what awaited them there, and they now wanted "to be among the transferred." Finally, Többens suggested that Jews put their trust only in the heads of the enterprises being transferred to the work camps of Poniatowa and Trawniki, and advised them to take their wives and children with them. (In fact, the Jews who were transported to these camps before the final destruction of the ghetto were murdered in a mass slaughter that took place in the Lublin area in November 1943 — the slaughter known as "the harvest festival.")

In addition to the transfer of Jews to the work camps, the German owners of the workshops and factories surreptitiously, but not always successfully, moved the equipment and stocks of materials to these camps. The Jewish Fighting Organization used fires and other methods of sabotage to destroy equipment and materials that the Germans intended to transfer.

During this period, the idea of resistance was on the rise, although people with means and connections stepped up their attempts to find hiding places in the Aryan part of Warsaw. Amost every remaining Jew in Warsaw participated in the construction of shelters and hiding places and in the preparation of equipment for survival in hiding. The shelters were readied in cellars and tunnels beneath the courtyards of buildings. The more secure were specially built for hiding, on the assumption that the enemy would find plans for all the houses and could then follow the outlines of existing cellars to find them.

The work of digging and preparing the bunkers was mainly done at night, mostly in rotation by the people who were to share the bunker. The earth that had been dug out was buried in the ordinary cellars, in order not to leave any trace of the work. Those individuals who formed a group to construct a bunker were obliged to pay a large sum of money to equip it adequately to be used as a hiding place. The work was done cleverly and with a great deal of thought. Wooden bunks were installed, sanitary arrangements made, and considerable attention was given to the stocking of foodstuffs. Smuggling provided for foods that would last.

A good bunker linked up with the central water supply system of the city, which passed under the ghetto and ensured the flow of fresh water. This applied to electricity as well. The organizers of the installation and occupation of the bunkers were very keen on having a medical doctor among them and on obtaining a supply of medicines. The best bunkers were not only well equipped but also had a camouflaged source of air. Exceptional bunkers also attached to a tunnel leading out of the ghetto or to the vacant area between the no man's land and the inhabited ghettos. Much thought was needed to plan the disguised entrances to the bunkers, which had to be completely invisible from the outside. Some professionals took part in their planning and construction, and frequently experts were hired for the purpose. Every bunker had its guiding group to ensure its efficient operation.

The number of houses in which there were no bunkers were few and far between, but there were courtyards in which two or three had been installed. At any rate, everyone tried to have a place in a bunker, just as they had a place to rest their heads above ground. And indeed, near the beginning of the final expulsion and destruction of the ghetto, almost the entire Jewish population of the central ghetto had places in bunkers. Seemingly overnight, the ghetto, particularly the central area, had become a city on two levels — houses above ground, and cellars and tunnels below.

Between January and April 1943, the Jewish Fighting Organization was unified; the hierarchy of personnel and the strategic plans were laid down for the inevitable struggle. The period between the two expulsions was one of marked change and preparation for the last battle. The organization did not delude itself that its resistance would prompt the Nazis to give up the idea of wiping out the ghetto and to leave them alone; instead, the imminent annihilation required swift preparations since it was the enemy who would determine the date of the battle.

The Jewish Fighting Organization and the revisionist ZZW had learned a great deal from the January conflict. A German surprise attack could take place at any moment. As a result, after January, there was a hasty organization of fighting groups into squads attached to dwelling places, which also served as the central posts of their concentrated force. There they kept their personal arms and trained, maintaining an ambiance of semimilitary discipline. Members of the squads were forbidden to leave without permission from the officer in charge. Yet an atmosphere of intimacy and friendship existed among the young men and women who made up these squads.

Much of the time, the members of the groups kept busy reading books and discussing social or political questions. As some of the survivors of the ZOB have described, they resembled discussion societies rather than fighting squads. The food was simple — rationed portions of bread and jam, with the morning drink sweetened by saccharine. Lunch consisted of soup. They did not deviate from this rather poor diet later, when they commanded larger sums of money. The funds raised voluntarily or by force were dedicated to acquiring arms.

According to available data, there were twenty-two fighting groups composed of youth movement members. The Dror movement had five groups; Hashomer Hatzaír, the Bund, and the Communists had four groups each; while Akiva, Gordonia, Hanoar Hazioni, Po'alei Zion C.S., and the Left Po'alei Zion had single groups. Preserving the youth movement framework of separate fighting units was necessary in order to maintain continuity and to strengthen the bonds among the fighters. Many considered their membership in the Jewish Fighting Organization the natural culmination of the long path they had taken in the ranks of their movement.

At the same time, close relationships were established between the squads. They visited one another, and occasionally individuals transferred from squad to squad. Commanders of the squads were appointed based on the youth movments they belonged to, but their appointments were founded on seniority rather than on ideological convictions or intellectual qualities, as they had been in the past.

The ghetto was divided into three sections: the central ghetto, the large workshop area, and the brushmakers' area. The central ghetto was the primary focus of the organization, and its head-quarters, led by Mordecai Anielewicz, was entrenched there. The commander of the local force, which consisted of nine fighting squads dispersed throughout the area, was Israel Kanal. In the workshop area, eight squads were led by Yitzhak Zuckerman, and in the brushmakers' area, five squads were under the command of Marek Edelman.

During the organization's formation, a strategic plan was developed that proved to be of great importance during the armed conflict. The members had no military experience and lacked understanding or knowledge of fighting methods, least of all military maneuvers in urban surroundings. Having no alternative, they had to base their strategy on a thorough knowledge of the area and on their recent experience. From the events of January, they knew that the organization could not engage in hand-to-hand battles in the streets or squares of the ghetto, as these would be decided by the crushing force of the Germans. In January this technique had worked, and changed the mood and stand of the ghetto, but in a calculated struggle over a period of time, different methods were required, including the deployment of forces in many places which could exploit the area and the element of surprise.

The organization's strategy was based on the reality of the situation. The houses in the ghetto were almost of equal height, between three and five stories, topped with tiled roofs that formed triangular attics. Between the roofs, passages were formed with ladders. At first, this route allowed for surreptitious movement from house to house. Over time, these passages were improved and became an element in the action plan. It was possible to appear at posts near the attics or the upper stories without moving about in the streets and to withdraw without being seen by the forces in the street. Clearly, in the familiar alcoves, on the narrow ladders, in the corners and crevices, the fighters had a marked advantage over the Germans, who feared entering the dark and little-known maze.

Positions were chosen from which to open fire, overlooking the crossroads through which German forces would pass to enter the ghetto. The weakest aspect of the plan was the lack of arms. In fact, after the events of January, many Jews sought to join the group but were refused due to the shortage of weapons. But by the beginning of April, every fighter in the fighting squads was armed with a revolver. In the interim the Jewish Fighting Organization "cleaned house." There were two fields of activity: the punishment and the execution of people in the ghetto who had collaborated with the Germans to the detriment of the Jews or had helped the Germans to carry out the expulsion. Emanuel Ringelblum named thirteen who were shot.

The ZOB did not prepare for withdrawal, and hence the strategy lacked a basic component of an ordinary battle plan. This was not accidental. Fighters planned to fight and fall in the streets and the neighborhoods. At their first meeting, according to Henryk Wolinski, "Jurek," or Arieh Wilner, the fighting organization's emissary, said, "We do not wish to save our lives. None of us will come out of this alive. We want to save the honor of mankind."

Unlike the Jewish fighting organization in Vilna (FPO), which planned an escape route after the fighting in order to continue the struggle, the ZOB refused every option for rescue and survival. Nor did the organization participate in preparing bunkers for its members, or tunnels leading to the "Aryan" side. In these respects, its concepts differed from those of the ZZW (the Jewish Fighting Union), although the lack of documentation makes it difficult to determine what its plans were.

During the three months that preceded the fighting and the great rebellion, the Germans focused their efforts on removing equipment from the factories and transferring workers. In their desire to achieve these aims in a reasonable and calm atmosphere, they reduced their intervention in the internal affairs of the ghetto. When the German authorities approached the Judenrat and urged them to act firmly, Marc Lichtenbaum, who had replaced Czerniakow as its leader, stated that he was unable to do so, as the real power rested in other hands. And indeed, despite the regulations concerning secrecy, the Jewish Fighting Organization was the actual ruler of the ghetto.

11

THE END

T HE ANNIHILATION of the last remnant of the Warsaw Jewish community was not unexpected. On the day in April preceding the final "action," information reached the ghetto from the Aryan side of the city. Police sources reported that an assault on the ghetto was imminent.

The Nazis launched the attack on Monday, April 19, 1943 — the eve of Passover. Although the Jews feared that catastrophe was approaching and unavoidable, they did not forgo their traditional holiday preparations. Passover was still Passover even in the Warsaw ghetto in 1943.

On Sunday night, the Jewish Fighting Organization ordered the guards at the posts overlooking the ghetto gates to be particularly vigilant, and after midnight messengers of the organization began alerting the residents. This time, there was less confusion than during the January action. Everyone seemed to know what to do. They took the bundles they had prepared for this emergency and descended into the bunkers. One survivor recalled:

It was a sleepless night for the Jews. We packed possessions, linen, bedclothes, food and took everything down to the bunkers. There was an enormous amount of movement in the courtyards and streets on that moonlit night. [Passover occurs at the full moon.]

A fighter from a ZOB squad in the central ghetto recounted the fighters' preparations:

Standby orders were given in the evening, and passwords were changed. Now we knew the Germans were preparing for an action in the ghetto. All the fighters were given the same password: "Jan-Warsaw." We started to fortify the posts. The entrance gate was barred by an overturned wagon with its wheels facing upward. We took out cupboards and other pieces of heavy furniture from the apartment and placed them in the entrance way. The windows were shored up with sand-bags. People dispersed to their various posts.

Aaron Carmi, from the ZOB unit attached to the workshops, wrote:

Movement beyond the wall became easier to discern. We saw that the Germans were passing along the wall and were being assigned to their posts. A vehicle carrying soldiers would stop from time to time, at intervals of approximately 50 meters, and some soldiers would get out, and then the vehicle would proceed to the next stop. Eliezer [Eliezer Geller, commander of the sector] would then turn up and check the guards. We were ordered to increase the number of guards and await orders.

Marek Edelman, the commander of the brushmaking sector, reported that information reached them at 2:00 A.M. and "we immediately alerted all the fighters' groups, and at 2:15, that is, after 15 minutes, they took up their fighting positions."

The commander of the SS and police in the Warsaw district, Oberführer von Sammern–Frankenegg, had not reported that he anticipated opposition. Von Sammern was evidently unwilling to admit that a Jewish force had sprung up under his nose and was making it difficult to execute the mission assigned to him. His reports and instructions dispatched after the events in January, and between January and April, make no mention of possible opposition in the ghetto. The reports from that period made by the governor of the region, Dr. Ludwig Fischer, also do not mention any opposition or tension in the ghetto. Yet von Sammern obviously expected a confrontation, for he had assembled a larger concentration of police and army troops than had been used in earlier anti-Jewish missions, even in the massive expulsions of July 1942. Still, he was unaware of the scope of the opposition he would confront.

Himmler apparently had little confidence in von Sammern and sent SS General Jürgen Stroop as a reinforcement to Warsaw. Before coming to Warsaw, Stroop had been in charge of SS and police security in the district of Galicia, where he had earned a reputation for establishing order in a harsh and violent manner against civilian populations and partisans. After the war, Stroop testified that he had been called to Cracow on April 17, where he was told by the senior commander of the SS and police in the General Government, Friedrich Wilhelm Krüger, to report to Warsaw and there von Sammern would tell him his assignment. In fact, after the first hours of the first day of the "action" Stroop took over the operation and von Sammern was dismissed. In reports sent to his superiors, Stroop refers to the action as a *Grossaktion* (a large operation). Even after the war, General Alfred Jodl, head of the Wehrmacht command staff, ridiculed Stroop as a braggart. Sitting on the defendant's bench at the war criminals trial in Nuremberg, Jodl bristled angrily at Stroop's description of the action, calling him an "arrogant SS pig" for boasting for seventy-five pages about his murderous assault on the Jews. As far as the great battle against the enemy was concerned, Jodl's report covered merely a few pages. His criticism came after the war. During the action itself, Jodl's superior and the supreme commander of the Wehrmacht, Field Marshal General Wilhelm Keitel, awarded Stroop the Iron Cross First Class for his execution of the "Murder Expedition," as Jodl accurately described it.

During the ghetto campaign, an average of 2,054 German soldiers and 36 officers a day were involved. These forces included an SS unit (an average of 381 soldiers daily) and units of the police, regular army, and supplementary troops (335 Ukrainians and camp guards). Their arms included 1,174 rifles, 135 submachine guns, 69 light machine guns, and 13 heavy guns, a cannon, a flamethrower, and three armored cars.

The term *military might* could hardly be used to describe the puny force that faced this powerful German fighting machine. Almost without exception, the courageous soldiers of the Jewish Fighting Organization and the Jewish Fighting Union were young people who had no military training whatsoever. According to estimates, there were 750 combatants in battle units, some 500 probably in the ranks of the ZOB, and 250 in the ZZW. The ZOB carried revolvers of various calibers and kinds. Every fighter had from ten to fifteen rounds of ammunition and four to five hand grenades, mostly homemade. The organization also had some 2,000 homemade Molotov cocktails, 10 rifles, and one or two submachine guns that had been taken from the Germans, along with an indeterminate supply of ammunition. The ZOB had mined the entrances to some key positions in the ghetto area.

The ZZW fighters also carried revolvers as personal weapons. The ZZW had a comparatively greater number of rifles and machine guns, including a light machine gun that was used during the fighting. Information is unavailable regarding any home production of arms within the ZZW.

When the German forces entered the central ghetto on April 19, the streets were empty. Most of the inhabitants were in their bunkers, with entrances sealed and camouflaged. There the ghetto's frightened people resolved to conduct their daily lives with the order and discipline needed to survive under such conditions. The entire quarter was like a ghost town. Meanwhile, the fighters awaited the enemy in well-fortified and camouflaged posts. As far as is known, the Judenrat was not in contact with those German officials in charge of the expulsion.

After the war, Stroop claimed that he had no contact with the people in the ghetto, but it is possible that Brandt of the Gestapo and Konrad of the *Werterfassung* (the SS enterprise that stored and classified movable Jewish property) had such connections. In his postwar trial, Konrad claimed that he had merely been a witness during the last expulsion and had not been involved. A unit of the Jewish Police was active during the invasion, but it dispersed immediately afterward and was not seen in the ghetto as an active unit thereafter. During the initial invasion, however, police members were used as hostages to screen the first attack of the fighters, but they had no part in executing the action itself.

At about 4:00 A.M., the German forces began moving in battle formation toward the ghetto. The fighters followed the Nazis' movements closely and with increasing tension. What they saw was recorded in their notes. Simha Ratajzer-Rotem, who was in the brushmakers' area, wrote:

At 4 in the morning, we saw a transport of Nazis moving toward the central ghetto on the Nalewki level. Some thousands were marching without end. After that, some tanks go by, armored vehicles, light cannons and hundreds of people of the SS units on bicycles. "They move as if they are going to war," I said to Zippora, a comrade on the post, and I suddenly felt how weak we were. What am I, and what is our strength against this armed and well-equipped army, against tanks and armored cars, and we merely have pistols and at best, hand grenades.

Tuvia Borzykowski, who was with the group that took part in the first battle, had a wholly different perspective in his book *Between Crumbling Walls*:

At 6 in the morning the siege around the ghetto was already completed. The first units already marched on ghetto ground in the direction of Nalewki, approaching the triangle of Nalewki, Gesia and Franciszkanska. We did not wait for the enemy to be the first to start the slaughter, and from all our posts we showered a hail of bullets and hand-grenades and bombs. Well, our home-made efforts were not so disappointing; they went off as they should and did their work well, leaving many slain and wounded Germans on the streets.

It was our first confrontation, and the bursting bombs proclaimed and told everyone that the uprising has begun! . . . German companies separated into smaller groups. They clung to the walls, fearing to take away their wounded comrades lying about on the roads . . . the first moments of shock passed and the German response was not long in coming. Under the open skies, they were exposed to our fire. As for us — the wall was our refuge and protection.

The fighter Haim Frymer was in one of four squads of the ZOB stationed at the corner of Zamenhof and Mila streets, the site of the major battle of that day:

At 6, a line of artillery soldiers entered. Part of the line turned in the direction of Wolinska Street and another part stayed on the spot, as if they were awaiting an order. Less than an hour passed when the Jewish police came through the gate. They lined up on either side of the street and were ordered to begin advancing along the street in our direction. I would pass on to Mordecai [Anielewicz] and Israel [Kanal] an account of everything that was happening through the fighter not far from me.

When the line of Jewish police reached our house, I asked how I should react: Should I attack or not? The answer was to wait, that the Germans would surely follow them, and they were most likely to be the target of our first fire, and that's the way it was: The order I received stated: When you can find the center of the line near the balcony, throw a hand-grenade at them and that will be the signal to begin the action . . . the tremendous crash that took place within the line was an indication to start the action. Hand-grenades were thrown at the Germans from all sides, from all the posts on both sides of the street. Out of the sounds of blast and firing, we heard the sounds of the German *schmeisser* [nickname for the submachine gun] being used by one of the neighboring squads.

I, myself, remained on the balcony and fired on the confused and embarrassed Germans with my Mauser. From my balcony, I could see them in all their helplessness and their loss of control.

The air was full of wails and shouts. Many of them tried to run to the walls of the houses for cover but everything was barred and beyond that, death was pursuing them. In the noise, the fluster, and the cries of the wounded, we heard the astonished outcry of one of the Germans: *Juden haben Waffen! Juden haben Waffen* [The Jews have arms] . . . The battle lasted for about half an hour. The Germans withdrew and there were many corpses and wounded in the street.

The Germans who entered the ghetto had been forced to engage in battles for which they were unprepared. Massive German forces had not intimidated the Jews. The Nazis would have to wage a long and stubborn battle. Jews behind the walls of the ghetto had routed Nazi soldiers, at least temporarily, and for a moment one heard the sound of freedom and expressions of vengeance. Flags flew from the roof of a house in Muranowska Street, which was held by the ZZW, a Jewish blue and white flag and the Polish national flag.

The enthusiasm reached its height when the Jews heard the brutal Nazi soldiers cry in fear. Mordecai Anielewicz wrote after four eventful days:

Something occurred that is beyond our wildest dreams. The Germans withdrew from the ghetto twice. One of our companies held out for 40 minutes, and the second for more than six hours.

The unexpected resistance caused an uproar among the Germans, and led to von Sammern's being summarily replaced. In the daily report of April 19, Stroop described the failure of the Germans' initial assault:

Immediately after the preparation of the units — a planned attack of fire from the Jews and the terrorists on a tank . . . and Molotov cocktails were thrown at two armored cars. The tank burst into flames twice. This attack of the enemy caused our forces to retreat at first. There were 12 losses in this first action (6 SS men and 6 people from Trawniki). At approximately

8:00, there was a second troop action under the command of the undersigned.

In postwar testimony, Stroop offered more details about the attack and von Sammern's role:

On April 19th, at six in the morning, Colonel von Sammern began the action. He retained command . . . with my approval, as he had made all the preparations and knew the area. We agreed that I should come to the ghetto at about 9 A.M., for until then I was unfamiliar with the place, not having been there until then. At 7:30, Sammern appeared at my residence and informed me that everything was lost. The forces that had entered the ghetto had retreated and there were already killed and wounded . . . Sammern said he would contact Cracow and ask for Stukas in order to bomb the ghetto from the air and thus put an end to the uprising that had taken place. I told Sammern not to contact Cracow, and that I wanted to survey the situation where it had taken place.

Casimir Moczarski, a member of the Polish underground, had been arrested in Communist Poland and shared a cell with Stroop before his trial. Moczarski related how Stroop decribed the situation:

The telephone in the command room rang. Dr. [Ludwig] Hahn [an SS colonel and a commander of the security police and special services, the S.D., in Warsaw] arrived. I spoke to Krüger three times and once to Heinrich Himmler. They were enraged. The Reichsführer [Himmler], who had always been polite, used the most vulgar language again and again. They ordered that von Sammern be dismissed from his command immediately as well as from his function as commander of the SS and Police in Warsaw.

They demanded that all the units should be taken out of the ghetto and that within two hours the action should begin again under my command. I did not have to give the order to retreat for von Sammern's soldiers had simply run away. Dr. Hahn was quiet during this tension and spoke of the political outcome of the failure in the ghetto. Krüger, however, cursed and shouted over the phone, saying that it is a "shame," a political and military "defeat," a stain on the SS' good name, caused by "this intelligent doctor of philosophy from the Tyrol" [von Sammern] and that the "stupid fellow" should be put in jail, etc. He ordered that, after a new order was decided upon and things should calm down, all the soldiers and SS in Warsaw should be sent into action.

In response to his comment that they were worried about the mood of the Poles, who may make some move, Krüger said: "All the forces of the SS should be directed against the ghetto. In order to deter the Poles, an emergency call-up of the German units should be issued, to include the Wehrmacht, the Party, the Railways, the Post Office, the Guards."

According to Stroop's account, noted by Moczarski, Himmler was more restrained. He objected to the punishment of von Sammern, predicting it could result in difficulties within the party in Austria. Nonetheless, he ordered von Sammern's dismissal and placed all the forces of the army and the SS in the General Government on standby.

Stroop claimed that after taking over the command, he reorganized the campaign using suitable tactics for street fighting. According to Borzykowski, the battle started again in Nalewki after a lull of three hours. The Germans put up a barricade of mattresses and, thus fortified, concentrated their fire on a house in which some of the fighters were positioned. The mattresses began to burn, but the house also went up in flames and the fighters had to abandon it.

Strong firing was also directed against the large concentration of Jewish forces at the corner of Zamenhof and Mila streets. There was a stubborn fight. The Germans' heavy arms could fire accurately and systematically at the windows and entrances of the houses from a distance. The Jewish fighters returned fire, but their pistols were not made for such distances. The fighters of the

ZOB abandoned their posts for the bunker in Zamenhof Street. Only at 5:30 P.M. did Stroop arrive with supporting forces in the Muranow area, where von Sammern and his troops had been unable to penetrate during the morning assault. The ZZW force of the central ghetto was ready. The firing power of the Jewish fighters was strong. Their machine guns prevented a German advance in the open area, and a prolonged battle developed. Stroop claimed, "A special fighting unit subdued the enemy, penetrated into houses, but did not catch the enemy. The Jews and the criminals defended themselves everywhere, post by post, and at the last moment, escaped thorough the attics or underground channels." Summarizing the battles under his command on that day, Stroop said, according to Moczarski:

> We achieved the enemy's retreat from the roofs and from the higher posts to the cellars, or to the bunkers or tunnels. During the combing, only 200 Jews were caught. Afterwards special units were operated against the bunkers which we knew about, and they were ordered to bring out the inhabitants of the bunkers and destroy the bunkers. In this action, some 380 Jews were caught. It appears that the Jews were in the sewerage tunnels.

The ZOB lost only one fighter on the first day of the struggle — a man known only as Yehiel, who belonged to Mordecai Grobas's squad. The ZZW had many more losses, including one of the commanders, Eliahu Halberstein. According to Stroop's report, one German was killed and thirty-two wounded, including twenty-four SS men, two gendarmes, six men from the supporting forces, and two Polish policemen.

There was more to the Germans' failure on April 19 than heavy fire, withdrawal, and their inability to capture the fighters. The Germans had expected to need just three days to capture the remaining Jews, almost the entire Jewish population of the central ghetto, and to transfer 16,000 temporary Jewish workers to the work camps, as well as to take over the equipment and materials stored throughout the ghetto. On the first day of the Uprising, however, they caught only 580 Jews.

In reality, the Germans had no intention of giving up their plans to eradicate the ghetto. Jewish resistance only inflamed their violence and determination. The Jew was no longer the downtrodden creature with whom one could do as one pleased. In this new confrontation the Jew was an enemy to be wary of; deporting the Jews would require a price in blood and lives.

While the Jews gave up the illusion that resistance would save them, they did not leave the bunkers either on the first day or in the days that followed. On the contrary, the fortification of the bunkers was an important element of their defensive campaign. At night, the ghetto was again free. People came out of the bunkers, and fighters appeared in the streets with their weapons. Even while the first houses had begun to burn, with no one there to extinguish them, there were displays of enthusiasm, and inhabitants shared their impressions of what had happened, most feeling that their desire for revenge had been realized. Sounds of explosives and shooting could be heard from afar.

In his memoirs, Borzykowski told of going to fetch an electric battery for his unit. On his way out, he found himself on the doorstep of the apartment of Rabbi Meisel, one of Warsaw's well-known religious leaders.

> When stepping into the house, I remembered that it was Passover. The first Seder. The glasses of red wine on the table brought to mind the memory of the Jews who were wiped out on the eve of the holiday. The Haggadah was read to the accompaniment of firing and bursting bombs of the night in the ghetto. Through the windows, the constant flashes of fire from nearby burning houses lit up the faces of those seated around the table in the dark room . . . when we parted from one another, the rabbi was very friendly and blessed me with success. "I am old," he said, "but you are youngsters; do not be afraid, fight and succeed. And may God go with you."

The commanders of the ghetto Uprising did not share in the exhilaration. German intentions were clear. The hundreds of Jews who were caught were too few to make up a transport so they were killed on the spot. Also, the burning of the houses indicated that the Germans' destructive wrath knew no bounds.

From the very first day of battle it was clear that the revolvers, the standard weapons of the fighters, were not suited to street fighting against an enemy equipped with fire-spitting semiautomatic weapons. A few days later, Anielewicz wrote in his last letter to Yitzhak Zuckerman, "You should know, the pistol is of no value, we almost did not use it. We need: hand grenades and rifles, machine guns and explosives." But it was too late, and the desperately needed weapons never arrived.

One wonders whether the experienced officers of the Polish underground knew that revolvers would be ineffective in a fighting campaign in the heart of the city. In his book *Those Seven Years,* Zuckerman recalled his first days as a representative of the Jewish Fighting Organization on the Aryan side. He arrived there on April 13, less than a week before the Uprising. After a few days, he met Henryk Wolinski, who was responsible for the Jewish department of the AK. Zuckerman found Wolinski to be sympathetic to the problem of the Jews but obliged to speak for AK's official position. Zuckerman wrote:

> He told me the harshest thing: he told me that a plan was being devised to transfer the Jewish Fighting Organization to the partisans. I expressed my astonishment at the idea. I told him that when we received their message that we must hurry lest the "salt will arrive after the meal" — I was certain that they were speaking of the updating and development of our mutual plans [initiated by Jurek] relating to the uprising in the ghetto. I told him that I understood there was a master plan, which was mainly [an attack by] the A.K. on the central ghetto when the uprising started . . .
>
> He said that they had reached the conclusion that in this period of increasing forces hostile to the Poles, they feared that should the uprising start in the ghetto, it would spread out beyond its borders . . . We knew the basic principles of their theory, which maintained that there is a major struggle between the two main powers: Germany and the Soviets, and that they must wait and see the outcome of this struggle . . . that Poland

had to wait and gather its strength, until the two powers bleed one another until they are exhausted. Then they [the Poles] would appear on the scene of battle.

On Monday, the twentieth of April, the major fighting arena was the brushmakers' workshops, the enclave of houses and partial streets near the central ghetto which contained about four thousand Jews, most of them employed in brush manufacturing. Five fighting squads under the command of Marek Edelman were stationed in the area, as well as a unit of the ZZW. The Germans quickly stormed those houses displaying flags. At the height of the battle, the ZZW commander, Leon Rodal, fell victim to the German assault. The Germans surrounded the central ghetto with weapons, including machine guns and light cannons.

In his daily report of April 20, Stroop indicated that he had decided to move the brushmaking industry out of the area, and consequently ordered its German manager to have the workers come forward voluntarily. It is likely that Stroop benefited from the agreement with Többens, who ran many shops inside the ghetto, and was supported by Globocnik, who headed the extermination camps in the Lublin area, first to relocate the factories to Poniatowa and only then to turn the ghetto into a field of death and scorched earth.

At 2:00 P.M., a German unit appeared at the entrance to the workshop area, detonating a mine and causing confusion and injuries. After an hour, the Germans retreated under fire from the Jewish fighters. An hour later they returned and tried to advance in small groups, moving along hesitantly. In the ensuing battle, the Germans rushed into the houses. Edelman described the scene:

We are suddenly surrounded in one of the attics. Nearby, the Germans are in the same attic and it is impossible to reach the stairs. In the dark corners of the attic we cannot even see one another. We do not notice Sewek Dunski and Junghajzer who crawl up the stairs from below, reach the attic and get behind the

Germans and throw a grenade. We do not even stop to consider how Michal Klepfisz jumped straight onto the German machine gun firing from behind the chimney. All we see is the cleared path after the Germans have been thrown out. Several hours later, we find Michal's body perforated like a sieve by a salvo from two machine-guns.

At 3:00 P.M. three German officers with white kerchiefs unexpectedly attached to the lapels of their uniforms called for a cease-fire and negotiations with the commander of the area. The Germans did not intend to negotiate with the fighters but only wanted a lull in which to persuade the workshop workers to make themselves available for deportation. The Germans evidently assumed that their strong show of force would intimidate the workers into agreeing to evacuation.

But according to Stroop's report, only a few Jews in the area responded: "Therefore I decided to evacuate the whole sector by force, or to blow it up." Thus, Stroop began the systematic destruction of the residential houses and of the brushmaking enterprise itself, arousing the considerable ire of its German owners. It is very likely that Stroop's extreme action, which consisted not only of the mass murder of Jews but also of the destruction of property that Himmler had ordered him to protect, was taken with his superior's permission and prompting.

From the very beginning, the campaign was described in articles and reports in the newspapers of the Polish underground. *Dzien Warszawy* (The Warsaw Daily), an underground paper published with the support of professional journalists and representing the Polish government in exile in London, wrote on April 20:

Considerable German forces which included battalions of the SS and some companies of the police, the gendarmes and supplementary forces, started a bloody action in the ghetto of Warsaw. Army troops and the blue Polish police [police in the service of the Germans] surrounded the Jewish quarter and the action began with a siege on the houses. The Jews hiding in the bunkers greeted the Germans with a concentrated barrage of machine-gun and pistol fire, and hand grenades. After a few minutes of fighting, at about 10 A.M., the attackers withdrew, taking with them their wounded (some twenty) and killed (seven) . . . It is impossible not to sympathize with and admire the Jewish population, who have set aside their passivity in order to carry on a heroic struggle which has no chance of succeeding, against the Nazi hangmen whose forces are a hundredfold stronger. We must express our deep and unspeakable revulsion to this battle of heavy arms being waged against a civilian population.

The next day, the paper reported:

The war of despair in the ghetto continues. The Germans have suffered many losses. Yesterday the Germans celebrated Hitler's 54th birthday. Throughout the world, in all advanced countries, the birthday of the head of government is generally marked by an amnesty. The Germans honor their leaders by the hangman's method — by the mass slaughter of Jews. . . . In the course of two wars, I participated in many battles. But none of them made such a moving impression as yesterday's. In the glare of the blazing flames, to the sound of the exploding field cannon and anti-armor fire, the throwing of hand grenades from the rooftops, the rattling of machine guns, the German sappers are advancing toward the Jews' fortified positions in order to lay mine traps. Flame-throwers were also used.

After these preparations, the German infantry moved to attack but from time to time were driven back by the Jews. I counted 15 dead and 39 wounded among the German soldiers in one sector alone. The Jews, using machine guns and a large quantity of hand grenades, are defending themselves with fierce bravery. Molotov cocktails are being thrown at armored vehicles and tanks. I witnessed a flaming tank from which its burnt crew was being extricated . . . yesterday, appeals appeared on the walls of houses bordering on the ghetto, which the Germans immediately removed, saying: Poles, Jews, we are asking for your help! Long Live Free Poland! The Germans called to all the Jews [of the ghetto] to appear at 6:30 A.M. at the *Umschlagplatz*. No one responded to the call. The battle continues.

Wiadomosci Codzienne (Daily News), published by nationalist right-wing circles, stated on April 22:

> The besieged are resisting stubbornly. They consist of some
> 20,000 armed men, led by someone named Jachman, a lieutenant
> in the Polish reserves. Even the women are fighting, pouring
> sulfuric acid, gasoline and benzine on their attackers. The Ger-
> man losses are quite painful. There are rumors that Soviet desert-
> ers have infiltrated into the ghetto where they are helping to
> organize the defensive . . . in the fighting in the ghetto, the cow-
> ardice of the SS people stands out, as they move "carefully"
> against the determined defense of the Jews.

Ludwik Landau, a Polish scientist of Jewish origin on the
"Aryan" side, who usually wrote in his diary dispassionately,
could not restrain the pathos in his entry of April 20:

> Life provides us with strange surprises at times. Now a war is
> being fought nearby, a real war, with shooting from both sides,
> setting fire to buildings, even with the aid of tanks and [small]
> cannons. In brief, "The War of the Jews," from which there are
> episodes which would merit the pen of a Josephus Flavius . . . a
> Jew bearing an automatic rifle is wounded and in the next mo-
> ment, the woman at his side takes over his weapon, and aims a
> round of bullets at the Germans.
>
> Alongside the walls, there is a group of SS men surrounded
> by curious spectators. A woman appears on the wall, waves a red
> flag and warns the civilians to leave and at the same time, a group
> of Jews move through the sewerage canals, throw hand grenades
> at the SS men and return to their posts by the same means. One
> or two tanks have been destroyed by setting them on fire with
> benzine, one of the cannons has been damaged. Vehicles full of
> dead Germans or wounded SS men were seen. Some prisoners
> were also taken by the besieged. Soldiers of the regular army
> were released while the SS men are being held.

Thus, amid many rumors and much exaggeration, the campaign was described by eyewitnesses and journalists. The entire

city was excited and amazed. To the confusion and embarrassment of German officials, Governor Hans Frank, who viewed
security as primarily the responsiblity of Himmler and his followers, sent a letter on April 20 to Hans Lammers, minister of the
Reich and Hitler's chief adminstrative officer, stating, "Since yesterday, we are experiencing a well-organized uprising of the Jews
of the Warsaw ghetto against which we must already use cannons."

If the Germans thought that the Jewish opposition would fade
after the first day, by the second day they soon realized they faced
a planned military campaign that encompassed all the ghetto and
the Jews. In the words of Ber Mark, one of the first to write about
the Uprising after the war, the "blitzkrieg" failed in the Warsaw
ghetto.

In earlier instructions, Stroop had been asked not to damage
the large area of workshops in and around Leszno Street. But on
the second day of the Uprising he encountered opposition in this
area. As a German army column accompanied by heavy equipment moved through Leszno Street, it was attacked by hand
grenades and incendiary bombs thrown by ZOB forces directed
by Eliezer Geller. A tank was hit and began to burn. In his report,
Stroop states that the area contained many nests of opposition
that prevented a nearby tank from passing through. Two units
were needed to subdue these rebels and clear the way for the tank
crew. In this operation, two SS men were wounded. The Nazi
forces burst into houses along the street where much of the
population of the workshop district lived. They destroyed everything in their path.

As reported by the AK, a group from the Polish organization
commanded by Captain Joseph Pszenny headed toward Bonifra-
terska Street to break through the wall and enable Jews to escape.
This was apparently an improvised plan meant to satisfy the
obligation undertaken by the AK command to aid the rebelling
ghetto. As this did not meet the needs of the Jewish side (Zuckerman does not even mention the action), and no simultaneous
move was coordinated with the Jewish fighters, it was no doubt
intended simply as a symbolic gesture. The Polish group was
equipped with mines and succeeded in getting near the wall with-

out interference. The area was full of curious Poles observing what was happening in the ghetto, which made it difficult to accomplish the task. Only one mine exploded, blasting a crater in the road but not damaging the wall. Polish police alerted the Germans, who exchanged fire with the Polish group. According to Polish sources, some Germans were wounded in the confrontation, as well as two of the AK fighters. On the same day, a group of men from the AL branch of the Communists attacked the German gun position opposite the ghetto in Nowiniarska Street. According to those involved, the gun was silenced and two German crewmen were wounded.

In his summary of the second day, Stroop reported that he sent 1,262 soldiers and 31 commanders into action and that nine bunkers were discovered whose inhabitants put up opposition. The special units caught 505 Jews, sending those fit for work to Poniatowa. On the second day, a group of 10 Jews, headed by a Jewish porter, Jacob Rakower, broke through the siege to a Jewish cemetery and across to the Polish side of the city. Most of the ZZW forces stationed in Muranowska Street also crossed over to the Polish side on that day, or the next, through a tunnel that had been prepared in advance. According to their reports, the fighters took the body of their commander, Leon Rodal, with them. Available documents suggest, but do not confirm, that the escape reflected a ZZW operational plan to fight with as much force as possible but, when the battle was clearly lost, to find ways of saving themselves. The group that escaped reached the woods on the outskirts of Warsaw where, either by betrayal or accident, they were met by a German force and caught.

There was a drastic change in fighting tactics on the fourth day. During the first days, the fighters conducted their attacks and defense from prepared and permanent posts. As the Uprising continued, however, the command evidently decided to use these positions as a base from which sorties and surprise attacks of mobile groups were to be conducted. The change in tactics was needed for two reasons. First, the Germans no longer moved in large groups but dispersed their units over the entire area, with only the heavy weapons stationed in permanent positions at some distance from the Jewish fighters. Second, the Germans had kindled a series of fires, and the conflagration was affecting the ghetto houses. The first fires actually had resulted from the Jews' attacks on the German barricade. The Germans made no attempt to put out the fires. From the third or fourth day onward, however, the Germans set fires sporadically, then began systematically burning all the houses of the ghetto.

It is unlikely that the fires were intended solely to get the fighters out of their posts in the higher stories of the buildings. Interest in eradicating the ghetto had already been made apparent in Himmler's instructions to destroy the ghetto after its systematic evacuation. Stroop's deviation from the original plan evidently stemmed from the Jews' stout resistance and the retreat of Jews to the bunkers.

It is astonishing that the Germans were unaware of the network of bunkers in the ghetto, in view of the many agents and traitors they placed within the ghetto. One can understand that the Germans were unable to gather reliable information about the underground and its preparations to fight, which very few knew about, but the construction of the bunkers was a mass phenomenon that went on in almost every house and, to a certain extent, quite openly in the central ghetto.

While the major defensive effort in the ghetto did not come as a complete surprise, after the war Stroop repeated the claim that the Germans had no knowledge of the bunkers. In a report summarizing the campaign for his superior in Cracow, Stroop said:

> The number of Jews taken from their houses in the ghetto during the first days was too slight. It turns out that the Jews hid in the sewerage canals and bunkers that were prepared especially for that purpose. During the first days, it was assumed that there are merely a few isolated bunkers, but in the course of the great action it became clear that the entire ghetto is systematically provided with cellars, bunkers and passageways. Each of these passageways and bunkers has an outlet to the sewerage canals. Hence, this allowed for undisturbed underground contact. This

effective network also served the Jews as a means of escaping to the "Aryan" side of Warsaw. We received constant reports that the Jews were trying to escape through the underground canals.

Soon, the focus of the campaign moved to the bunkers, which formed a kind of fortress for the remaining Jews. In the fierce "battle of the bunkers," the Nazis relied on fire. The area became a burning battlefield. During the day the sky was filled with smoke, and at night with an enormous wheel of fire.

On the third day, skirmishes continued in the streets of the central ghetto, and the German forces turned to attack the brush-makers' area, an attack that did not end until nightfall. In his April 21 report, Stroop stated that a reinforced battle unit of the Engineers Corps was in action in the area:

> After combing a large block of houses, where it was evident that there were a large number of underground passageways and bunkers, some 60 Jews were caught. Out of the 700 to 800 Jews living in this block, it was impossible to apprehend more of them, despite all our efforts. These Jews withdrew from cover to cover through these underground passageways while being fired on from time to time. I therefore decided to blow up these passages, if I could discover their whereabouts, and afterwards set everything on fire.

In his notes of the same day, he pointed out that "the enemy is fighting today [the Jews were now raised to the level of 'the enemy'] with the same weapons as yesterday — home-made explosives . . . this is the first time that women members of the Jewish Fighting Organization can be seen on the battlefield." A fighter from the brushmakers' district, Simha Ratajzer-Rotem, described the situation at the height of the Germans' massive attack:

> The fighters' stand was so determined that the Germans finally had to forgo the possibility of suppressing them by military

means and look for a new and seemingly more certain way of handling the situation. They set fire to the brushmakers' area from every side. For a moment, the flames enveloped the entire neighborhood, black smoke congested one's throat and irritated one's eyes. The fighters don't want to be burned alive, so we take the only chance left to us and decide to burst out of the ghetto.

Enveloped by fires, in flame-lit darkness, the fighters and the units filed out one by one, from passageway to passageway, from house to house, and from courtyard to courtyard, with the units covering one another. Reaching the stretch of the central ghetto was only possible through a narrow opening in the wall, which was guarded by gendarmes, Ukrainians, and the blue police. There were twelve guards alongside a two-meter-wide passage. Five units had to break through the narrow outlet. Ratajzer recalled:

> In shoes wrapped in rags to stifle the sound of their tread, under fire, and in a state of considerable tension, the units of Gutman [Hanoch], Gerlinski, Grinbaum make their way and pass through. Jurek Blones' group covers them from behind. When the first members of the group reach the street, the Germans illuminate the place. It seems that no one would pass through after this. Romanovitz extinguishes the light with a single shot. Even before the gendarmes managed to understand what was going on, all of us were already on the other side.

The fighters reached one of the bunkers in a house with many courtyards in Franciszkanska Street, in which the workers of the supply center were located. On the following day, as a result of a confrontation with the Germans in one of the attics of this house (this was evidently the first time the German forces penetrated a house after sundown), the house was also set on fire. Fighters from the brushmakers' block joined the fighting in the central ghetto.

Stroop was particularly interested in a mass evacuation of the Jews. On the second day, he noted in his report that he tried to persuade the larger enterprises (Többens, Schultz, and Hoffmann) to be ready to leave the following day.

> The man in charge of the Többens workshop took on the responsibility for leading some 4,000–5,000 Jews to the transport gathering point willingly. If the voluntary evacuation does not succeed, as in the instance of the manager of army supplies [the brushmakers], I shall also purge this part of the ghetto by force.

The owners of the factories did their best to convince the workers and even tried to get those who occupied key posts in the workshops to assist them. They argued that the destruction and slaughter in the central ghetto did not affect the workshop area, and that if the local population would refrain from joining the revolt, they would be taken to better conditions in Poniatowa, where a work camp awaited them under the supervision of Többens and other workshop owners.

On April 21, Többens, in collaboration with Stroop, issued an order addressed to workers in the large workshops in the principal factory area. This directive stated that "workers without special permits who will be found in the closed area after the evacuation, will be executed [on the spot] in accordance with military law."

In his report of April 21, Stroop claimed that "5,200 Jews from the former munitions factory were caught and were brought under guard to the loading station assigned to transports, that is, the *Umschlagplatz*." Evidently Stroop had some reason for saying that the Jews who actually arrived at the transport center voluntarily had been "caught." In reality, the major part of the transport had been slyly surrounded when they were assembling in the workshop area. There was, however, a real difference between the behavior of the people in the workshop area and other ghetto residents. The number of bunkers was limited in the workshop area, and did not suffice for all the inhabitants. In addition, some of the workshop employees assumed that they had an alternative not available to the inhabitants of the central ghetto. As occurred on more than one occasion during the period of Nazi domination, the Jews were victimized by fate and lack of understanding of the Nazis' methods. The Jews who were brought from the workshops in Warsaw to the camps in Poniatowa and Trawniki before and during the last expulsion were all murdered within a few months, in November 1943. Those who were taken during the final stages of the Uprising were not sent to Trawniki but to the concentration camp of Majdanek. After enduring immense torment in the harsh conditions of concentration camps such as Majdanek, Auschwitz, Mauthausen, Buchenwald, and others, only a few had the luck to survive the terrible "death marches" of the final stages of the war. Of these, some hundreds survived.

Stefan Grayek noted in his memoirs that after the transport of April 21, the workshop sector was no longer protected by the owners of Többens and Schultz, and, as with the rest of the ghetto, complete control of the enterprises was transferred to Stroop's soldiers. On April 21, Ludwik Landau wrote:

Warsaw continues to be the center of the struggle nearby — the Jewish-German war. "The Third Front," as it is commonly referred to. The emotional attitude to the fighting differs: Among some it is characterized by a sympathy for the Nazi victims who are bravely withstanding the Nazis; among others, the foreboding element of anti-Semitism in what is happening leaves its imprint. And perhaps the majority represent the view of the neutral bystander. But even among the indifferent or even antagonistic, one hears a tone of admiration and everyone is interested and even tense . . .

At night one sees increasing fires over the ghetto, one hears echoes of the rumbling sound of cannon . . . Today one saw, it is told, 20 tanks moving towards the ghetto. Georgian units were seen being transported there. And it is said that regular army units were being sent to this "front." The struggle is going on with unusual fierceness — at any rate, on the part of the defenders. One says that houses are changing hands a number of times in the course of the fighting, that the Jews hold their positions and continue the fight from the higher stories even when the

Germans are already in the lower stories . . . the beleaguered population has had their water cut off by order of the authorities, but there are wells in the ghetto area.

The worst aspect of the situation is the [shortage of supplies], especially of arms and munitions. One has to take into consideration that despite German efforts, contact has not been severed altogether and there are passageways and tunnels that the Germans do not know about. The optimists assumed that the ghetto would continue to defend itself for another few weeks, and there were those, it was said, who wished to stimulate the war front against the Germans. By the way, now there are said to be alleged German deserters there . . .

On the fourth or fifth day of the Uprising, the Germans strengthened their hold over the ghetto, and the Jews began going on sorties and fortifying their positions in the bunkers. In his report of the twenty-second, Stroop said:

The fire that had been burning throughout the night caused those Jews who, despite all the combing exercises, were still hiding under the roofs, in cellars, and other hiding places, to penetrate to the front yards of the blocks of houses in order to evade the fire in one way or another. Gripped by flames, the Jews jumped out of the windows in great numbers — whole families — or tried to wrap themselves in bedsheets attached to one another and the like. We saw to it that these and other Jews would be immediately destroyed.

Edelman wrote that with the change in fighting tactics, the fighters of the ZOB sought to

defend the larger concentrations of people hiding from the Germans in their bunkers. Thus, for instance, two ZOB units (those of Hochberg and Barak) transfer some hundreds of Jews from the blocked shelter at 37 Mila Street to 7 Mila Street during the day. This position, in which some thousands are hiding, succeeded in holding out for more than a week.

The fighters rescued hundreds of Jews whom Franz Konrad had assembled from the *Werterfassung* employees and tried to bring to the *Umschlagplatz*. More and more, from a stubborn attempt to defend the ghetto or part of it, the fighting was turning into a struggle over bunkers and isolated houses. The fires blocked the entrances and passageways and made the bunkers utterly useless. The arrangements made when the bunkers were set up had fallen to pieces, and Jews seeking a place to hide wandered despondently in the night with their last possessions wrapped in a bundle. The lack of fresh air, water, and edible bread caused many to collapse. In his last letter of April 23, Anielewicz expressed his sense of personal fulfillment and the feeling that he and his comrades had engaged in an event of historic significance on the brink of destruction. He wrote:

> I cannot describe the conditions in which the Jews of the ghetto now live. Only an unusually determined person could hold out. The remainder will die sooner or later. Their fate has been decided. In almost all the bunkers in which thousands are hiding it is impossible to light a candle because of the lack of air.

The most terrible calamity the bunkers had to endure was the fires. Most of the bunkers had been constructed under the houses in existing cellars or tunnels that were built for this purpose. The buildings were burned to their very foundations, and within the bunkers the concrete, bricks, and smoldering embers created a dreadful heat. One memoir described the events in a bunker beneath a burned building:

> We can think of nothing but a breath of air. The heat in the bunker is unbearable. This is not simply a burning heat. The seething walls exude odors, as if the mildew of decades was released and spread out under the influence of the temperature.
> I sit with my mouth open and everyone around me does likewise, with the illusion and effort that we are swallowing air. One does not talk in the bunker. When one talks, it is even more difficult to breathe. But from time to time there is shouting,

quarrels, nervousness and tension without end, and generally the quarrels are nonsensical. We have not eaten now for twenty-four hours. Only rusks can be gnawed at, and the water is still more or less possible to drink.

All the food supplies have been spoiled. The moldy smell has seeped into the food and it cannot be used. Some try to console themselves with the fact that when the house cools down, it may be possible to save some of the food stores. But the talk of cooling down is just an illusion. The house was burnt down two days ago and the heat has not only not subsided, but increases hour by hour. Everyone has taken off their clothes and no one gives a thought to the fact that the men and women sitting about are almost naked. . . .

This afternoon, an argument started which implicated almost everyone in the bunker. Someone went to the entrance, moved the hidden cover, and started to swallow the fresh air coming in from outside. To do this in the middle of the day was like committing suicide. The Nazis above us are poking around and looking for us — at any moment they may be just above our heads. Frequently, the sound of their heavy boots can be heard above us. They sniffed round, searched, and went off, without finding anything. But we know that many bunkers have been penetrated and we must be very careful. The sounds and stifling air escaping from the entrance can lead to our discovery.

The entire ghetto was ablaze. Thousands of people near physical and mental collapse — virtually on the verge of madness — not only maintained this way of life but viewed its disappearance as a great catastrophe. We know of no instances in which the inhabitants of an entire bunker capitulated. There were many cases, however, in which, when a bunker was discovered and the Nazis called to surrender, the inhabitants responded with bullets.

The Polish press ignored "the war of the bunkers," nor was there much evidence in the survivors' accounts that were sent abroad at the height of the war. In fact, even after the war, not much was revealed on the subject. Paradoxically, alone among those retelling the story of the Warsaw Ghetto Uprising, Stroop was greatly concerned with the campaign against the bunkers and the efforts required to conquer them.

On April 23, the fifth day of the expulsion, Stroop was convinced that the Uprising had come to an end. He divided the ghetto into twenty-four sectors and assigned a special unit to comb the sectors thoroughly. "The units were informed that the action would come to an end today," he reported, noting that the mission would have to be completed by 1600 hours. But his units encountered opposition from Jews using ingenious means to avoid falling into his hands. Again it was reported that Jews were discovered in the sewage canals and hiding in the wagons that took the dead to the cemetery.

The continued resistance forced Stroop to delay ending the mission until the following day. He again put twenty-four units into action, ordering them not to advance but to attack every corner of the ghetto area simultaneously. Such pressure was necessary, as Stroop put it, because despite the surrounding inferno, the Jews "preferred to return to the fire than fall into our hands."

On April 25, Stroop put together seven special units and issued an order stating: "A further combing of all the houses. Locate the bunkers, blow them up, and get hold of the Jews. Wherever there is opposition or it is impossible to reach a bunker, the house should be set on fire." Nearly all the special units concluded their missions by igniting large fires to force the Jews to abandon their hiding places. In all, some 1,690 Jews were captured, 274 were shot, and, as was the case earlier, hundreds more were buried in the blown-up bunkers or perished in the flames.

"According to my estimate," Stroop reported, "in addition to today's spoils, a large number of the bandits [a term used frequently when referring to the fighters] were caught together with the lowest element of the ghetto. The immediate destruction was not completed until sundown." And, he added, "there were also incidents of repeated armed opposition, and in one bunker three pistols and bombs were taken."

On April 26, Stroop returned to the original plan of the

mission and announced that the time had arrived to deal with the most stubborn Jews. Almost all the special divisions reported encountering opposition, which was silenced by setting fires and blowing up bunkers. The bunkers were often entered by force, and their inhabitants had not come out from under the ground since the beginning of the action. In a series of instances after a bunker had been blown up, the inhabitants were almost unable to crawl out. According to accounts of the Jews who were taken in this manner, many of the bunkers' inhabitants "went out of their minds because of the heat, the dense smoke, and the successful bombing."

Stroop no longer proclaimed that the action had been completed. Every day he noted the number of Jews who had been caught and sent away. The tally reached nearly thirty thousand on April 26, according to his estimates. The previous day he estimated his casualties of fifty wounded (twenty-seven of the SS) and five dead. On April 27, Stroop stated that "the outward appearance of the Jews who were caught indicates that it is now the turn of those who led the uprising. Cursing against Germany, the Führer, and the German soldiers, they threw themselves out of the windows and balconies."

On the same day, there was a report of a fierce battle in a house outside the area where Jews were permitted to live and where Jews had entrenched themselves. This report also mentioned the capture of a large number of Poles, including two Polish policemen who knew of the entrenched Jews. On the twenty-eighth, Stroop spoke about continuing the battle against the nest of the "Jewish Military Organization," reporting that a group of fighters again appeared in the area that had been searched earlier on: "In some places, there was strong armed opposition today as well, and it was broken up."

In the announcement evidently published on April 27, Zegota, the Council for Aid to Jews among the Poles, stated:

> The opposition of the Jewish Fighting Organization now continues for nine days, which at first was fought from defensive positions and has now adopted partisan tactics, and has made a tremendous impression among the Polish population of Warsaw.

The Poles now call the ghetto Ghettograd [after the prolonged siege of Stalingrad].

However, the dying ghetto did not have the chance that Stalingrad had. Neither supporters nor rescuers from the outside world, from other armies or from the population, came to aid the Jews. The Jews fought until the end in total isolation, accompanied by words of praise and pronouncements of encouragement — words, but no actual assistance.

On April 30, 1943, the Polish underground paper *Polska Zwyciezy* (Poland Will Conquer) reported:

> In the British Isles, on the American continent and countries outside the German hell, the flames rising above Poland are not seen — the symbol of the torture and suffering of man abandoned to criminals . . . Those of you on "the other side" *do not see or hear.* Every sound that reaches us from the burning ghetto affects our conscience and causes us pain. There, horrible crimes are beyond our comprehension. We read bulletins from the war fronts — from Africa, Russia and China, the Pacific. There, too, people are being killed, and acts of bravery and indifference to death go on. But there they are fighting and dying under different circumstances.
>
> In the battle going on behind the ghetto walls, people die "differently." This is a battle of the lost versus wild beasts of prey. One must read bulletins from this battlefield as if they come from the front of struggling humanity, in order that the soldiers of this front can be proud [of] their comrades-in-arms who are being killed today in the houses and streets of the ghetto. The smoke clouds over Warsaw cannot disappear without a trace, for then all that was considered courageous would also disappear and the horrors which cry out for vengeance would also vanish.

Similar sentiment was expressed in *Trybuna Wolnosci* (Freedom's Platform), the journal of the Communist PPR, in the May 15 issue: "The battles have enormous political significance. This is the most important expression of organized self-defense in the occupied countries." But there were also publications that, despite the tragedy of the last days of the ghetto, reported events in hostile and skeptical terms. A popular thesis was that the Communists and members of the Soviet army were directing the rebellion. Such falsehoods evidently found willing ears, for in June 1943 the minister of security of the Polish goverment-in-exile, General Marian Kukiel, in a message from London to Warsaw, asked "whether there is any truth in the claim that the opposition of the Jews of Warsaw during the destruction of the Jewish ghetto was led and organized by Soviet officers and other ranks, who were parachuted from the air, and whether arms, munitions and anti-tank guns were supplied in the same way."

Even those who acknowledged the bravery and greatness of spirit of the ghetto fighters did not call on the Poles to help the Jews. Official statements by political bodies in the underground, which backed the government in exile, were confined to condemning Polish assistance to the Germans and demanding an end to the practice of informing on Jews and handing them over to the Germans. The Polish press in London focused on the recently revealed murder of Polish officers in Katyn, which caused considerable embarrassment and uncertainty, and virtually ignored events in the Warsaw ghetto and the war behind its walls.

In early May, the Polish underground press published a declaration by Jan Stanislaw Jankowski, the deputy responsible for those elements of the Polish underground subordinate to the London-based Polish government-in-exile. In an address to Poles on the Nazis' oppressive policies, Jankowski noted:

> During the last few weeks, the capital of Poland has been the scene of the bloodthirsty annihilation of the remaining Jews in the Warsaw ghetto by the German police and their Latvian mercenaries. Their cruel persecution and the destruction of these Jews who are hiding is taking place in the ruins of the ghetto and outside its walls. The Polish people, immersed in the Christian spirit and who are not given to double standards of morality, are repelled by the German savagery. Since April 19, a conflict has been raging between unequals and we respect and sympathize with the Jews who are defending themselves bravely while detest-

ing the German murderers. The political leadership of Poland has already expressed its profound condemnation of the anti-Jewish acts of the Germans and stresses this condemnation once again. The Polish population are right to feel sympathy with the persecuted Jews and the help they offer them should be continued.

Jankowski suggested no practical action in his declaration but merely generalized about the past and cautioned that one should not stray from the ways of the past.

Even more prominent was the statement by Wladyslaw Sikorski, leader of the Polish government-in-exile, on May 5, sixteen days after the desperate struggle began in the ghetto. Addressing the Poles in their homeland, he said:

The greatest crime in the history of mankind is being enacted. We know that you are assisting the tortured Jews as much as you can. I thank you, my countrymen, in my own name and that of the government. I beg you to render them the maximum assistance and with it, to diminish this terrible cruelty.

This was evidently a clear call asking the Poles to provide help to the fighting Jews. Even then no action to aid the Jews was taken. The strange silence of the Polish press in London also continued. On April 29, the *Biuleatyn Informacyjny,* the AK journal in the Polish underground, published the nearest thing to an open call for aid to the Jews:

The spirit of the future obliges humanity to put an end to the mass murders regardless of who is responsible, otherwise the Second World War is lost, and the world will not free itself from the vicious circle of blood-letting. Helping the Jews escaping from the burning ghetto is a Christian obligation, until the days when liberated Poland will return to this part of Europe its security, real freedom, and its ancient European cultural sovereignty.

What is missing from this humane document is the simple and basic statement that Polish Jews are citizens of Poland and not just the proposed beneficiaries of a "Christian obligation," and that the Polish citizen has a patriotic duty to aid his countrymen who have been subjected to racist discrimination.

In his work on relations between the Poles and the Jews, Emanuel Ringelblum included a collection of conversations with Poles in Warsaw concerning events in the ghetto. Ringelblum may paint too dark a picture with comments taken from anecdotal random conversations. Nevertheless, a member of the PPS (the Polish Socialist party) noted that the party was not prepared to take military action:

> We sympathize with the Jews in this tragic situation. It would be right to supply them with weapons, but active collaboration is impossible. For the principle matter, for the liberation, everyone has to suffer. The party must choose the right moment to begin the struggle and not be driven by emotions, no matter how noble they are. Some noble spirits have become bitter about the indifference and ignorance allotted to this great tragedy which is being enacted before the entire population: we remain as we were, as if nothing has happened. We eat well, and afterwards we go out to the balcony to watch the fires in the ghetto from above. We hear the thunderous echoes of bombs and explosives blowing up the buildings and the shelters — and we keep silent.

There was often a hint of antisemitism in the conversations reported by Ringelblum, as well as satisfaction with the happenings in the ghetto. Finally Warsaw was to be *Judenfrei* (free of Jews), and the dream of the Polish antisemites — a Warsaw devoid of Jews — had been realized. Some expressed open satisfaction that the Germans had murdered the Jews, while others kept such opinions to themselves. Sympathy was expressed by saying "that although the victims were Jews, they are after all human beings." Some Poles regretted the burning of the buildings more than that of the human beings inside of them. They feared only that the Germans, after disposing of the Jews, would turn their attention to the Poles; this marred their appreciation of the ethnic purification of Warsaw. Antisemites considered that the Jews flew the Polish flag only to please the Poles; they refused to believe that the Jews were capable of defending themselves and rebelling against the enemy.

On May 6, an article entitled "Preying on the Greatest Tragedy," in the Polish underground journal, *Rzeczypospolita Polska* (Polish Republic), stated:

It is well known that wherever there is a war, there are hyenas . . . the last year had brought with it another sort of wartime hyena. They exploited the Jewish tragedy in order to blackmail and pressure the Jews in hiding or persecuted by the Germans. The majority of our population, healthy morally and with a true Christian spirit, viewed and view with repulsion the crimes of the German brutes towards the Jews and their attitude towards the victims of this crime is one of sincere and profound sympathy. But there are exceptions to the rule, who are regretfully too often members of the police, who do not hesitate to exploit the tragedy of the persecuted Jews who are subjected to acts of blackmail and considerable ransom. These people lacking self-respect or conscience who go in for this blackmail are fortunately very few in number. They are but one step away from the criminals who also do not hesitate to hand over the Jews to the Germans.

Sunday, April 25, was Easter. In the square bordering the ghetto, a crowd of gay holidaymakers in their festive dress had gathered. Close to the walls, the clouds of smoke, and the pervasive acrid smell, carousels turned and spirits were high. Helena Balicka-Kozlowska, a Polish woman who helped the Jews and the Jewish underground, wrote in her memoirs, *The Wall Had Two Sides*:

The square looked like a market: there were many hawkers of water and sellers of sweets and cigarettes. The place was filled with shouting and laughing exchanges. Near the carousel with the loud orchestra, there were field cannons. Their crews did not necessarily repel the curious crowds. They evidently felt more secure from Jewish attack among the Polish crowds.

The Polish poet and Nobel Prize winner Czeslaw Milosz, who witnessed both fear and joy on this stretch of land divided by a wall, wrote the poem "Campo dei Fiori":

In Rome on the Campo dei Fiori
baskets of olives and lemons,
cobbles spattered with wine
and the wreckage of flowers.
Vendors cover the trestles
with rose-pink fish;
armfuls of dark grapes
heaped on peach-down.

On this same square
they burned Giordano Bruno.
Henchmen kindled the pyre
close-pressed by the mob.
Before the flames had died
the taverns were full again,
baskets of olives and lemons
again on the vendors' shoulders.

I thought of the Campo dei Fiori
in Warsaw by the sky-carousel
one clear spring evening
to the strains of a carnival tune.
The bright melody drowned
the salvos from the ghetto wall,
and couples were flying
high in the cloudless sky.

At times wind from the burning
would drift dark kites along
and riders on the carousel
caught petals in midair.
That same hot wind
blew open the skirts of the girls
and the crowds were laughing
on that beautiful Warsaw Sunday.

Deportation of Jews during the Warsaw Ghetto Uprising,
April 20, 1943. The photographer was a Polish firefighter and
member of the resistance named Leszek Grzywaczewski.
(United States Holocaust Memorial Museum, Washington, D.C.)

German troops using heavy artillery during the Warsaw Ghetto Uprising. (Myron and Ally Friedman/United States Holocaust Memorial Museum)

Jews discovered in a bunker during the Warsaw Ghetto Uprising. *(Stroop Report*, National Archives, Washington, D.C.)

SS troops walk through the burning Warsaw ghetto.
(Stroop Report, National Archives, Washington, D.C.)

The ruins of the Warsaw ghetto.
(Stroop Report, National Archives, Washington, D.C.)

Ukrainian SS volunteers view corpses of Jews during the Warsaw Ghetto Uprising. (National Archives, Washington, D.C.)

Corpses of Jews lying in the street during the Warsaw Ghetto Uprising. *(Stroop Report,* National Archives, Washington, D.C.)

Ruins of the Warsaw ghetto, 1945.
(Central State Archive of Film, Photography, and Documents, Moscow)

Researchers of the Jewish Historical Institute in Warsaw examine documents of the Ringelblum Archive which were hidden in milk cans in the Warsaw ghetto. Warsaw, 1950.
(Yad Vashem, Jerusalem, Israel)

Someone will read as moral
that the people of Rome or Warsaw
haggle, laugh, make love
as they pass by martyrs' pyres.
Someone else will read
of the passing of things human,
of the oblivion
born before the flames have died.

But that day I thought only
of the loneliness of the dying,
of how, when Giordano
climbed to his burning
he could not find
in any human tongue
words for mankind,
mankind who live on.

Already they were back at their wine
or peddled their white starfish,
baskets of olives and lemons
they had shouldered to the fair,
and he already distanced
as if centuries had passed
while they paused just a moment
for his flying in the fire.

Those dying here, the lonely
forgotten by the world,
our tongues of an ancient planet.
Until, when all is legend
and many years have passed,
on a new Campo dei Fiori
rage will kindle at a poet's word.

During the last days of April, Jews continued their struggle. In one report, Stroop mentioned that "in most instances, the Jews put up armed opposition before leaving the bunkers." For the Germans, uncovering hundreds of bunkers located throughout the courtyards and under the ruins was a slow and tiring process. They used police dogs and sound detectors to trace the presence of human beings. When a bunker was discovered, and the Germans were convinced that people were hiding there, they had to remove them.

In the very few instances when they did not find the bunker entrances, the Nazis used explosives to create an opening, or relied on information from informers who were coerced into revealing the hideouts. To gain this information the Germans would stand a bunker's captured inhabitants against a wall, promising clemency to those who would reveal the existence and location of the openings to other bunkers. In this way, they managed to blow up quite a few openings to the bunkers; people inside heard someone speaking Yiddish or Polish stating that they were surrounded and that if they left the bunkers willingly, no harm would come to them. Generally, the inhabitants of the bunkers refused to leave even after the bunker and its entrance were "burned."

During the last stages, the Germans used asphyxiating gas to force people out. Stroop claimed that his soldiers used smoke rockets, not gases, but evidence from Jewish survivors confirmed that some kind of gas had penetrated the bunkers, forcing them to leave. In fact, many Jews sent to Majdanek and other camps near Lublin had infected lungs and died shortly after arrival.

Beneath the blazing ghetto, the bunkers, which had been planned and equipped to provide refuge for months, became burning cages without air, water, or food. The inhabitants were forced to abandon their hiding places at night to seek shelter in other bunkers. Some changed bunkers two or three times, occasionally moving into a bunker that had been discovered earlier and whose inhabitants had fled or had been removed.

In his report of April 28, Stroop said:

In the afternoon, a fighting unit was stationed in a block of houses that had been combed and set on fire. Today, as on former days, masses of Jews are revealed because of the heat of the fire and the very strong smells. At another place, an officer-engineer of the Wehrmacht succeeded after considerable effort in opening a bunker which had been set up in October of the previous year and which was equipped with water pipes, a toilet, electricity and other accessories. 274 Jews were taken out of the bunker and they were from among the wealthier and more influential Jews. Today the opposition in various places was broken by using arms . . . the results were: 1655 Jews caught and transported, of whom 110 were shot during the fighting.

On April 30, Stroop reported:

In the course of blowing up a large bunker, a whole house collapsed and all the bandits within were killed. In the increasing fire which ensued there were enormous eruptions and outbursts of flames which indicated that there were certainly large quantities of ammunition and explosives there.

Although enormous blocks of houses have been burnt to the ground, there are still Jews in bunkers located some two to three meters under ground. In many cases, it is possible to discover the bunker only after Jews who have been caught there, show it to us.

On the same day there was an armed skirmish involving German units.

On May 1, Stroop stated that it was impossible to subdue the bunkers, that the Jews would not leave without the use of force. A large number of Jews were taken out of the sewerage canals by bombing them and blocking the exits. "Since the beginning of the *Grossaktion* [great action], 150 Jews who had evidently escaped from Warsaw were shot by gendarmes outside the ghetto in the vicinity of the city," Stroop noted.

From the beginning of May, Stroop's reports claimed that he was eliminating nests of hard-core rebels. About five hundred police and soldiers searched and purged the ghetto. A similar number formed a tight ring around the ghetto in order to prevent escape. General Friedrich Wilhelm Krüger, commander of the police and SS forces, arrived from Cracow to survey the Warsaw ghetto front.

On May 3, the Germans overcame one of three bunkers in a house at 30 Franciszkanska Street where a company of fighters from the ZOB had fortified themselves. Seventeen-year-old Shanan Lent was killed and twenty-three-year-old Zippora Lehrer also fell. Altogether, about half the fighters on the spot died on that day. Some of the remainder squeezed into the bunker at Mila Street number 18.

The next day, Stroop mentioned that a special unit of sixty men assigned to unearth bunkers was being reinforced by members of the Engineers Corps of the Wehrmacht. Evacuating the bunkers had become increasingly difficult. Only the use of smoke rockets would force the Jews out.

On May 6, Stroop reported that his forces returned to search the houses that were burned on the fourth. Although it was unlikely that people remained in the area, a number of bunkers were discovered in the burning heat. On the seventh of May, an unknown number of Jews who refused to leave their bunkers attacked the Germans, and died in subsequent bombing.

Stroop stated on May 8 that the command bunker was taken and that the deputy commander and the head of staff of the organization were caught and executed. His report, however, lacked the identifying initials of the organization and data on the capture of commanders which fit the facts. But smoke rockets were thrown into the bunker, as Stroop says, or gas had penetrated the bunker.

The command bunker at Mila 18 had not been erected by the ZOB. The organization was not involved in preparing bunkers. This well-constructed and well-equipped bunker housed successful underworld smugglers, and they took in the ZOB commanders and a large number of fighters. In its final hours Mila 18 contained three hundred people, among them an odd mixture of military commanders, ideological leaders, street fighters, and crooks. As tactical headquarters for the underground, Mila 18 became the center of the Uprising.

Zivia Lubetkin described the atmosphere of Mila 18 in her memoirs:

A company of fighters were stationed at the bunker in Mila 18 — and perhaps its owners were really people from the underworld of Warsaw, among them thieves of some repute. Their leaders had dug deep into the earth along a stretch of three blocks of enormous buildings which had become ruins [during the Uprising] and had constructed a large and spacious bunker. A long and narrow corridor ran down the entire length, with many rooms extending from either side. Electricity had been installed and a well was dug; there was a well-arranged kitchen and even a reading and recreation room, and dozens of their followers and henchmen from their gangs stayed in this "inn."

Shmuel Asher, or Shmuel Issachar, a manly, broad-shouldered, awkward Jew, was head of the gang and behaves here in the bowels of the earth like king of the roost and reminds me of Haim Nachman Bialik's [the Hebrew poet] "Arieh, the Able-bodied." He runs everything in this place: our nourishment, sleeping arrangements, and decides when it is possible to go out on sorties and obtain necessities. At first there were all sorts of luxuries here, special rooms and even beds. Their confederates on the Aryan side [from the gangs] would supply them with fresh bread and liquor via the sewerage canals. The common folk were unbelievably loyal to their leaders and ready to go through fire and water for them.

Purely by chance, a command company of the Jewish Fighting Organization landed up here and later on, additional companies came under the same roof, and the bunker that was intended for dozens of gangsters housed 300 people densely crowding all the rooms. On the first day, the leader welcomed us warmly — we were already known in the ghetto and he and his pals treated the fighting organization with great respect. Everything we have is yours, he said, and we are at your disposal. We are strong, we're skilled in undoing locks, we can move around at night unnoticed, climb over fences and walls, and we know by heart every lane and crevice in the ruins of the ghetto. You'll soon learn how useful we can be. And indeed they were our guides in many respects, by day and by night. Especially for spying on German positions. Afterwards, when the ghetto went up in flames and it was difficult to make out the names of the streets, a notorious thief led us safely through. Like a supple cat, he would crawl, climb, disappear into stairways, holes and cellars. And thus we would pass through the streets without being seen by the enemy . . . This bunker housed 120 Jewish fighters and the command.

Vladka Meed, who was an underground courier for the Jewish Fighting Organization, noted in her memoirs an account of the bunker's last moments based on what she heard from its survivors:

On the morning of May 8, the Germans surrounded the bunker at Mila 18. They demanded that everyone come outside. The collection of rag-pickers [meaning the owners of the bunker] obeyed and went out. The fighters remained within, with the weapons in hand. They were ready for the battle. The Germans were afraid to enter the bunker (the fact is that the Germans were generally unwilling to enter the bunkers), and injected poison gas while beginning to bombard them with hand-grenades.

The fighters returned fire. They could not withstand [this] for any length of time. The gas continued to penetrate the bunker and the fighters began to suffocate. But there was not a single one who was ready to fall into the hands of the enemy alive. A shot was heard from the bunker. The fighters had shot themselves. The first to call for suicide was Arieh Wilner. The rest followed suit. Miraculously, there were a few who found a way of getting out through an unnoticed opening. Thus ended the lives of people who incited the Jews of the ghetto to rebel with fearless determination. They had directed the course of the struggle by means of their courage and noble spirit.

Of those who escaped from Mila 18, seven to eight fighters suffered poisoning, including the outstanding figure in the underground and the fighting organization, Tosia Altman. None of them survived to witness the day of liberation.

The fighting in the ghetto did not end with the collapse of the bunker at Mila 18. During the next few days, Stroop's daily reports recorded the discovery of many bunkers, with the opposition and skirmishes continuing as before. On May 10, Stroop mentioned three wounded SS men among his troops; on May 11 he noted one SS soldier was wounded. In his last reports, Stroop refers to Jews who stayed hidden in the sewerage canals and others who abandoned the bunkers and burrowed into holes and hiding places among the ruins.

On May 12, Stroop reported that the Germans discovered thirty bunkers and captured 663 Jews, of whom 133 were shot. Also on May 12, Stroop stated that two buildings in Prosta Street which were used by the Többens workshop were attacked and set on fire. "One can assume," he said, "that a large number of Jews died in the flames." On the thirteenth of May, Stroop pointed out that in the category of losses, "there were two SS men killed, and three SS men were slain as a result of the bombing from the air." From another source we learn that there was indeed a Soviet air attack, but it is doubtful whether they died as a result of this attack; it may simply have been more convenient to report them as victims of the bombing.

On May 14, Stroop added to his daily report that on the next day he would decide whether or not to end the action against the ghetto. On the fifteenth, there was another wounded policeman, and at the end of the report Stroop stated: "I will end the *Grossaktion* on May 16, 1943, in the evening, with the blowing up of the synagogue which we have succeeded in destroying today."

As the Warsaw ghetto was coming to its end, Shmuel Zygelbojm, a Bund activist and party representative to the National Polish Council in London, found little to ease his mind and spirit. His family and friends were gone. They had taken what weapons they could and begun a more than justified battle, which was unique in the inequality of its combatants. He had heard eyewitness reports from Jan Karski, the Polish courier who relayed firsthand impressions of the Warsaw ghetto and who requested Western action. Zygelbojm had also appealed for American help. On May 12, he met with Major Arthur J. Goldberg, who later was to become a Supreme Court justice and American ambassador to the United Nations, but who was then working for the OSS in London. Goldberg brokenheartedly informed Zygelbojm that no American aid would be forthcoming. Zygelbojm weighed the odds of getting help for the Jews who were vanishing in the flames of the ghetto. He chose to become one with the ghetto fighters, setting himself on fire in front of the British Parliament on May 13, two days before Stroop announced the end of the action in the ghetto. "In my death," Zygelbojm wrote, "I wish to express my strongest protest against mankind, which looks on and accepts the annihilation of the Jewish people."

Zygelbojm left behind letters to friends, to the world, and to the Polish authorities. In one, he wrote,

From the news coming from Poland, it appears that the Germans are now annihilating the Jewish remnant of Poland in the most cruel way. The last act of a tragedy which has no parallel in history is being enacted behind the walls of the ghetto. The responsibility for the crime of murdering the entire Jewish population of Poland falls first and foremost on the murderers themselves, but indirectly, this responsibility also falls on all of mankind, the nations and the governments of the Allies, who have until now made no real efforts to stop the crime . . . I would also like to declare that although the Polish government contributed to a large extent to awakening public opinion throughout the world, it did not do enough. It did not do anything which could measure up to the proportions of the drama now taking place in Poland . . . I can no longer be silent. I can no longer live while remnants of the Jewish people in Poland, whose representative I am, are being destroyed. My friends in the Warsaw ghetto fell with their weapons in hand in the final battle. I did not succeed in dying in the same way or together with them. But I belong to them and the mass graves there.

On May 24, Stroop answered a series of questions about the destruction of the Warsaw ghetto which were put to him by Krüger, the head of the SS and the police:

Out of the overall number of 56,065 Jews who were caught in the former Jewish quarter, 7,000 were wiped out in the great action on the spot. Via the transport to TII [Treblinka], 6,929 Jews were finished off, so that a total of 13,929 Jews were annihilated, apart from the 56,065. According to our estimate, 5–6 thousand Jews were slain by bombing and fires. 631 bunkers were destroyed.

As for spoils, these consisted of: 7 Polish rifles, 1 Russian rifle, 1 German rifle, 59 revolvers of various calibers. A few hundred hand grenades, which included Polish and home-made grenades, a few hundred Molotov cocktails, home-made bombs and detonators, and quantities of explosives, and munitions. Among these there were also munitions for MGs. One must take into account that in most instances it was impossible to get hold of the fighters' weapons, because before the fighters and the bandits were caught, they generally threw them into hiding places which were difficult to pinpoint. They were also difficult to take possession of because the bunkers were filled with smoke from the rockets that had been thrown into them. As the bunkers had to be blown up immediately, it was impossible to take the weapons into account . . . Apart from eight structures (the police hostel, the hospital, the hostel for factory guards), the former ghetto was completely destroyed. What was not accomplished by blowing up the place were a few burnt walls. What could be retrieved from the ruins were quantities of bricks and scrap-iron.

Not surprisingly, Stroop tried to justify the lengthy military campaign he was forced to undertake — tying up so many troops and arousing attention — against an enemy that had no real weapons. The number of Germans who fell in the struggle was exaggerated to hundreds and thousands by the Jews and the Poles. It is clear that after the first few days, the German forces encountered considerable difficulties. There are discrepancies between Stroop's figures in his daily reports and his summary in the survey forwarded to Cracow. In the latter, Stroop reports sixteen killed and eighty-five wounded. Stroop's announcement about ending the assault on the sixteenth and blowing up the great synagogue outside the ghetto was intended to symbolize the victory of the Nazis' mission. But this did not end the opposition of the last inhabitants of the ghetto. The Jews hiding in the ruins were not aware, of course, of Stroop's plan to end the mission. Nor did they know that their exact number was not known and that some estimates ran into the thousands. They continued to struggle for their lives within the ruins, as we know from Jewish and non-Jewish witnesses and documentation.

Reports by the Polish police, who were responsible for the abandoned area of the ghetto, describe what was happening in the area. A report on May 18 noted that "Jewish units emerge from under the earth and attack the Germans . . . There is not a single German in the ghetto area at night. The SS people claim that hundreds of Jews are hiding in the underground haunts and ruins." On the twentieth, a report said that "there are shots in the ghetto in the daytime and at night . . . and the throwing of hand grenades by both sides." Skirmishes and heavy fighting were reported between May 27 and the thirtieth, and on June 1 and 2 "it seemed as if the situation in the ghetto had become worse."

Arieh Neiberg was one of the survivors from the ruins, or the *malinas* (shelters), as they were called, after the "great action" was over (he now lives in Israel). Neiberg kept a diary in which he described events in the ghetto from the beginning of the Uprising until September 26, 1943, the date on which he escaped via the Jewish cemetery to the Aryan side of Warsaw. Through his notes, we learn of the fate of the last of the bunker dwellers, who did not know what the Germans were doing and thought that the passage of time had proved that the last few bunkers would never be discovered. Jews living in underground caves struggled to find food and drinking water. These living shadows were also fighters, and they continued to battle with all their bodies and souls. Neiberg described the scene on May 26:

Near the wall of the house, near the waste bin, there were women and children lying in pools of blood . . . a tangle of arms and legs was evidence that only a short time earlier, there were living and breathing creatures here . . . we stare at the scene and cannot hold back our tears. We speak in Yiddish in whispers.

Suddenly there is a movement among the bodies. Someone is trying to stand up. We hurry over. A child about 7 years old, with a blindfold over her eyes, says to us in Yiddish: "Jews, have no fear . . . give us water." And she immediately picks up a little girl of 5 from the ground: "She is also alive, not even wounded." When she has quenched her thirst, she introduces herself: "I am Irka Rubinstein, and the other girl is Halinka Eizenstadt."

Afterwards, Irka tells us what had happened: "After the Germans took us out of the bunker, everyone was stood up in the courtyard of Walowa 2." They were ordered to take off all their clothes; a search was made, and they stole the watches, and jewelry, etc. Irka's older sister refused to undress, and she was violently beaten and her clothes were torn off her. They had to stand naked from 3 in the afternoon until 6:30 in the evening.

One of the SS people told them that they would be killed in the evening. Only if someone would tell them where the Jews were to be found, would they be taken to the *Befehlstelle* [the building that housed the German command of the evacuation forces]. Mundek, the wagoner, volunteered, and the Germans immediately took him away with them.

The mothers taught the children to fall to the ground as soon as they heard shooting. Afterwards, they were all moved from the courtyard to the hallway and from there taken away in groups of five. Irka went with her mother, holding her hand. Behind her there was the rumbling sound of shots; she fell, someone pressed down on her with their entire body, and blood flowed over her face. She did not know whether she was wounded or dying. Her heart was pounding. Her eyes dimmed and there was a buzzing in her ears. And whatever was pressing down on her troubled her so.

Germans passed by and kicked them. Whoever moved or

shouted would be a target for their revolvers. Irka held her breath and lay still as she could. Then she heard them leaving and marching off singing. She lay awhile longer and then pushed aside the body lying on top of her. And then she discovered that the corpse lying on top of her — was her mother. "It's my mother," she cried out and burst into tears. "It was her blood that was flowing over me." Irka kissed her and started to search among the dead; perhaps her sister had survived. But they all lay still without showing any sign of life.

By chance, she stepped on Halinka Eizenstadt's foot and the foot moved. She felt her pulse — her heart was still beating. She pushed aside the corpse covering her — it was Halinka's mother. She removed Halinka's blindfold, took some water from the bunker and brought her to life. Suddenly she heard footsteps. The two little girls returned to the dead bodies and lay among them as dead. They thought that the murderers had returned and held their breath. "We lay still and listened — perhaps there would be some more shooting. Suddenly, I heard someone speaking Yiddish, and I knew it was one of us!"

In reports on other days, Neiberg describes the Jews' weapons and their armed clashes with the Germans, as well as the constant alert maintained by all the groups in the remaining bunkers. On June 14, Neiberg wrote in his notebook:

For some days, there has been no water in no-mans-land. However, there have been heavy rains. Until now, we only exploited the rains for "showers," but now we collected it for drinking water. We took planks from Greenbaum's shelter and made a small roof with a tiny gutter from burnt tin, beyond the nearby balcony to the "malina" [shelter], where we set down a series of broken pots to collect the rainwater. When this experiment succeeded, the enthusiasm was tremendous, and people vied with one another in coming up with all sorts of innovations. Whenever there was rain in the days that followed, we would accumulate the water and keep it in whatever containers were at hand.

On September 25, 1943, the day before he moved to the Aryan side, Neiberg described the survivors:

> Out of the original 45 who made up the group — four remained alive. Zamsz' wife is bloated from hunger and utterly despondent. Czarno-Czapka is feeble and indifferent. Shorshan prays to God and awaits a miracle. My body is swelling too. I think we ought to go up on the wall and escape to the Polish side. And if this does not succeed — a bullet will solve everything.

The time had come to escape. In September forced laborers, accompanied by armed guards, were sent to demolish the burned framework of the walls still standing in the ghetto. The ruins had been the site of executions of Polish prisoners, as well as of many Jews who had tried to live on the Aryan side, among them Emmanuel Ringelblum. Later, Polish workers and prisoners were sent into the ruins to collect bricks and scrap iron.

On April 19, 1944, exactly one year after the final expulsion began, Dr. Hans Kammler, the SS man responsible for planning and construction, reported 22.5 million bricks had been collected from the ruins and that 4,675 people had been engaged in the effort.

Missions were launched to rescue the fighters after the Uprising had passed its climax. But there was no prearranged plan with the Polish underground. The Jewish Fighting Organization had worried that setting down rescue scenarios would undermine the fighters' resolve to resist until the very end. The Poles, however, had been interested in transferring the fighters from the ghetto to regions far from Warsaw before the Uprising even began — a proposal that was categorically rejected.

After the fighting was over, there were no contacts with the Polish underground, which made no offers to rescue the remaining fighters. The little documentation that survived suggests that contacts and plans of this sort were worked out with the ZZW, which evidently supported the idea of a bout of serious fighting followed by escape to the Aryan side. The tunnel that linked Muranow Square to the Polish side, apart from its use as a pipeline for arms and materials, was intended to serve this purpose.

But the ZZW did not have contact with Polish underground leaders, and the elements of the AK with whom they were in contact did not have sufficient influence with the organization's command. Nonetheless, ZZW members tried to escape to the Aryan side, and a number of such sorties were carried out. Unfortunately, because the ZZW did not have many contacts there, several of these attempts ended tragically. None of the higher-ranking ZZW members, nor those familiar with its organizational problems, nor activists of the organization in contact with the Polish underground, survived.

One of the successful escapes took place on April 30, when a large company of ZOB fighters, including its commander, Eliezer Geller, left the workshop area and moved through the sewerage tunnels. The courier leading them was Reginka Fuden, one of the oldest and most experienced couriers in the ZOB. In addition to the fighters, the group of forty people also included bunker dwellers and other civilians.

Some of those who escaped in this fashion managed to stay alive, and provided detailed descriptions of the hazardous journey via the tunnels to the Polish side. The fighter Aaron Carmi, who was part of this group, described the moment they reached the neck of the tunnel on the Aryan side of town:

> We went out one by one, helping one another to ascend to the street. The picture as we had imagined it the previous day when we learned that we were leaving was quite different from the situation we found ourselves in . . . ! Yesterday, we visualized being met by many people coming to our aid, armed to the teeth, keeping an eye on our exit point, bringing us food, and a large truck would be awaiting us to take us to the forest.
>
> But what we actually saw was so paltry and disappointing — there was not a soul to be seen, the night was misty, hunger gnawed at our insides, and we are in the middle of the street. Not far from us, standing at the corner at Zelazna and Ogrodowa

streets, was a German check-post, but they did not even notice us.

Reginka Fuden did not stay with the fighters but returned through the tunnels to the large workshop area in order to free the remaining fighters. She evidently succeeded in gathering together a group for departure, but while leading them through the tunnel, she was hit by a German bullet and the mission failed. Only a few fighters' groups managed to make their way through on their own. The first group was taken through with the aid of an AL member, Vladislav Gaik, and the courier of the ZOB, Tuvia Scheingut (Tadek). They reached the Lomanki woods near Warsaw and became the nucleus of a partisan group of former fighters which bore the name of Mordecai Anielewicz.

During this period, Zalman Friedrich (Zigmund) and Simha Ratajzer-Rotem (Kazik) were sent from the central ghetto in order to renew contact with Yitzhak Zuckerman and to inform him of the rescue efforts. Organizing this campaign advanced very slowly and encountered many problems. Only on May 9 did two members of the ZOB, Ratajzer-Rotem and Rysiek Moselman, together with some Polish sanitary workers, set out for the central ghetto. Going through the tunnels was difficult and tiring, and after the group started to go back without anything to show for it, they encountered a group of some ten ZOB fighters who had tried to get through on their own. From what they said, it became clear that the rescue mission had started too late — a day after the main force and command heads of the ZOB had fallen in the bunker at Mila 18.

Two fighters returned to the central ghetto in order to locate the last of the ZOB fighters still in the area. Dozens of people, among them Tosia Altman and Zivia Lubetkin, were spotted and brought together, and they made their way through the tunnels and reached the opening in Prosta Street. They were to be picked up from there, but the promised vehicle did not arrive. Then Gaik finally turned up with a vehicle. Although the day was already at its peak, the leaders of the rescue were urged to let the others in the stifling tunnel escape, and they too were rescued despite the extreme danger involved. But there was a tragic setback. Perhaps because of the lateness of the hour and the weariness of the travelers, or perhaps owing to the appearance of a suspicious individual who appeared in the tunnel, which added to the tension, some of those in the tunnel were not saved. After replacing the cover on the tunnel, the escapees realized that some fifteen people had been left behind.

The attempt to rescue them was thwarted because the Germans had been informed of the rescue mission and placed the area under siege. According to Borzykowski, one of those who succeeded in getting through, "Afterwards we received news that they had tried to get out of the tunnel on their own but had encountered some Germans and all of them perished in the ensuing skirmish."

Conditions on the Aryan side did not permit an effort to rescue all ZOB survivors and their relatives. There were many obstacles to rescue. Survivors were not concentrated in one place, and the daily struggle to stay alive depleted almost all of their energy. Yitzhak Zuckerman represented the organization among the few survivors who lived among the Poles. But various groups and individuals, among them such outstanding personalities as Israel Kanal and Eliezer Geller, were active independently. The group that concentrated in the forests around Vishkov also did not enjoy the protection of the Polish underground, despite all of Zuckerman's efforts, and many Jews died in very questionable circumstances.

Zuckerman and his immediate circle, together with the group from the Bund, managed to provide financial aid from abroad from money received through the Polish underground. Some fifteen thousand to twenty thousand Jews are estimated to have gone into hiding or lived with borrowed or fictitious papers in Polish Warsaw and its environs after the Uprising and the wiping out of the ghetto. This remnant would have been unable to find a refuge and shelter had it not been for the honorable Poles who offered them help, at times endangering themselves and their families in the process.

The help rendered by the Zegota to those in hiding also carried considerable weight. However, there were still gangs of blackmailers and informers who betrayed many of those who had escaped from the ghetto. No one knows with certainty how many Jews who escaped to the Polish side survived until the end of the war. It is known, however, that at the height of the Polish rebellion in Warsaw in August 1944, a company of Jews under Zuckerman's command, among them former members of the ZOB, actively participated in the campaign.

In his reports, Stroop frequently stressed that the German authorities were unaware of what was happening in the ghetto, that they were unprepared for the Uprising and knew nothing of the maze of bunkers and the extent of the tunnels. During his interrogation in a Polish prison, Stroop claimed that his predecessor, von Sammern, the man who planned and prepared the last evacuation from the ghetto, "did not take into account even the slightest opposition." He assumed, Stroop said, that the final expulsion would go as smoothly as former actions of this kind.

According to Stroop, it was only on the eve of the nineteenth that von Sammern received news of the impending opposition, and the forces he recruited for this purpose seem to indicate as much. But he did not ascribe any importance to this revelation. Perhaps he thought that armed Jewish opposition within the ghetto could be interpreted as insanity and also could undermine the status of the governor under whose rule this curious phenomenon had developed. Obviously, von Sammern had not imagined the trial awaiting his troops, nor the extent of the network of bunkers and tunnels that had been prepared.

The campaign in the ghetto was a source of embarrassment to the Germans, who feared that the Jewish example would be emulated by the Poles, who were only too anxious to fight. As with many other matters, the eradication of the ghetto and the Uprising were not mentioned in the German press and official media. News reached officials and others in the Third Reich via secret channels. The Polish underground press, however, gave wide coverage to the Uprising, its progress, and significance. While the Polish government-in-exile distributed considerable information on the expulsion, only limited news of the Jewish Uprising was passed on to the free world.

The Uprising was also used as a weapon in the power struggle between the Germans responsible for Poland. Himmler, who wrote frequent letters and issued orders about the liquidation of the ghetto, did not mention the Uprising in his correspondence. One can assume that Himmler, who was responsible for security and order in occupied Poland, preferred to be silent about events in the Warsaw ghetto. On the other hand, Himmler's rival, Hans Frank, hastened to inform Hans Lammers, head of Hitler's office, of the "well-organized uprising in the ghetto," on the assumption that Lammers would bring the matter to Hitler's attention.

On April 23, Himmler pressed Krüger not to worry about the effect on the munitions industry and to use whatever means were necessary to destroy the ghetto, although he had earlier demanded that the property be safeguarded. Stroop also claimed that he had received the order from Cracow to destroy the synagogue.

Joseph Goebbels wrote in his diary a few days after the beginning of the Uprising that

> a really grotesque situation had arisen in Warsaw . . . notably hard battles between our police, including also parts of the army, and the rebelling Jews. Indeed, the Jews had managed to fortify the ghetto in order to defend it . . . it has even reached the point where the Jewish senior command issues daily military bulletins [referring to the reports and proclamations published during the uprising by the ZOB representatives on the Aryan side] . . . This emphasizes only too well what one can expect from these Jews when they have weapons in their hands. Unfortunately they also have good German weapons and particularly machine guns. Only God knows how they obtained them.

On May 7, Goebbels noted in his diary that the situation in the General Government had deteriorated to such an extent that "there is no point in keeping Dr. Frank on." He wrote that the Uprising was the straw that broke the camel's back and questioned the status of the governor. So, while Frank was trying to shift responsibility for events in the ghetto to Himmler, Goebbels was attempting to place the blame on Frank.

The governor of the Warsaw district, Dr. Ludwig Fischer,

worried particularly about the Polish reaction. On May 13, Fischer published a declaration, addressed to the Polish population of Warsaw:

> Lately there have been a series of murderous attacks in the city of Warsaw. The same force stands behind these attacks as those who hope one day to bring to this country the bloody rule of Bolsheviks. Everyone's task now is to frustrate the provocation of the Communist and Jewish agents. Every Jew and Bolshevik who is still alive and free is the most dangerous enemy of the population . . . Whoever informs the authorities where such a Jewish or Communist agent moves about freely, is thereby fulfilling his obvious duty to himself and to his neighbor.

In an internal report of events in the Warsaw district in April and May 1943, Fischer wrote, "In Warsaw, 126 attacks were carried out in April, while in May, there were 163 attacks in which many Germans were killed." The report stated:

> During the annihilation of the ghetto, more than 1000 buildings were destroyed. Thus the possibility of erecting industrial enterprises here has gone forever together with the storing of materials in the area. To a marked extent, Warsaw's ability to absorb industrial enterprises is limited by the Reich with increasing insistence. Despite the battles in the ghetto which continued for many weeks, economic life in Warsaw has gone on undisturbed. There was no sabotage at work places because the Polish workers and employees have displayed admirable discipline.

The Warsaw Ghetto Uprising resolved one of the persistent questions raised by the Holocaust: Was the annihilation of the Jews made possible by the passivity of its victims? The Germans accomplished their goals all too easily. Serious challenges in other ghettos, towns, and villages, or even in the Warsaw ghetto when it was the home of more than 350,000 Jews, might have forced them to act with fateful results. Yet, faced with an organized armed opposition, German authorities did not cancel their plans for the complete evacuation of the ghetto. Instead, their rage intensified and their savagery grew. The Uprising confirmed that Nazi ideology and definitive plans for the destruction of the Jews fueled the "final solution," not Jewish passivity.

The Uprising in Warsaw undoubtedly influenced German authorities but it did not reverse their attitude toward the Jews and the process of extinction. The lesson learned by the Germans was to anticipate the possibility of armed opposition by Jews.

Among the pragmatists in the General Government and army officers, the destruction of the ghetto was frequently associated with the loss of a sizable Jewish work force that they had previously had at their disposal. At a conference attended by many General Government officials in Cracow on May 31, 1943, at which SS Obergruppenführer Dr. Ernst Kaltenbrunner was a guest, the expulsion and struggle in the ghetto came up for discussion during a session on security. It was said that many Jews fled to the forests during the expulsion and joined the partisans. SS General Krüger claimed that the "ethnic purification" had undoubtedly helped calm the situation. It was one of the most difficult and unpleasant tasks for the police forces.

> The Führer's instruction had to be carried out and the matter was essential to Europe's well-being . . . In the factories, the Jews employed there, called Maccabees [this usage does not appear anywhere else, as far as we know], were in a better state and were excellent workers; in addition to which there were also women who proved to be physically stronger than the men. Incidentally, the same experience was encountered during the evacuation of the Warsaw ghetto. This task was indeed more difficult. The losses in the police force reached 15 dead and 88 wounded. Armed Jewish women were also fighting against men of the SS and the police.
>
> Continuing our preoccupation with the purging of Jews appears to be undesirable. For some time now, the foreign press and propaganda abroad has been making much of this issue. Unrelated to this, we should try to catch the Jews who evaded the expulsion and who now wander about everywhere in disguise. As one can see from security police reports, the Jews in Warsaw continue to carry out attacks and murder.

Some news of the Uprising spread despite the wall of silence erected by the Germans. The story of the rebellion in Warsaw and the heroic people who led it became legendary. As the Warsaw Ghetto Uprising moved from history to legend, it took its place alongside the stories of Leonidas and his army who refused to retreat at the siege of Thermopylae. In Jewish legend the Warsaw Ghetto Uprising often recalled Eleazar ben Yair and the men and women at Masada who fought the Romans on the heights in the year 73 C.E. They refused to surrender. "Only a free life is worth living" is how Josephus retells the final speech of the Zealot leader.

In Warsaw, the few had stood against the many, the pure of heart against the wicked power. They were armed by their courage. They were emboldened because they had no choice. And if victory eluded them, honor and dignity did not. One thousand years of Jewish history had come to an end in Poland not with a whimper or with the cries of cowering masses, but with the courageous acts of young fighters who stood to defend their honor — who resisted despite the overwhelming power of the foe.

Rumors and half-truths about the Uprising reached survivors in other Polish ghettos, in work camps, and in concentration camps throughout the occupied areas, as well as the fronts in Eastern and Western Europe, the Jewish population in Palestine, and the free world. Many identified with the fight in the ghetto and were moved to join in the struggle. At Treblinka, where the Jews of Warsaw had been murdered by the hundreds of thousands, planning for the uprising began only after news of Warsaw's last stand penetrated the death camp. The underground began to acquire weapons and plan a strategy for taking over the camp. The Uprising reverberated even in Treblinka.

The image of the Jew as a submissive, passive, pious man was transformed into that of the young warrior. The transformation of the image of the Jew continued in the emergent State of Israel. Some Israeli leaders looked back on the Holocaust with fear and sometimes with shame. The only usable past, the only history of that period that they adopted for the image of the future was the heroic chapter of resistance. Thus, eventually, the law for Yom

Hashoah, Israel's Holocaust Memorial Day, was called Yom Hashoah V'hagevurah, Holocaust and Resistance Day, as if the two were synonymous, equivalent.

Yitzhak Gruenbaum, the notable leader of Polish Jewry between the wars and of the Jewish community in the early days of the state, also criticized the Diaspora Jews for failing to behave with dignity and not knowing how to defend themselves. Moreover, Gruenbaum, who headed the Rescue Committee of the Jewish Agency, which was formed to rally help for Jews in the occupied countries, claimed that their lack of opposition cost the Jews the support of the rest of the world. In July 1943, in an article entitled "From Destruction to Destruction," Gruenbaum said:

> It is said that the martyrdom of the first Christians who were tortured by the Romans and thrown to the beasts in their circuses, was what brought the emptied hearts of the intelligentsia and the masses nearer to Christianity . . . while the torture and martyrdom of generations of Jews in the Diaspora and its influence on the spirituality and hearts of the Christian nations was less than nil . . . Does the self-defense, the effort to sell their lives dearly, to stand up for the people's honor — isolated and tortured — does all this not merit the sympathy of the world? We have not yet been tried in this manner, we have not yet trod the path of heroism, except during the last days of Warsaw, in the last hours of the surviving remnant in the Polish ghettos. And now our hearts are beginning to beat on hearing of the splendid heroism and the terrible depression is beginning to vanish.
>
> For two thousand years, we have lived on the legend of the war against the Romans . . . and now again a wondrous and glorious legend is being enacted which sheds a glowing light on the Diaspora in Poland, on its great day, and ours.

David Ben Gurion said in mid-February 1943, on the day when Palestinian Jews honored the defenders of Tel Hai, the Jewish settlement in the Galilee that fought to the last man rather than surrender:

However, for this tortured exile as well, the death of the defenders of Tel Hai was not in vain. Six days ago news reached us that our comrades in Warsaw — the tiny remnant of Jews still there, decided to fight for their lives and organized small groups to rise up and defend themselves. They could not obtain weapons from the Polish underground, and only a few had them, but they still decided to fight, and yesterday the first report reached us that the Jews of Warsaw have rebelled [referring to the opposition in the ghetto in January 1943] and dozens of the Nazi hangmen have been killed by our comrades. Although hundreds and perhaps thousands — who knows how many — paid for it with their lives, they have learned the new lesson of death which the defenders of Tel Hai and Sedgera have bequeathed to us — the heroic death.

The Uprising of the Warsaw ghetto, the rebellion of other ghettos, and the role of the Jewish partisan movement erased the stereotype of the passive Jews of the Diaspora. The stereotype was widely held and false. It no longer reflected the attitude of modern society in Europe on the eve of the Holocaust.

Though we expect an innocent man who is attacked by a mob to fight in his own defense, the extreme violence of the twentieth century has shown such expectations to be naive. Within totalitarian regimes, human society abandoned the principles and values of Judeo-Christian civilization, triggering a moral breakdown that undoubtedly influenced both the murderer and his victim. The victims of extreme Nazi violence and murder — prisoners in concentration camps, prisoners of war, and forced laborers — the people with the greatest motivation to rebel, did not generally resist or fight. The same phenomenon occurred under the Stalinist regime in the Soviet Union. During both regimes, the passivity of even veteran revolutionaries, daring activists of the underground, and experienced fighters shows that human beings are able and ready to resist and revolt when their struggle and death has some chance or could influence many others. Under circumstances established by totalitarian regimes, abandoned and without any hope or chance, victims as a rule did not resist or rebel.

Thus, the Uprising in the Warsaw ghetto was a rare exception. It demonstrates the depths to which humanity can sink and the heights to which it can soar.

On May 6, 1944, a year after the struggle and destruction of the Warsaw ghetto, the following appeared in a publication of the Polish underground:

> On April 19, 1944, the British Broadcasting Company's World Service broadcast to Europe a special program in a number of languages in commemoration of a year from the day of the uprising in the Warsaw ghetto. This memorial day was marked throughout the world. It significance in our country is stressed by the fact that the Polish National Council in London included the fighting of the Jews of Poland as part of Poland's struggle for freedom and independence and the high command of the Polish armed forces have bestowed the military cross (Virtuti Militari) on the late commander of the Warsaw ghetto uprising.

A biography of Mordecai Anielewicz, which was published in Israel, ends with these words:

> The war ended in May 1945. Millions of people returned from every part of Germany, from the countries in which they had been held as prisoners, from the camps and the fronts. In the Red Square in Moscow, the joy mounted and lessened the sorrow of the victims. The flags of victory were borne on high and the abominable flags of the Nazis were thrown to the ground. London, Paris, and Amsterdam celebrated. On the lanes and highways, on every possible roadway, there was an endless stream of people. An army of returners. Homeward, to their homeland, city, and their people awaiting them with trembling and joy. The bells of liberation rang out. The Jews are also on the move. They come from the Aryan side, from the city, the camps. Shamed and awkward shreds of existence, strangers to themselves and their city . . . those who came to Warsaw did not find a city or a house, or a relative. They climbed onto the heaps of ruins. Nothing was recognizable. One could not tell where a certain street had been or where a house had stood. However, they discovered the spot,

the hole where the house on Mila 18 had stood. They took a great black stone, a mass of dull rock, and placed it there. In simple lettering, in three languages, the following was etched on the stone: *Here on the 8th day of May 1943, Mordecai Anielewicz, the commander of the Warsaw ghetto uprising together with the staff of the Jewish Fighting Organization and dozens of fighters, fell in the campaign against the Nazi enemy.*

The State of Israel enacted the law of Yad Vashem, creating Israel's national memorial to the Holocaust and Resistance in memory of the Holocaust, and established the twenty-seventh of Nisan as the day commemorating the anniversary of the Uprising of the Jews of Warsaw — the memorial day of the Holocaust and its heroism. On this day there are gatherings throughout Israel in addition to an official assembly on the Hill of Remembrance (Mount Herzl) in Yad Vashem in Jerusalem. There are two mass rallies: one in the north at Kibbutz Lochamei Hagetaot (the ghetto fighters' kibbutz), established by survivors of the fighters in the Warsaw ghetto, including Yitzhak Zuckerman and Zivia Lubetkin; and the second in Yad Mordecai, the kibbutz in the south named after Mordecai Anielewicz where a monument stands in his memory.

Memorial Day is now commemorated by official assemblies in Warsaw, in Washington, in Jewish congregations throughout the world, and in an increasing number of towns, settlements, kibbutzim, and youth groups. On this occasion, the thoughts of survivors and public leaders return to those dark and torturous days and to the courage that will forever stir the soul. In the darkest hours of the Warsaw ghetto, when all hope was lost, when none had a chance to survive and the end was certain, young Jews arose to fight. They chose to die in freedom rather than cower before an overpowering enemy. They refused to surrender, preferring instead to fight to the death and thus preserve their honor even when they could no longer defend their lives.

BIBLIOGRAPHICAL NOTES

INDEX

BIBLIOGRAPHICAL NOTES

Throughout the ages, Jewish life in Warsaw has been the topic of numerous important works. Emanuel Ringelblum, who chronicled the last days of the Jews in the Warsaw ghetto, also published an important study on the early years of Warsaw's Jews until their expulsion in 1527: see Emanuel Ringelblum, *Zydzi w Warszawie, od czasow najdawniej-szych do ostatniego wygnania w r. 1527, Warszawa, 1932.*

In 1881 Hilary Nusbaum published his book *Z zycia Zydow w Warszwie,* containing pictures of Jewish daily life and important historical events in the life of the city's Jewish community. Special note should go to Jacob Shatzky's work, *The History of the Jews in Warsaw (Geschichte von Yidn in Varshe),* published in Yiddish in three volumes by YIVO, in New York, during the years 1947–53. The work covers the period from the beginning of Jewish settlement in Warsaw until 1896.

Numerous works deal with the city of Warsaw and its inhabitants. Among the authors of these works are several outstanding contemporary historians of Poland. Similarly, Warsaw's city life has been a popular subject for many writers in Poland for generations. The most relevant in terms of the Jews of Warsaw is the in-depth series published by Panstwowe Wydawnictwo Naukowe and edited by Stefan Kieniewicz, which includes the following volumes:

Maria Bogucka, et al., *Warszawa w latach 1526–1749.*
Stanislaw Kieniewicz, *Warszawa w latach 1749–1914.*
Marek Drozdowski, *Warszawa w latach 1914–1939.*
Krzysztof Dunin-Wasowicz, *Warszawa w latach 1939–1945.*

In Israel, a book was published by Avraham Levinson entitled *History of the Jews of Warsaw (Toldot Yehudei Varsha),* a comprehensive survey of the city's Jews and Jewish life (second publication in 1953). Much material can be found on the Jews of Warsaw in the three-volume *Encyclopedia of the Diaspora (Encyclopedia shel haGaluyot),* published in Jerusalem (volume 1, 1953; volume 2, 1959; volume 3, 1973). Information can also be found in *Warsaw Memorial Book (Pinkas Varshe),* published in Yiddish in Buenos Aires in 1955.

A number of comprehensive works on Warsaw have recently been published in Poland. Especially noteworthy is the anthology edited by Wladyslaw T. Bartoszewski and Antony Polonsky entitled *The Jews of Warsaw* (Oxford, 1991).

The literature on the Jews of Warsaw during the Holocaust is extremely rich and includes original journals, diaries, memoirs, scholarly articles, and beautiful stories and poems. This work relied primarily upon the abundant archival material on the Warsaw ghetto in the collection established by Emanuel Ringelblum, as well as Warsaw's Jewish underground newspapers.

The greatest importance must be assigned to the diaries kept in Warsaw during the Holocaust, especially the chronicle of Emanuel Ringelblum, published in part and in full in many languages. The most complete is the two-volume Yiddish edition, published in Warsaw (1963) and in Tel Aviv (1985), entitled *Writings from the Ghetto (Ksovim fun Geto).* Recently a multivolume work was prepared in Hebrew, with accompanying notes and explanations. The first volume was published in 1993.

The diary of Adam Czerniakow, chairman of Warsaw's Judenrat, was published in English and edited by Raul Hilberg and others: *The Warsaw Diary of Adam Czerniakow* (New York, 1979). Another valuable diary concerning ghetto life in Warsaw is that of Chaim Aaron Kaplan. A complete volume has been published in English: *The Warsaw Diary of Chaim A. Kaplan,* edited by A. L. Katsh (New York, 1973). The diary of Abraham Levin has been published in English and edited by Antony Polonsky: *A Cup of Tears* (Oxford, 1988). Also translated into English is the diary of Stanslaw Adler, officer of the Jewish police in the Warsaw ghetto: Stanslaw Adler, *In the Warsaw Ghetto, 1940–1943* (Jerusalem, 1982).

A separate place is given to the memoirs and many articles published by survivors of the Warsaw ghetto, especially those by members of the underground and of fighting organizations. Some of these have been translated into English: Yitzhak Zuckerman (*Antek*), Marek Edelman, Zivia Lubetkin, David Wdowinski, Bernard Goldstein, and others.

Among the general scholarly works dealing with Warsaw during the war or containing material on Warsaw's Jews during this period are the many books of Ber Mark, as well as Israel Gutman, *The Jews of Warsaw 1939–1943* (Bloomington, Indiana, 1982). Also included are:

Wladyslaw Bartoszewski, *Warszawski pierscien smierci* (Warszawa, 1967).
Wladyslaw Bartoszewski, *1859 dni Warszawy* (Krakow, 1984).
Tomasz Szarota, *Okupowanej Warszawy dzien powszedni* (Warszawa, 1988).

INDEX

Adamowicz, Irena, 106
Admor of Ger, 35
Agudath Israel party, xii, 6, 23, 26, 27, 29, 35
AK (Armia Krajowa, Polish Home Army), 106, 110, 171, 172, 173, 186, 212, 217–18, 231
Akiva, 46, 122, 152, 155, 197
Aktion Reinhard, 111, 134
AL (Armia Ludowa, Polish People's Army), 110
Alberstein, Eliahu, 169
Alter, R. Abraham Mordecai, 35
Alter, Victor, 6
Altman, Tosia, 107, 240–41, 249
American Jewish Joint Distribution Committee (the Joint), 43, 46, 64, 65, 66, 68, 69, 94, 95
Anders, Wladyslaw, 109
Anielewicz, Mordecai, xviii, 165, 180, 198, 259; on Uprising success, xx, 207; on German doctor scout, 106; and weapons, 108, 212; returned from Soviet-occupied territory, 123; bare-headed custom begun by, 125; and Jewish Fighting Organization, 152–53, 166, 167; Berlinski on meeting with, 182; accounts passed on to, 206; on bunker conditions, 225; partisan group named for, 249; biography of, 258–59; kibbutz named for, 259
Anski, S., xiii
Antek. *See* Zuckerman, Yitzhak
Anti-fascist bloc, 112, 113–14, 115
Antisemitism: in interwar Poland, 19, 21, 22, 32, 39, 44–45; and emigration, 22, 24; as stereotyping, 40; German, 75; and Warsaw struggle, 223, 232–33
Arbuz (OBW owner), 152
Archives, 65–66, 116–17, 151–52, 155
Arendt, Hannah, xiv
Arlt, Fritz, 68
Artstein, Zechariah, 183
Asch, Sholem, 31